SETTING THE PEOPLE FREE

JOHN DUNN is Professor of Political Theory at the University of Cambridge and Fellow of King's College. He is the author of a number of titles, among them *The Cunning of Unreason: Making Sense of Politics* and *The Political Thought of John Locke*. He is also the editor of *Democracy: the Unfinished Journey* and a Fellow of the British Academy.

'One of the strengths of *Setting the People Free* – alongside clarity and erudition – is the way in which its author's confidence in democracy allows him to analyse both its detriments and its exploitation by unscrupulous politicians… In short, democracy alone is not enough – essential to liberty though it is. The demonstration of that – often regarded as heretical – truth is what makes *Setting the People Free* important.'

Roy Hattersley, *The Times*

'Ambitious… thoughtful and illuminating.'

Shirley Williams, *Independent*

SETTING THE PEOPLE FREE

The Story of Democracy

JOHN DUNN

Atlantic Books
London

First published in hardback in 2005 by Atlantic Books,
an imprint of Grove Atlantic Ltd.

This paperback edition published by Atlantic Books in 2006.

Copyright © John Dunn 2005

The moral right of John Dunn to be identified as the author of this work
has been asserted in accordance with the Copyright, Designs and Patents
Act of 1988.

10 9 8 7 6 5 4 3 2 1

A CIP catalogue record for this book is available from the British Library.

ISBN 1 84354 213 7

Text design: www.carrstudio.co.uk
Printed in Great Britain by Bookmarque Ltd, Croydon

Grove Atlantic Ltd
Ormond House
26–27 Boswell Street
London WC1N 3JZ

For Ruth

ACKNOWLEDGEMENTS

This book is no one's fault but mine. But many people have put them-selves out to help me as I wrote. I am extremely grateful for the patience, lucidity and directness of Gill Coleridge throughout my efforts to plan and complete it. At Atlantic Books, I should like to thank Toby Mundy, who brings to publishing a combination of consideration and zest of which authors vainly dream, and Bonnie Chiang, who has been consistently encouraging and helpful. I have had prompt, generous and effective aid over particular points from many colleagues in Cambridge and beyond: notably Robin Osborne, Simon Goldhill, Stephen Alford, Paul Cartledge, Basim Musallam, Gareth Stedman Jones, Tim Blanning, Bela Kapossy, and Michael Sonenscher. The experience of writing it has reminded me vividly of old intellec-tual debts which can never be repaid, above all to Moses Finley and Bernard Bailyn, of the intellectual companionship over decades of Michael Cook, Quentin Skinner and Istvan Hont, and of the help and encouragement in a variety of settings of many friends: Bianca Fontana, Bernard Manin, Pasquale Pasquino, Adam Przeworski, Tony Judt, Richard Tuck, Cynthia Farrar, Sunil Khilnani, Sudipta Kaviraj, Tom Metzger, Ian Shapiro, Andrew Barshay, Takamaro Hanzawa,

Takashi Kato, and most recently Guillermo O'Donnell, who has devoted his life to fathoming democracy's fate. I owe very special thanks to Raymond Geuss, with whom I have taught now for over a decade, and who has been the truest of friends.

My colleagues in the Department of Politics have shouldered many burdens to give me the chance to work on it. I am especially grateful to Helen Thompson and Geoffrey Hawthorn for their help and solidarity. The University of Cambridge gave me the sabbatical leave which enabled me to begin it in reasonable calm; and the Arts and Humanities Research Board, once again, gave me the final term of research leave which I needed to complete it.

Three figures particularly have given me hope and nerve over the last few years in pressing the questions which I try to answer. Edward Said by his warmth, his glowing vitality, and his unforgettable generosity of spirit, as the shades closed in. Janet Malcolm by her grace and luminosity on the page, and by the ear of the Recording Angel. Dr Kim Dae-Jung, the one unmistakably great political leader with whom I have had the privilege to talk at length, to whom his country owes far more than it has yet begun to realize, by his singular courage.

King's College, Cambridge, October 2004

We used to go down on our knees before the people in power, but now we have got to our feet.

NADIA BEREZOVSKA

(middle-aged postmistress, amongst the crowds in central Kiev who forced the holding of a fresh election on Ukraine's incumbent President)

[Stefan Wagstyl & Tom Warner, 'We used to go down on our knees before the people in power, but now we have got to our feet', Financial Times, 21 December 2004, p17]

CONTENTS

P r e f a c e

WHY DEMOCRACY?

This book tells an astonishing story. It is the story of a word of casual origins, and with a long and often ignominious history behind it, which has come quite recently to dominate the world's political imagination. Over the course of the book I try to show how little we yet understand that remarkable ascent, but also how we can learn to grasp its causes and significance altogether better.

Why does democracy loom so large today? Why should it hold such sway over the political speech of the modern world? What does its recent prominence really mean? When America and Britain set out to bury Baghdad in its own rubble, why was it in the name of democracy of all words that they claimed to do so? Is its novel dominance in fact illusory: a sustained exercise in fraud or an index of utter confusion? Or does it mark a huge moral and political advance, which only needs to cover the whole world, and be made a little more real, for history to come to a reassuring end?

This book sets out to explain the extraordinary presence of democracy in today's world. It shows how it began as an improvised remedy for a very local Greek difficulty two and a half thousand years ago, flourished briefly but scintillatingly, and then faded away almost everywhere for all but two thousand years. It tells how it came back to life as a real modern political option, explaining why it first did so, under another name, in the struggle for American independence and with the founding of the new American republic. It shows how it then returned, almost immediately and under its own name, if far more erratically, amid the struggles of France's Revolution. It registers its slow but insistent rise over the next century and a half, and its overwhelming triumph in the years since 1945. In that rise we can see how strong the continuities remain, but also how sharp the breaks must be, between its Greek original and any modern democratic state. We can grasp what it is about democracy which equipped it to evoke such vital allegiance, but which also guarantees that it will continue to arouse intense fear and suspicion, and open intellectual and moral scorn. Within the last three-quarters of a century democracy has become the political core of the civilization which the West offers to the rest of the world. Now, as never before, we need to understand what that core really is. As do those to whom we make that offer.

In this book, accordingly, I try to answer two very large questions. The first concerns an extremely strange fact about modern politics. The second concerns the single most unmistakably momentous political outcome of the last three-quarters of a century. I know of no serious attempt to answer the first question. Few even care to pose it in a clear and reasonably frank way. Answers to the second question, by contrast, are two a penny. They litter the pages of serious newspapers and form a commonplace of contemporary political commentary. Most, however, are plainly wrong; and once the question is considered with care, it becomes all too clear that it is exceedingly hard to answer. I believe that the answers to these questions are closely connected, and that, between them, they show something of immense importance about modern politics. But readers may judge otherwise, and still, I hope, learn for themselves from the challenge of trying to answer each.

The first question has two distinct elements: the existence of a single cosmopolitan standard, and the term selected to express it. Why should it be the case that, for the first time in the history of our still conspicuously multi-lingual species, there is for the present a single world-wide name for the legitimate basis of political authority? Not, of course, uncontested in practice anywhere, and still roundly rejected in many quarters, but never, any longer, in favour of an alternative secular claimant to cosmopolitan legitimacy. This is a startling fact, and clearly requires explanation; but in itself it is not necessarily any stranger than much else about the world in which we now live. What is very strange indeed (in fact, quite bizarre) is the fact that this single term, endlessly transliterated or translated across all modern languages,[1] should turn out to be the ancient Greek noun *demokratia*, which originally meant not a basis for legitimacy, or a regime defined by its good intentions or its noble mission, but simply one particular form of government, and that a form, for almost two thousand years of its history as a word, which, it was overwhelmingly judged by most who used the term, had proved grossly illegitimate in theory and every bit as disastrous in practice.

The first question, therefore, is in part a question about the history of language (the vocabulary of modern politics, and its historical antecedents). But it is also a question about the history of political thought and argument, and about the history of political organization and struggle. Why should it be this word that has won the verbal competition for ultimate political commendation across the globe? What does it carry within it to gain it this smashing victory? How did the ideas we now take it to imply, in the end and after so very many centuries, face down the variety of ideas which for so long dominated it with such apparent ease? How did it shake off its lengthy notoriety, adjust its register from dispassionate or disabused description to confident and committed commendation, and pick up the oecumenical allure which its Athenian inventors never intended, and could not distantly have imagined?

At the core of this story is the intensely political history of a very political word. But the word itself cannot answer our questions. Once it was there (as far as we know, summoned into existence precisely to name the regime form which Kleisthenes pioneered for Athens, for his now largely inscrutable reasons, very late in the sixth century BC), that word could be carried laterally in space, and aimed backwards as well as forwards in time. It could be deployed to designate communities which had never heard of Kleisthenes, or even Athens, and practices, whether earlier or later, which were clearly quite unaffected by anything the Athenians ever did, or anything else which we know them to have said. But for over two thousand years it remained a noun designating a system of rule. Not till very late in the eighteenth century, very close to France's great revolution, and apparently largely in and because of it, did *democracy* transform itself into a noun of agency (a *democrat*), an adjective which expressed allegiance and did not merely allude to it (*democratic*), and a verb (to *democratize*), which described the project of refashioning politics, society, and even economy in their entirety, to meet the standards set by the idea of popular self-rule. Ancient Greece had partisans of democracy as a regime. But, as far as we know, it did not exactly have democrats: men (or women) who did not just favour democracy in a particular setting within a given conflict, but were also confident of the clear illegitimacy anywhere of every rival political form, and relatively clear just where the superiority of democracy lay. Certainly, no Greek thinker or political actor ever either defended or explained their political aspirations as efforts to raise distinct aspects of political, economic or social arrangements to the exacting standards which democracy implies.

Athens gave democracy a name, and worked out an elaborate, highly distinctive and astonishingly thoroughgoing interpretation of the political conditions required to achieve it. But it took the French Revolution, well over two thousand years later, to turn *democrat* into a partisan label and a badge of political honour, and first lend imaginative credibility to the idea of transforming human collective life, anywhere and everywhere, to fit those requirements. Only after 1789, as far as we know, did any human beings begin to speak of *democratizing* the societies to which they belonged.

For us, democracy is both a form of government and a political value. We quarrel fiercely, if confusedly, over how far the value vindicates or indicts our own practices of government; but we also quarrel over how far the same value is practically coherent, or desirable in its prospective consequences in different circumstances, on any scale between an individual family or domestic unit and the entire human population of a still painfully disunited globe. When we do so, we largely recapitulate Greek arguments between local partisans of democracy as a form of rule, and intellectual critics who invented political philosophy, alongside other genres of critical reflection on politics, in their attempts to call its merits into question.

With the French Revolution, democracy as a word and an idea acquired a political momentum that it has never since wholly lost. Its merits, both moral and practical, have been contested vigorously throughout, as they still are today. But despite these blatant and endlessly reiterated vulnerabilities, it has become ever clearer that, whatever its limitations, there is something irresistibly potent about democracy as a political rallying cry, and that any hope of halting it permanently in its tracks is utterly forlorn. The political potency of democracy as a word is no guarantee of its intellectual potency as an idea. But its political force is no standing miracle. It cannot issue merely from a meaningless or unintelligible buzz of sound. Democracy has won its present prominence, and even the degree of reluctant deference which it now enjoys, in ferocious competition with very many other words, and not a few other ideas. Today, it is plainly a source and embodiment of political power in itself; and its cumulative victory, however disappointing or hollow if judged against loftier aspirations of its own or others, has itself been a sustained display of political power.

In this book I tell the story of democracy's passage from parochial eccentricity and protracted ignominy, seek to capture its main metamorphoses along the way, and show what its long, slow and wholly unexpected victory really means for the political world in which we all now have to live. In tracing that vast arc across space and through time, I try throughout to do full justice to two clear perceptions which most students of democracy have found it uncomfortable to combine: the startlingly insistent power lurking in this apparently drab word and in the ideas which it has come to evoke, and the speciousness of applying it at all literally to the organizational and governmental structures of any human population early in the third millennium. It is easy to grasp democracy by suppressing either perception. But, if you do, what you grasp must always be drastically other than what is really there: a cynical truncation of that reality, or a stupidly ingenuous gloss upon it. (It is not hard to be an idiot in politics. We are all strongly tempted to political idiocy quite a lot of the time.)

The citizens of Athens in the fifth and fourth centuries BC, to a now bewildering degree, governed themselves. What they meant by democracy (which was originally their word) was the extraordinary complex of institutions which enabled them to do so. No modern population can govern themselves in the same sense; and we lose all feeling for political reality when we strive today to see in America or Britain, as they prepare for war or draw up their public budgets, instances of either people governing itself in even a mildly opaque way. When any modern state claims to be a democracy, it necessarily misdescribes itself. But that is very far from rendering the misdescription inconsequential, and cannot credibly be viewed merely as deliberate self-deception. There is every reason for today's citizens to insist that their own state describe itself in these terms, and choose its friends and commit its power and resources largely alongside other states which also choose to do so. There are, as we shall see, very practical advantages to doing so over time, even if most of them might be furnished just as reliably for a bit under a more clinical vocabulary.

But the label of democracy does more than affirm a clear duty for states to provide their citizens with these practical advantages. It also expresses symbolically something altogether different: the degree to which all government, however necessary and expeditious, is also a presumption and an offence. Like every modern state, the democracies of today demand obedience and insist on a very large measure of compulsory alienation of judgement on the part of their citizens. (To demand that obedience and enforce such alienation is what makes a state a state.) When they make that demand in their citizens' own name, however, they do not merely add insult to injury, or perpetrate an evident absurdity. They also acknowledge their own permanent potential for effrontery in levying any such demands, and offer a slim measure of apology for the offence inherent in levying them. With that offer, they close the circle of civic subjection, and set out a framework of categories within which a population can reasonably think of itself over time as living together as equals, on terms and within a set of presumptions, which they could reasonably and freely choose. Everywhere that the word *democracy* has fought its way forward across time and space, you can hear both themes: the purposeful struggle to improve the practical circumstances of life, and to escape from arbitrary and often brutal coercion, but also the determination and longing to be treated with respect and some degree of consideration. What we mean by democracy is not that we govern ourselves. When we speak or think of ourselves as living in a democracy, what we have in mind is something quite different. It is that our own state, and the government which does so much to organize our lives, draws its legitimacy from us, and that we have a reasonable chance of being able to compel each of them to continue to do so. They draw it, today, from holding regular elections, in which every adult citizen can vote freely and without fear, in which their votes have at least a reasonably equal weight, and in which any uncriminalized political opinion can compete freely for them. Modern representative democracy has changed the idea of democracy almost beyond recognition. But, in doing so, it has shifted it from one of history's hopeless losers to one of its more insistent winners.

My second question, then, is what exactly it is, embodied in or centred upon this novel state form, that has given this very old and much reviled word the stamina and drive to win through in the end.

This book, then, tells three remarkable stories. It tells in the first place the story of a word. But it also tells alongside it the story of an idea, by turns inspiring and ludicrous, and the further story of a range of widely varying practices associated with that idea. One broad family of those practices, the governmental forms of the modern representative capitalist democracy, now dominates the world through its wealth and confidence, and through the quite unprecedented powers of destruction which it has at its disposal. The first two stories are long, complicated, and closely intertwined. The first two sections of the book, accordingly, tell them in the boldest outline. The third is far briefer, but also much denser and more complicated: the very core of the political history of the globe over the last half-century. It is not clear that it could yet be told as a story at all, let alone told convincingly at endurable length. In this third section, therefore, I attempt not to record what has happened, but to explain why it has done so.

This is a story, all too obviously, about us: the story, at the very least, of the historical backcloth to the lives of an ever-growing majority amongst us.[2] The question I try to answer here, the book's second question, is why this particular state form, the modern representative capitalist democracy, has for the present won the global struggle for wealth and power. This is a hard question; and I cannot claim to have answered it conclusively. What I hope to show is why its answer cannot be either of the two conclusions which we are endlessly urged to draw from it (because it is evidently just and because it works reliably in practice), and where, instead, that answer must lie. If these judgements are right, they imply at least one simple conclusion: that our own need to understand the political reality of the world in which we now live is still every bit as urgent as the need which prompted the Athenians to invent and deepen that very distant system of self-rule. For them, it was a price they chose to pay to protect their freedom, as well as an expression of that freedom in itself. We cannot protect our freedom in the same way. But we too, if we care to, can see how pressingly that freedom still needs protection, judge how best it can be protected amongst the many claimants who volunteer their services for the purpose, and choose for ourselves the price we are or are not willing to pay to protect it as best we can. We too, if we choose, can use this antique word, not in theft and mystification, but to focus the challenges which history sends us, and face them alertly together.

Chapter One

DEMOCRACY'S FIRST COMING

Out of the dark and from very long ago has come a word. Like every word which carries authority for human beings, it began its life somewhere in particular. Today that word reaches out almost everywhere on earth where humans gather together in any numbers. Wherever it goes, it presses a claim for authority and a demand for respect. Everywhere, still, these claims remain sharply contested. In some settings they are brushed effortlessly aside, and all but cowed into silence. In others they are affirmed sonorously enough, but heard by most listeners with a hollow groan. Virtually nowhere any longer, even in the most brutal of autocracies, are they merely unintelligible as claims; and in remarkably few sites by now are they simply and permanently inaudible: excluded or erased from public speech by the sheer ferocity of repression. (Note, for example, what was first to respond even for Iraq in the summer of 2003 when the United Nations Security Council demanded its submission, before America launched its invasion. It was not the tyrant who had ruled the country with such murderous brutality and for so long, and whose image dominated every Iraqi public space, but what passed for a national representative assembly: a Parliament. It was they, not their real master, who showily declined to submit. Within the week, their real master, less showily, had decided quite differently. Or so, at least for a time, it seemed.)

As it travels through time and space, the word democracy never travels all on its own. Increasingly, as the last two centuries have gone by, it has travelled in fine company, alongside freedom, human rights, and perhaps now even, at least in pretension, material prosperity as well. But unlike these companions, democracy stakes a claim which is disconcerting from the outset: the claim to be obeyed. Every right constrains free action. Even freedom necessarily intrudes on the freedom of action of others. But democracy is itself a direct pressure on the will: a demand to accept, abide by, and in the end even submit to, the choices of most of your fellow citizens. There is nothing enticing about that demand, and no guarantee ever that accepting it will avoid fearsome consequences and may not involve hideous complicities. In many ways, and from many different points of view, the authority won by this far-flung word is strange indeed.

This is a story with a beginning. Democracy began in Athens. Not anything whatever which anyone today might reasonably choose to call democracy,[1] but something which someone first in fact, as far as we know, did. Today democracy has come to be used, with sufficient gall, to refer to almost any form of rule or decision making. But when it entered human speech, it did so as a description of an already existing and very specific state of affairs, somewhere in particular. That place was Athens.

What exactly did democracy describe when the Athenians first used the term as a description? What did they mean by describing it in this way? To see what was happening in that first act of naming (or labelling), it helps to begin by listening to the Athenians as they addressed one another about the experience which they hoped to capture. Consider two voices, one very much speaking on democracy's behalf, the other writing of it without enthusiasm and in a more confiding and enquiring fashion.

The first is famous and imposing, the voice of Pericles himself. The grandest celebration of ancient democracy comes not from a poet or philosopher (or even a professional orator),[2] but from the great political leader who led Athens into the war which all but destroyed her. It evokes, and claims to report, a single momentous historical ceremony, held late in the year 430BC. True, we do not know that Pericles himself ever spoke a single word of it. But Thucydides, the mesmerizing historian who certainly composed virtually all of it, assures his readers that it, like the many other speeches of his *History*, conveys not merely what Pericles should have said but also what he would have meant.[3] Thucydides, as he tells us himself with some pride, intended his story to last for ever;[4] and Pericles by that point had led his city state in war and peace for longer than Abraham Lincoln or Winston Churchill, and done so under conditions which often tested the skills of domestic political leadership as exactingly as America's devastating Civil War or the grim struggle to withstand and overthrow the Third Reich. He also led it (and could only have led it), to a degree that has never been true in any modern Parliamentary or Presidential regime, by convincing, time after time, a majority of the citizens present on the occasion by the speeches which he made. He held power by oratory,[5] and did so steadily and tautly enough for Thucydides himself to describe Athens at the time as being ruled by a single person.[6] We need not be surprised at the lasting power or resonance of this remarkable witness.

It was a speech for a proud sad occasion: a eulogy to the war dead of Athens in the opening year of the long drawn-out Peloponnesian War, delivered, as at every Athenian public funeral of its fallen (with the single exception of the victors of Marathon),[7] before their common grave beside the loveliest approach road to the city walls. In it, Pericles spoke not at all of the individual exploits or daring of his heroes,[8] though he left his hearers in little doubt that many had done finely. What he spoke of, incomparably, was Athens itself, the community for which each had made their final sacrifice. He spoke of its singular glories and its unique claim to such ultimate devotion. Thucydides was no sentimentalist, and no one since he wrote has judged the political conduct of the Athenians in those years more searchingly. What he makes Pericles say in praise of Athens at that point, in vindication of the choices of those who went out to die on its behalf, begins from and centres on its political regime, and the political and spiritual lives which it freed and prompted the Athenians to live together:

> *We live under a form of government which does not emulate the institutions of our neighbours; on the contrary, we are ourselves a model (*paradeigma*, or paradigm) which some follow, rather than the imitators of other peoples.*[9]

This regime, which is called democracy (*demokratia*), because it is administered with a view to the interest of the many, not of the few, has not merely made Athens great. It has also rendered its citizens equal before the law in their private disputes, and equally free to compete for public honours by personal merit and exertion, or to seek to lead the city, irrespective of their own wealth or social background.[10] Pericles praises it for the mutual politeness and lack of spite it fostered between those citizens, for the deep respect for law it inculcated, and for drawing to the city the fruits and products of the whole world. He praises it, too, for the military superiority it had mustered, for its determined openness in face of every other people, and the stalwart courage nurtured by its way of life. But he praises it, equally, for its taste and responsiveness to beauty, its sobriety of judgement and respect for wisdom, its pride in its own energy, discretion and generosity. Athens, he boasted in summary, is an education for the whole of Greece.[11]

Democracy for the Athenians began (and even acquired its name) before the category itself carried or expressed any clear or special value. Yet within a few decades of picking up the name, it had come to mean for some not just a way of organizing power and political institutions, but a whole way of life and the inspiring qualities which somehow suffused it. At the core of that way of life lay a combination of personal commitment to a community of birth and residence, and a continuing practice of alert public judgement on which that community quite consciously depended for its own security:

> *For we alone regard the man who takes no part in public affairs, not as one who minds his own business, but as good for nothing; and we Athenians decide public questions for ourselves or at least endeavour to arrive at a sound understanding of them, in the belief that it is not debate which is a hindrance to action, but rather not to be instructed by debate before the time comes for action.*[12]

There has never been a fuller or saner expression of the hope which lies at the very centre of democracy as a political ideal.

The speech which Thucydides gives us is a historian's presentation of a dutifully partisan and highly political performance. It is also an epitome of the ways in which the citizens of Athens had come to wish to conceive themselves as a community.[13] To other Athenians at the time, just as earlier and later, democracy naturally meant something very different, as it presumably did to many inhabitants of Attica – slaves, women, *metics* – who could never become full citizens.[14] With the critics of democracy there is a wider range of voices to listen to, not all of them cultured despisers like Plato.[15] Especially striking is the figure whom British classical scholars, for reasons now largely forgotten, have come to call the Old Oligarch, author of a terse study of *The Constitution of Athens*, long attributed to Xenophon.[16] For the Old Oligarch, writing in all probability before the Peloponnesian War even began, Athens's democracy was no occasion for applause;[17] but it certainly was a coherent political order, with many elements well calculated to sustain and strengthen it over time. It gave power to the poor, the unsavoury and the unabashedly popular,[18] and did so quite deliberately at the expense of those of wealth, nobility of birth or social distinction.[19] This distribution of power[20] had entirely natural consequences,[21] benefiting the former mercilessly at the expense of the latter. What made the distribution viable was the main source of the city's military power, its citizen navy, drawn overwhelmingly from the poorer sections of Athens's population, unlike the heavily armed hoplites who dominated its land armies.[22] In the eyes of the Old Oligarch, it was true in every country that those of greater distinction[23] oppose democracy, seeing themselves as repositories of decorum and respect for justice, and their social inferiors as ignorant, disorderly and vicious.[24] In the face of these attitudes, the poorer majority of Athens's citizens are very well advised to insist on their opportunity to share the public offices of the city, and their right to address their fellow citizens at will,[25] and especially well advised to allocate those public offices on which the safety or danger of the people depended,[26] the roles of general or cavalry commander, not randomly across the citizen body but by popular election of those best equipped to hold them (inevitably, the wealthier and more powerful).

For Pericles, as Thucydides makes him speak, the democracy of Athens was a way of living together in political freedom, which ennobled the characters and refined the sensibilities of an entire community. It opened up to them lives rich with interest and gratification, and protected them effectively in living out these lives with one another. It would be hard sanely to ask for more from any set of political institutions or practices. For the Old Oligarch, in stark contrast, the democracy of Athens was a robust but flagrantly unedifying system of power, which subjected the nobler elements of its society to the meaner, transferred wealth purposefully from one to the other, and distributed the means of coercion clear-headedly and determinedly to cement this outcome and keep the nobler elements under control.

> *For the people do not want a good government under which they themselves are slaves; they want to be free and to rule.*[27]

No one could miss the clash between these two views. What is harder to assess is how far they really conflict in judgement and not merely in taste, and, where they do conflict in judgement, which better conveys the way democratic Athens really was.

Anyone who tries to see that reality for themselves faces three very different obstacles. The first is intrinsic to assessing the politics of anywhere at any time. It comes from the ambiguities of politics itself, above all the permanent tensions between its two principal components.[28] Every political community is an elusive and unstable blend of human purposes and the (principally unintended) consequences of human actions. Those purposes can be extremely narrow or very widely shared. They can flicker for a day or two, or congeal into well-defined institutions or rules of action, and carefully interpreted conceptions of why both institutions and rules are or are not appropriate. Any picture of politics which focuses principally on institutions, practices and values starts off from the official face of a political community, and registers its aspirations and pretensions. A picture which attempts instead to pin down what actually happens as a result of how particular men and women choose to behave is all but certain to present that community in a less sanguine or generous light. It is likely to conclude that the aspirations enunciated on its official occasions are often bogus, its institutions grossly at odds with their official justifications, and the values invoked within it to sanction one line of political conduct against another little more than tools of deception.[29] What must be true, however, is that neither picture can ever be adequate on its own and neither, therefore, ever wholly beside the point.[30] With Athens, more clearly perhaps than with General Mobutu's Zaire or the Wahabite Kingdom of Saudi Arabia, the need for each is very clear.

The other two impediments to seeing Athenian democracy the way it really was are less intimidating but every bit as inconvenient. The first is the sporadic and often capricious character of the evidence which is still available to us. Much of this does not consist of elaborate descriptive texts.[31] But all of it is still very much in the shadow of a relatively small number of extremely striking texts, above all works of history, philosophy, drama or oratory. All of these, in one way or another, press upon us their own picture of that very distant reality, and do so for purposes of their own, many hard, or even impossible, now to identify. We have works of painstaking institutional description, like Aristotle's *Constitution of Athens*, comedies and tragedies from Aeschylus to Aristophanes, probing histories from Herodotus and Thucydides, passionately engaged speeches by prominent political advocates like Demosthenes or Isocrates, unexcelled enquiries into the meaning of human life and the place of politics within it from Plato and Aristotle. Between them these disparate texts make some things arrestingly clear; but they also leave a great deal which is now wholly out of view. These large gaps in our knowledge do nothing to blur the realities of the distant past,[32] or weaken our reasons for straining to grasp them as best we can. But they offer a salutary warning of how easy it will always remain to deceive ourselves about the sources of our own views of those realities: why we see them, and feel about them, the way we do.

The third obstacle is the lengthy and surprisingly continuous history which has led us to see them this way, a history largely carried by the historical transmission of exactly the same texts. There is, as we shall see, little direct relation between the political institutions and practices of ancient Athens and those of any human community today. But there is unmistakably at least one connecting strand, which runs without interruption from the texts of Aeschylus to the present day. What is transmitted along this strand is seldom, if ever, firm structures of power or definite institutional practices. What travels along it, often with great vitality, is conceptions of what to value and aim for, and why and how to act on the basis of those conceptions. Conceptions of this kind (values, ideals, visions of life) never determine the outcome of the politics of any community, and change constantly as they shape and reshape purposes along the way. But no community can exist even fugitively, let alone persist and extend across long spans of time, except by courtesy of just such conceptions, and the complicated tissue of institutions and practices which they inform and sustain. (The law of any society is an ideal setting in which to see the weight of this simple consideration: an endless battleground of contending force, but also and just as necessarily a seamless canvas for enquiry and interpretation, the play of intelligence and even the impact of scruple.[33]) As we peer back towards the democracy of Athens, through the murk of history, and quarrel endlessly about what was ever really there, we largely recapitulate Greek arguments. We do so partly because of an obvious continuity in subject matter: because the reality we are trying to grasp was to such a large degree what those arguments were about; and partly too because recapitulating Greek arguments was what for almost two thousand years Europeans, and later North Americans, were tirelessly trained to do. But we also do so because of the enduring power of some of those arguments, itself a testimony to the power of the way of life from which they first came.[34]

What then was Athenian democracy? Of some things we can be quite certain. For the Athenians themselves what it was remained fiercely contentious from its beginning to its end. It could scarcely have been less like the anodyne political recipe which democracy readily seems today, an almost wholly unreflective formula for how things ought to be politically almost everywhere and almost always (anywhere and any time, at least, at which it does not very urgently matter).[35] What the Athenians disagreed about, of course, was what happened in and through and because of their democracy, and what their regime therefore meant. They had far less doubt about what its principal institutions were, or when it had come into existence, or when, eventually, it had come to an end. What divided them, as it divides every human community, was how they saw one another's political actions, and the purposes which lay behind these, and the forces and interests (conscious or otherwise) which in turn lay behind those purposes.

Throughout its history, the democracy of Athens had bitter enemies as well as committed partisans, both at home and abroad. It may have come to be, as Pericles boasted, a proudly shared way of life in a conspicuously splendid setting; but that way of life itself attracted hatred and scorn as well as love and admiration; and the hatred and the love flowed out over and enveloped the institutions and practices of the democracy itself, and the balance of competing groups, social interests and political energies which it reflected and secured.

Democracy in Athens arose out of struggles between wealthier landowners and poorer families who had lost, or were in danger of losing, their land, and who therefore risked being forced into unfree labour by their accumulated debts.[36] It did not arise, directly and self-consciously, through that struggle itself, by unmistakable victory of the poor over the rich, but through a sequence of political initiatives which reshaped the social geography and institutions of Athens, and endowed it with a political identity, and a system of self-rule which equipped it to express and defend that identity. The most important of these initiatives, the reforms of Solon, were put in place before Athens had in any sense become a democracy.

Solon was an Athenian nobleman (*Eupatrid*), chosen magistrate (*Archon*) for the year 594BC, and given full power to reorganize the basis of land ownership, credit and personal status amongst the Athenians, and give it lasting legal form. He codified the laws, revised the levels of property on the basis of which wealthier Athenians were eligible to hold public office,[37] modified the structure of law courts, greatly improving access for the poor, freed those already enslaved for debt and abolished debt bondage for the future. He firmly refused to redistribute the land.[38]

By these means Solon tamed the brutal dynamics of appropriation, land hunger, debt and potential enslavement amongst the Athenians themselves, and showed them how Athens could hope to conceive itself, and keep itself together as a community, while the world changed round it. What he failed to do was to establish a political mechanism through which the Athenians could act together to realize that hope. His reforms were a remedy for a dire trouble between the Athenians themselves. It was yet to become a remedy in their own hands.

The next key initiative, the conventional date for democracy's inauguration, came almost a century later and after much intervening political turmoil. Solon was a real historical person; but he was also a figure of legend, one of the two great Lawgivers (Legislators) who haunted the political imagination of Greek communities, and have obsessed their would-be successors ever since.[39] What the Lawgiver did was to focus the fundamental challenges facing a particular community clearly in his mind's eye,[40] set out a framework which provided a durable solution for those problems and define this through the medium of law. Kleisthenes, who brought to Athens in 507BC what the Athenians in due course came to call democracy, was also a historical figure, a nobleman (*Eupatrid*) like Solon; but he has never become a figure of legend. None of the historical sources presents him as setting out from a clearly articulated conception of the fundamental challenges Athens faced, or carefully selecting democracy for their remedy. Democracy, indeed, was not merely as yet unnamed.[41] It was not even a pre-specified formula, applied to solve a clearly defined problem. What Kleisthenes did, as Solon had done before him, was to reorganize Athenian social geography and institutions to resolve a set of immediate problems and build a stable framework for Athens as a community around that would-be resolution. To do so, he needed to win power in the first place; and democracy, as it turned out, was both an initial means to do so, and in due course a consequence of having done so. What was different about his solution was that the framework he established was from its outset a way of organizing political choice which took it outside the ranks of the well-born and relatively wealthy, and assigned it clearly and unapologetically to the Athenian *demos* as a whole.

Herodotus presents Kleisthenes's adoption of this approach, not as an instance of intellectual or moral conviction, but as a practical expedient to muster support against his aristocratic rivals and their Spartan allies.[42] But even at the time the motives and aspirations which led him to select it may not have greatly mattered, once he had done so. What mattered more even then, and still matters to this day, is that in many ways and for a surprisingly long time the expedient worked.

As it continued to work, it acquired a name of its own (*demokratia* – rule of, or by, or, more literally, strength or power in the hands of, the *demos* – the people as a whole, or, in the eyes of its enemies, the common or non-noble (non-*Eupatrid*) people). It also fashioned a developing institutional form to express that rule, and a steadily deepening sense of its own identity and point. Pericles's speech was delivered (in some form) some three-quarters of a century after Kleisthenes won power in Athens through and for democracy; and Athens remained a democracy, with two brief but destructive interruptions, for a further century afterwards. When democracy came to an end in the city, what ended it was not Athenian political choices (or even their unintended consequences). It was foreign military power: the armies of the kingdom of Macedon.

Throughout this century and three-quarters, Athens, a community of some third of a million inhabitants with a large and increasingly resplendent urban centre and a substantial rural hinterland, was very often at war, initially against the Persian empire, but usually against other Greek city states (above all, its great rival, the warrior kingdom of Sparta), and eventually and decisively against the only quasi-Greek kingdom of Macedon. There were close ties, as there were in every Greek community, between its military (or naval) organization, its political institutions and the balance of social groups within it which supported or threatened these institutions. The Athenians liked to think of themselves as more historically continuous and more firmly rooted in their own territory than other Greek city states,[43] contrasting the depth of their commitment to the more opportunistic and nomadic attitudes induced by more fertile parts of Hellas.[44]

By the time that Pericles had finished with it Athens had become a rather grand city, full of fine new public buildings (many still there to be admired) and magnificent statuary (much of which, for one reason or another, is now elsewhere). But except when directly threatened in war, when most of its rural inhabitants chose to retreat behind its Long Walls, the majority of Athenian citizens did not live permanently in the city itself but continued to own and farm land elsewhere in Attica. The citizen population of Athens was never very large, perhaps 100,000 in all,[45] of whom about 30,000 would have been full citizens, all adult males and most of them Athenian by descent for several generations. In addition there were some 40,000 resident aliens (*metics*), men, women and children, a few of whom could hope in due course to become citizens themselves, and a much larger number of slaves (perhaps 150,000 in all).[46] The full citizens therefore represented little more than a tenth of the population.[47]

Most of these citizens, naturally, did not spend all their time attempting to rule the city, or fighting in its endless naval or military campaigns. Many, for the century after Kleisthenes,[48] could not conceivably have afforded to, since they did not own slaves themselves, and drew such income as they had, and secured much of their household's food supply, from the produce of their own small farms. Some lived too far away from Athens to attend the meetings of the Assembly with any frequency. But all had the right to attend whenever the Assembly met, as it did with increasing frequency as the democracy evolved over time, whether at pre-arranged intervals or to deal with particular eventualities – a diplomatic or military emergency, a major trial.[49] They also had the right not merely to vote on all proposals coming before it, and thus to determine together its outcome, but also to address it themselves, if they could muster the nerve, on any issue which came under discussion. They held these rights as equals, whatever their own level of personal wealth or education, the social standing of their families, or the prestige of their occupations. We do not know how many mustered the nerve, or just what emboldened them to do so. But we certainly know that a majority of them for nearly a hundred and thirty years remained firmly committed to, and took a deep pride in, the conspicuous core of personal equality which these arrangements expressed and asserted. For success in Athenian politics personal wealth, family background and even costly education were just as helpful as they are in the United States today (or most other wealthy capitalist countries). As far as we know, no Athenian was surprised that they should have proved so, or embarrassed when they did. What was surprising, and remained disconcerting to some throughout Athens's history as a democracy, was how robust the assertion of equality eventually became, and how clearly it set the terms on which the pressures of wealth, family background and educational embellishment could continue to exert themselves.

Besides the Assembly itself, which took all the great decisions of state for the Athenians, made war or peace, despatched armies or navies, and passed or rejected each new law, there were several other key institutions, which kept the main direction of Athenian political life firmly in the hands of its citizens as a whole. There was the Council (the *Boule*), 500 in number, which drew up the agenda for every Assembly meeting.[50] This met each weekday, co-ordinating other public bodies and effectively conducting the foreign relations of the *polis* throughout. It was drawn from all the 139 territorial units (the *demes*) into which Kleisthenes had divided the Athenians for political purposes, its members selected by lot from those who chose to offer themselves for the purpose.[51] Within the Council a tenth of its members served as a continuing executive body, rotating throughout the year, chaired on each occasion by a fresh individual, selected again by lot from the tenth in question for twenty-four hours at a time.[52]

There were also the popular Law Courts, in effect juries drawn from an annual panel of 6,000 citizens, all of whom had volunteered for the service and sworn a formal oath to do justice within it, and who were paid a modest daily fee for providing it. These courts heard every significant case brought to trial in Athens and decided its outcome by their verdict, without benefit of (or impediment from) professional judicial advice. They held every magistrate to account for the conduct of their office, most decisively of all in the great political trials which any prominent Athenian political leader might have to face at any point, and which often endangered not merely their reputation or personal fortune but their very lives.

It is not hard in this picture to pick up some of the fierce directness of Athenian democracy, and the formidable dispersion of personal power and responsibility across the citizen body which it made possible. What remains hard to see clearly is quite how this startling immediacy in Athenian politics, and the permanent and intensely personal accountability which it enforced, nevertheless fitted with and modified the continuing role of its political leaders. If Pericles ever in any sense ruled Athens as a single person, he certainly did so by continuing courtesy of, and with the clear consent of, most of his fellow citizens who took an active interest in the matter; and even Pericles in due course found himself the target of a menacing prosecution, and sentenced to pay a heavy fine.[53] Where the leaders made their mark, and laid themselves open to such acute personal danger, was by setting themselves forward to champion major changes in the law, or defend one line of policy against another, principally in the field of foreign war, and by competing to lead the armies or fleets sent off to fight in these incessant struggles. To do the first, they had to win the consent of the Assembly, and do so without the backing of an organized personal following which could ever have mustered a substantial proportion of the votes required. (Contrast any modern legislature in action.)[54] To do the second, they had to get themselves elected for the purpose. The election of the Generals, strangely to our eyes, was widely recognized as the least democratic feature of Athens's political arrangements, a clear concession to the massive importance of warfare, and the dire potential costs of losing at it.

We can picture this political regime most clearly when at its most public and dramatic, in the great set-piece debates in the Assembly at which it took its most momentous decisions. We see it above all, whether we wish to or not, through Thucydides's glittering portrayal of the trajectory of the Peloponnesian War: in the savage punishment willed upon Mitylene and almost immediately regretted, or the launching of the Sicilian expedition which ensured Athens's ultimate defeat. We know almost nothing of the ceaseless mustering of influence or flow of persuasion which gave its main leaders their followings and helped them sway their huge audiences. In so far as it did work, we do not really understand why, or quite how, it did so. All that we can plainly see is that in many ways and for a long time it just did.[55]

Looking at it from today, what we most want to believe is that Athenian democracy somehow worked because it should have done so, because, within its own narrow confines,[56] it organized power in essentially the right way, assigning it, within those terms, on the right basis, and allocating it in the right way. It is above all that conviction, however confusedly, which we locked into place, when we turned the noun which initially described it into our own name for the sole basis on which it is decent to claim political power over time in any modern political community. Quite how and why we chose to effect that transformation is what this book is about. Most of the answer must lie very far from ancient Athens either in time or in space. It might in principle even be true that none of the answer had any real connection with that vastly distant experience. The passage of the word itself might mean no more than that. It might be just an accident in the patterning of letters or sounds, across languages and territories, over a huge span of time. But that at least we clearly know to be false. The survival of democracy as a word, its penetration from ancient

Greek into a wide range of later languages, and still more its enforced translation over a much briefer time-span into the language of every other substantial human population across the globe, came less from its continuing capacity to elicit enthusiasm than from its utility in organizing thought, facilitating argument and shaping judgement.

This is extraordinarily important. It means that democracy entered the ideological history of the modern world reluctantly and facing backwards. It won its vast following not by evoking a golden past, or reminding its hearers of a glory for which they consciously longed, or with which they already urgently identified. It did so just by referring, and in less than seductive terms, to possibilities now opening up before them. Initially at least, when it did this, it helped them not merely to talk more clearly to one another about these possibilities, and the rewards and hazards which they might carry, but also to think more clearly about whether to pursue these possibilities, and at what prospective cost. Two millennia and more later this is not a role which the term can still readily play. Today the term democracy has become (as the Freudians put it) too highly cathected: saturated with emotion, irradiated by passion, tugged to and fro and ever more overwhelmed by accumulated confusion. To rescue it as an aid in understanding politics, we need to think our way past a mass of history and block our ears to many pressing importunities.

What survived from ancient democracy, for at least the next two thousand years, was not a set of institutions or practical techniques for carrying on political life. It was a body of thinking which its creators certainly envisaged (whatever else they may have also had in mind in fashioning it) as an aid in understanding politics. Its most powerful elements can be found principally in three books, by three separate authors who overlapped with one another in time: the historian Thucydides, and the philosophers Plato and his pupil Aristotle. All three spent an appreciable portion of their lives in Athens itself. None was an open partisan of democracy as a system of rule; and Plato was as harsh a critic as it has ever encountered. But all were evidently more concerned to understand what democracy was and meant than they were to sneer at it or try to subvert it.[57]

The least explicit of the three in his ultimate judgement, Thucydides, was also in some ways the most informative, and still gives by far the best sense of what the democracy was like in action. (Aristotle's most informative text on ancient democracy was not his systematic treatise the *Politics*, but his historical study of the *Constitution of Athens*, which made little or no attempt to reach an overall assessment of its merits.)[58] It was Thucydides's *History* above all on which the most committed and influential modern interpreters of Greek democracy have drawn for their most evocative evidence of what it was like, from George Grote in mid-nineteenth-century England up till today.[59] Plato and Aristotle make little attempt to convey anything of the kind. For all their differences with one another, each viewed the democracy at work through an elaborate and enormously ambitious conception of what a political regime is, or should be, for. Each, accordingly, judged the democracy of Athens and found it to some degree wanting, because its principal elements and natural operating dynamics laid it wide open to purposes of which they keenly disapproved, and largely closed it to considerations and forces which they valued far more highly.

Much of the continuing political and moral thought of the western world has been a sequence of arguments about what conclusions to draw from these three writers: naturally about many other matters too, but increasingly over the last two centuries about democracy in particular. What claims should we and should we not accept about it? In what respects should we place our trust in it, or decline to do anything of the kind? For far the larger part of this span of time, the conclusions drawn remained more or less sharply negative. Democracy, on the Athenian evidence, was not a set of institutions or techniques for conducting political life in which any community would be well advised to trust. The experience of Athens, no doubt flamboyantly misreported, was grossly discouraging. It was an experience, too, which had ended in humiliating and permanent defeat. And well before this, less than halfway through its political lifespan, it passed through the long trauma of the Peloponnesian War, staged, by a writer of superlative political intelligence and literary force, as a story of the due punishment of overweening pride, greed and deeply corrupted judgement.[60] Scholars disagree to this day over how far Thucydides was in the end an enemy to democracy itself, and how far he was merely a particularly subtle and clear-sighted analyst of how it operated in Athens over one of its darkest times and in face of its single most unnerving challenge.[61] What is certain is that many later European thinkers read his *History*, as Thomas Hobbes did as he worked through his translation in the anxious decades before England's mid-seventeenth-century Civil War,[62] as the definitive diagnosis of the malignity of democracy as a political regime. To see in Thucydides a case for democracy you had to look for it, as the great Victorian historian George Grote did, with some care. To find that case today is as hard as ever, not least over democracy's suitability as a way of conducting the foreign relations or choosing the defence strategies for a community in immediate peril, as Athens was, and we are sure to continue to be.

But it was not the text of Thucydides which preserved democracy as a format through which generation after generation of Europeans sought to understand politics. What preserved it for this purpose, and kept it durably available as an instrument of practical thought, were the more politically explicit and intellectually demanding texts of Plato and Aristotle. It is not, of course, because Plato so detested it that we have all become democrats today (however sheepishly, however evasively). To reject democracy today may just be, sooner or later, to write yourself out of politics. It is definitely to write yourself more or less at once out of polite political conversation. But there is a deep connection between Plato's open scorn and the salience of this term in all our political vocabularies. The connection is not obvious, and it is far from clear what it means. It does not run from democracy,

either as an idea or in the forms in which the Athenians institutional-
ized and realized that idea, to a set of conclusions which the idea or
its institutional embodiments simply enforce upon anyone. Instead it
runs from the experience of democracy over time, to the occasion
which that experience offered them, and the opportunity which it
provided them, for reflecting more or less accountably with others on
just what it does mean to institutionalize power in one way rather
than another, and seek to realize particular political goals through
one such institutional form rather than another. More bemusingly, it
runs from the drastic force of the conclusions reached about each
question by these two remarkable thinkers. When they gravitated
back to the vocabulary of ancient Greek classifications of forms of
government (democracy, aristocracy, oligarchy, monarchy), what
pulled successive generations of Europeans back, time after time, was
the imaginative tug of these two political assessments.

At face value, Plato's *Republic* is not a book about democracy.
Perhaps, as it says itself, it is principally about justice, or acting as one
should, or about the nature of goodness and why human beings have
sound reasons to try to see that nature clearly and respond to it with
all the imagination and energy at their disposal. It certainly discusses
good and bad forms of government for a city state (*polis*) community,
ending up by defending the exotic conclusion (as implausible then as
it remains to this day) that in the best form of government philosophers would rule. But it at least appears to do so principally in order
to clarify the grounds which every individual human being intrinsi-
cally possesses for living well rather than badly: as they should, and
not as they emphatically shouldn't.

Except in its physical setting and its cast list, furthermore, the
Republic is not obviously even a book about Athens: more a book, in
aspiration, for everywhere, as Thucydides's *History* was to be a book
for all time. But, despite the modest portion of the text devoted to
democracy and what it means, it is no distortion to see the *Republic*
as a book against democracy, and at least in part therefore in the last

instance against Athens precisely because it was so ebulliently a democracy.

There are many reasons why Plato might have disliked democracy, and held his dislike against his own community of birth and residence. It might have been simply a matter of social background, since Plato himself came from one of the grander Athenian families, forced collectively to surrender power to it over the preceding century, very much against their will. He belonged unmistakably in the ranks of the losers from democracy, as the Old Oligarch saw them: *to beltiston* (the best bit).[63] But this must be too simple, since the same was true of Pericles, as it had been of Kleisthenes before him, by no stretch of the imagination enemies to the democracy. It might have been a more immediate matter of personal milieu, the circle of friends, or even lovers, some of whom proved their enmity towards democracy in all too practical and conspicuous ways. It might, more narrowly still, have been a response to the bitter fate of his great teacher Socrates, sentenced by a democratic court to kill himself for his impiety, and for corrupting the city's youth (once more drawn principally, if not exclusively, from its grander families). Probably, it was partly all three. But none of these, not even the judicial murder[64] of Socrates, that primal stain on democracy's honour, does much to explain what Plato held against democracy, what he saw as ineliminably wrong with it.

Socrates himself had been a deliberately disturbing presence at Athens for many decades, before the Athenians at last turned on him and chose to kill him. He disturbed by challenging the terms in which his fellow citizens thought, above all about how and how not to live. As a citizen he carried out every duty required of him (above all on the battlefield) over the course of a long life; and at the end, when only deserting Athens could still save that life, he elected to stay in prison instead and kill himself as ordered, because he had no wish to go on living anywhere else, and saw the very idea of taking flight as the betrayal of a lifetime's commitment to a place, a group of fellow citizens and his deep respect for the community to which he had belonged throughout that life and striven to serve to the utmost of his own courage and imagination.[65]

This proud choice was the clearest message which Socrates left behind him; and Plato turned it, with whatever embellishments, into a text of singular power, the *Apology*.[66] In so far as Plato's case against democracy was merely a denunciation of the killing of Socrates, that denunciation is carried far more clearly and directly in the *Apology* and the *Crito* than in the *Republic* itself. The Athenians chose to kill Socrates, as far as we can tell, for a number of different reasons. One was the affront which he gave to their religious sensibilities in the hectic conditions at the end of the Peloponnesian War. Another, almost certainly, was his intimate relations with some of those who most harmed Athens during those terrible years: above all with Alkibiades and Kritias. Alkibiades was the glittering, haughty, ruthless orator and general most responsible for launching the disastrous invasion of Sicily, who eventually betrayed his fellow citizens most flamboyantly by deserting to the enemy. Kritias was the most brutal and domineering of the oligarchic leaders who crushed the democracy at the war's close and tyrannized over their fellow citizens, until they too were overthrown in outrage in their turn. These were not, in retrospect, friendships which it was easy to excuse. But Socrates himself was no advocate of tyranny or treason. When Plato set out the lessons which he had drawn himself, in the more elaborate and searching explorations of the *Republic*, what he too offered was in no sense a defence of tyranny,[67] or even of the social, political or economic privileges of the loftier elements in any existing society.

In all its elusiveness and power, that offer centred on a defence of the need for rule and order, and the steady recognition of what genuinely is good, and on an uncompromising rejection of the democracy's claims to provide any of these, except by sporadic and fleeting accident. *The Republic* is a book with many morals. It is also a deliberately teasing book, and open to an endless range of interpretations. But no serious reader could fail to recognize that it comes down firmly against democracy.[68]

Plato makes many charges against democratic rule, and the way of life which forms around it and arises out of it. He sees it in essence as an all but demented solvent of value, decency and good judgement, as the rule of the foolish, vicious, and always potentially brutal, and a frontal assault on the possibility of a good life, lived with others on the scale of a community. The principle of democratic rule is equality, the presumption that, when it comes to shaping a community and exercising power, everyone's judgement deserves as much weight as everyone else's. That presumption in turn implies that there can be no lasting shape to a democratic community, and nothing reliable about the ways in which power is exercised within it. What this means, as Thomas Hobbes pointed out two thousand years later, is that in a democratic community there can be no real security for anyone or anything except by sheer fluke.[69]

Exactly the same principle applies, with equally calamitous effects, within the individual personality and in the individual life.[70] For the democratic man (the individual personality formed by and appropriate to a democracy) there is neither order nor compulsion (*taxis oute anagke*) in his life.[71] For him it is precisely this shapeless unconstraint which makes a life free and sweet and blessed (*makarion*: the key word of the Beatitudes in the Sermon on the Mount).[72] Plato acknowledges the vitality of this way of life, and sees how enviable its colour and diversity can readily make it.[73] But for him the rage for liberty[74] which accompanies and corresponds to its commitment to equality ('Anyone free by nature could see only a democratic *polis* as fit to live in')[75] will infallibly undermine democratic rule and dissolve every form of authority within it. It disrupts and in the end destroys the ties between teacher and taught, father and son, children and parents, young and old, foreigners (*metics*) and citizens, free persons and slaves, even human beings and animals.[76] Any constraint at all comes to be seen as slavery.[77] The chaos which this unleashes must end ineluctably in arbitrary rule (tyranny): a precipitous descent from democracy, the height of liberty, to the fullest and harshest slavery.[78]

Plato's assault was not an astute prediction of the democracy's future over the next two generations. It captured nothing of what in due course brought democracy to an end in Athens itself. But it raised the stakes in assessing political regimes to an unprecedented height. Democratic Athens shrugged Plato himself aside without discernible effort. But the challenge which he levelled at the democracy's preferred conception of what it meant remains as potent as ever today, in a world which has chosen to embrace at least the word and some aspects of the idea in preference to any of its innumerable competitors across the ages. How can this of all political ideas in the end make any stable sense? How can it claim allegiance and win loyalty, while it endlessly takes to pieces every other form of order or basis of inhibition around which groups of human beings have tried to organize their lives?

Plato saw democracy above all as a presumptuous and grossly ugly idea, whose demerits could be read clearly in its erratic passage through the Greek world. The chaos of the idea itself was realized in the political disruptions of the communities to which it came, and the disorder of the ways of life which it sanctioned. While not a reliable recipe for the worst life, as tyranny was,[79] it all but guaranteed a bad life to any community that chose to adopt it, and effortlessly subverted every attempt to lead a good life together in close association with a community of others. This was an extreme view, and clearly derived not from careful study of what did or did not occur in many places over a long period of time, but from brooding on the idea itself.

Aristotle, Plato's most gifted and least dependent pupil, had far less confidence in what can be judged about the human world merely by considering ideas in themselves. He set himself as well to assess the merits of contending political formulae by identifying what did and did not occur in most cases in the human world when they were applied to it. The lessons about democracy which he drew from these enquiries were far more extensive and complicated than Plato's verdict in the *Republic*.[80] They are also far less conclusive in their ultimate implications. Plato loathed democracy and did so without inhibition. Some have seen, in his entire conception of knowledge, a systematization of that overwhelming distaste. Aristotle was more sober, less carried away by his feelings and more open to the judgements of others in the conclusions which he eventually drew. For him democracy (*demokratia*) was not itself one of the good forms of rule,[81] since it amounted to government not in the interest of the community as a whole but merely of the poor (*ton aporon*). But government by the many (*to plethos*)[82] could nevertheless prove a good form of government, provided only that it was exercised for the common good. When he thought it was, Aristotle himself chose to call it not democracy but *politeia* (polity or, more informatively, constitutional government). *Politeia* was distinguished from democracy not merely by a difference in purpose and disposition (a commitment to collective good rather than group advantage), but also by a different and more elaborate institutional structure. The purpose of this structure was not to enforce the will of some upon others at the latter's expense (like oligarchy, or at the extreme tyranny), but to distribute powers and responsibilities as far as possible in accordance with capacities, and thus draw on a far wider range of energies and skills, and elicit a correspondingly broad range of sympathy and loyalty by doing so.

Politeia is not the only form of government which aims at the common advantage[83] and is therefore compatible with justice. Monarchy and aristocracy, the government of a single person or a superior group, might in principle set themselves the same goal and vindicate their claim to justice in so far as they contrived to reach it. But their success or failure depended quite directly on the virtue, discernment and luck of the rulers themselves. Only in the case of *politeia*, Aristotle suggests strongly, does the prospect for realizing justice in practice in the government of a community depend largely on the institutional organization of power and the resulting division of responsibilities within it.

Aristotle does not seem ever to have supposed, as later followers of Thomas Hobbes or Jeremy Bentham often did, that the institutional organization of power, or the predictable workings of individual interest within it, might somehow furnish dependably just outcomes, without the need to pass through and engage the purposes of human agents, who took justice for their own goal and accepted the constraints which it inevitably imposed upon them. He did not think of political institutions as a substitute for personal virtue, but more as a way of eliciting and sustaining it, and a means for economizing on what might always prove a very scarce good.

Aristotle, it seems clear, did not draw the distinction between democracy and *politeia* from current common usage. He developed it to bring into focus a key contrast. The point of that contrast was to answer two large and pregnant questions: what is the point of human beings living together in substantial numbers? And how exactly must they organize their lives together to best secure that point? The point, as he saw it, was to explore and define together compelling conceptions of how it does and does not make good sense to live, a search that depended profoundly upon language, imagination, and the balance of sympathy and antipathy between human beings; and then, to realize the more compelling of these conceptions to the highest degree possible in the living of real lives. Even as Aristotle himself envisaged it, this proved an open-ended and somewhat centrifugal task.[84] It has lost greatly in imaginative force, and ceded much ground in recent centuries to the very different enticements of the quest to enhance material comforts and multiply personal amusements. But, like the latter, the principal dynamic of our own economic energies, Aristotle's goal too can, without mistranslation, be described as the pursuit of happiness.[85] What is striking for us in how Aristotle saw that quest is not the value he attached to experience and the will to shape a life, but the extent to which he viewed a system of participatory self-government as an aid in its pursuit, and the peculiarities of the Greek *polis* as a special opportunity for attaining it.

Because of the massive impact of his book *The Politics* on the thought of Europe, and then the world, both idiosyncrasies have proved to matter. The special eligibility of the *polis* as a setting in which to pursue the good life together is an elusive and confusing theme[86] which need not concern us. But the idea that a system of participatory self-government will aid its pursuit provides the central strand of the story we need to follow for most of the next two thousand years. Two elements in Aristotle's view are especially important. One is the far juster and more careful assessment of the merits of government by the multitude, where this is based on the acceptance of a common good, and on some willingness to pursue it together, and where it is also organized in a way that uses the capacities of its citizens and restrains their more malevolent and dangerous characteristics in an effective way. The second, in the end less decisively, but for a very long time every bit as consequentially, was Aristotle's decision not merely to contrast a healthy with a pathological version of rule by the multitude, but also to reserve the term *demokratia* for the pathological version.

The Greek champions of democracy praised and fought for rule by the multitude (*to plethos*), by a broad array of political arrangements. But, unlike Aristotle, they either did not choose to write books, or failed to ensure the preservation of any books which they did write. Their picture and their case have largely passed from the earth, leaving the scantiest traces behind.[87] *Politeia* for Aristotle we might say (using a device of Hobbes) was simply democracy liked, while *demokratia* (democracy to you and me) was democracy keenly misliked. Not only was the word itself marked negatively; still more insistently, it was marked in a way and through a set of thoughts that explained all too evocatively just why it deserved such suspicion.

Democracy in Aristotle's final vocabulary, the vocabulary he eventually handed on to medieval Europe and thus to modern understandings of politics, was a form of government which simply did not aim at a common good. It was a regime of naked group interest, unapologetically devoted to serving the many at the expense of the wealthier, the better, the more elevated, the more fastidious or virtuous. As they took their bearings through the vocabulary which Aristotle had passed on to them, it is not hard to see why generation after generation of European thinkers shied away from this word. Not only was democracy violent, unstable and menacing to those who already held wealth, power or even pretension, it was, Aristotle taught many centuries of European speakers to mean, ill-intentioned and disreputable in itself through and through.

Why then have we now, so recently and yet so completely, changed our mind? (Or, if not our mind, at least our verbal habits, and the feelings which we attach to them?) The first of those questions is blunt, and perhaps not too difficult to answer (though it is hard to pluck a plausible answer off the library shelf). But the second – just what lies behind our selection of the term *democracy* itself as privileged vector for political legitimacy and decency across the globe – is more elusive. To grasp this, we need to see a good deal more than how and why we have reversed the values attached to that word, shifting it back from pejorative to neutral, and then, more tentatively, onward to all but untrammelled enthusiasm. Such shifts in the evaluative connotations of political words occur during most protracted political struggles and often serve to register their outcomes.[88] The real question is not why we feel more warmly towards democracy today, or why our greater warmth has crept into our vocabulary choices. It is why we have chosen, somehow, out of the entire prior history of human speech, this single, for so long so baleful, Greek noun to carry this huge weight of political hope and commitment. Why should we have chosen a Greek word at all? Why should we (that large majority of us who are not Europeans) have chosen a European word? Why should it be this of all Greek words? Why is it this set of letters and this loose blur of sound on which we have come to place this vast gamble?

No doubt, if we see the matter quite like this, we must be grossly in error, either in understanding what we are doing, or in placing the bet itself. It cannot possibly be sane to entrust the destiny of the species[89] to an arrangement of letters or a set of sounds. But that, of course, is not what we suppose ourselves to be doing. What we believe ourselves to be doing (no doubt correctly enough) is to place our trust in what that word picks out, however vaguely, in the world: in a more or less coherent approach to assigning power and acknowledging responsibility within the ever more complicated network of political, economic, social and legal communities to which we belong and on which we have no real option but to depend.

Democracy has come to be our preferred name for the sole basis on which we accept either our belonging or our dependence. We may not embrace either with joy, or even ease; but, at least on this proviso, these might be communities which on balance we can accept rather than repudiate. It is, above all, our term for political identification: we, the people. What the term means (even now, when that so clearly is not how matters are in the outside world)[90] is that the people (we) hold power and exercise rule. That was what it meant at Athens, where the claim bore some relation to the truth. That is what it means today, when it very much appears a thumping falsehood: a bare-faced lie. Much of the history of modern politics has been a long, slow, resentful reconciliation to this obvious falsehood, a process within which democracy has often proved a far from preferred term for political identification.[91] Across this struggle, with all its swirls and eddies, and stagnant backwaters, the vicissitudes of democracy have often been of negligible importance. There is no special reason to believe that to focus on it will give either clear or economical guidance on what exactly has been at stake or why the battles have come out as they have. Where there has proved to be something very special about democracy is in the lonely eminence it has now won. In that outcome, however temporary or precarious it may prove, we can see quite clearly, there is something of immense importance which we reasonably can (and perhaps now must) set ourselves to try to understand.

One side of the story, the embrace of this one word, has, for all its intricacy, a single relatively clear shape in space and time. It is, we have already noted, a story with a beginning. It is, too, a story with a single heroine. (*Demokratia* is a feminine noun.) Or, if that seems too literal-minded a way of putting it, a story with a single collective hero, the *demos*, first of Athens and now, potentially, of anywhere in the world where a set of human beings cares to think of themselves as belonging together by right and responsibility, and through and because of who they are.

The other side of the story, the words not chosen, has no shape at all. It has no discernible beginning and no self-identifying sites: not even a definite cast list, let alone a manageable array of heroes or heroines. Much of it, obviously, is too unheroic and inconsequential to bear telling. There cannot be a story of all the myriads upon myriads of unchosen words which fall by the wayside.

We cannot think about the casting aside of potential rivals, or passing them by on the other side, all at once and through a single evidently appropriate structure. Still less can we sift consecutively through all these interminable rejections or evasions in any coherent way. All we can readily do is to recognize the different shapes of enquiry appropriate to these three questions we have already raised. Why firstly a European word? Why secondly a Greek word at all? Why thirdly this of all Greek words?

The main brunt of the answers to the first and third of these questions falls clearly on the last two centuries or so of world history. They are facets of the answer to a very different type of question: why is it that one way of organizing and competing for power, the capitalist representative democracy, has had such overwhelming competitive success over the last sixty years? It was this Greek word, of all

Greek words, because it names something about that now dominant political format which is closely (if perhaps misleadingly) tied to what gave it that awesome competitive edge. It was a European word because, in the end, it was European powers and not China which forged the world capitalist economy, and built the successive empires within and through which that economy was largely shaped, and because, once their power had ebbed, it was the United States of America, very much an heir to the language of European politics, and in no small part built through that language, which stepped commandingly into their abandoned shoes.

To get beneath this somewhat glib level of understanding, we would need to view the history of human life on earth as a single blind amorphous struggle between human beings to get their own way, and see right across it and with steady detachment why exactly the balance of advantage has tilted endlessly towards some and against others along the way. It is not hard to see why the global name for legitimate political authority does not come from the language of the San Bushmen or Evans-Pritchard's Nuer in the Southern Sudan,[92] their homeland now seared by decades of repression. But there is no crisply convincing way to see why it should have been Europe rather than China[93] which made the world a single crowded painful common habitat for our species, and so made Europe's bigotries and parochialisms a global world-historical force, instead of a mere local deformity or a continental stigma. To see the place of the words not chosen we must take many things as given, above all the densely overlapping histories of capitalism and imperialism, the shapers of the world in which we all now belong.

The odd one out in these three questions is why the privileged European word which has come to enjoy this startling world-historical destiny should have been a Greek word at all. It might have come instead from further north or further east, from a Norse or Teutonic or Turkish language. It might, still more plainly, have come from slightly further west, from the language of Greece's Roman conquerors, or the later Romance languages which in due course stemmed from these. All of these languages recognize some form of authorization through popular political choice. Some for a time loomed large within Europe itself, and even beyond it in the global struggle for wealth and power. But, whatever would have happened by now if the Third Reich had somehow won the Second World War, only one of these languages looks today like a truly formidable rival, the Latin language of Rome's great empire. That language still gives us a large proportion of our vocabulary of political evaluation: citizenship, legality, liberty, public and private, constitution, republic, union, federation, perhaps, directly or at one remove, state itself.

What it does not give us is the word *democracy*. And that, not because *democracy* does not happen to be a word which the Romans themselves went to the trouble of borrowing. Not only is democracy not a classical Latin word. It is not a Roman way of thought. It does not express how the Romans (any of them, as far as we know) envisaged politics. It is not that the Latin word *populus* (people) is at all a bad translation for the Greek work *demos*. Nor is it that the Romans in no sense conceived the Roman *populus* as the ultimate source of Rome's law, and hence of political authority within Rome. It is simply that they never conceived that *populus* as ruling directly itself, unimpeded, and within a framework of authority which it was permanently free to revise for itself.[94] The unit of political authority in Roman public inscriptions (of which there were many) was the Senate and People of Rome (*Senatus Populusque Romanus: SPQR*). In that formula (and by no means only in that formula), the Senate came first.

There is much else to say on this question, some of it powerfully argued over the last few decades in Oxford and elsewhere.[95] There were, perhaps, other possible futures for the Roman Republic than the military subversion and imperial subjection in which it came to its bitter end.[96] There could perhaps have been another outcome to the struggles of the champions of the *populus*, the brother Tribunes,

Tiberius and Gaius Gracchus, than the political murders to which they succumbed. Perhaps it might even have been possible to keep the Republic in being, alongside the armies with which it conquered most of the world it knew, and for Rome's empire to have been an empire only for the rulers whom it overthrew.[97] For almost fifteen hundred years the political thinking of European communities repeatedly circled back to brood on these possibilities, and try to summon them back into life.[98] But that was not the history which in fact occurred. It was not the history that forged the world in which we live. It has nothing to tell us about why democracy should now be our name for duly exercised political power.

The Romans themselves, as far as we know, never used the term democracy to interpret or assess their own political arrangements,[99] or indeed anyone else's. It was, however, used about them by at least two sophisticated Greek analysts of Rome's historical development as a political community, Polybius and Cassius Dio.[100] Of these two, Polybius was the loftier thinker. He drew systematically on the accumulated resources of Greek political thought to analyse the basis of Rome's rise to mastery over the Mediterranean world and explore its future prospects.[101] In many ways his *Histories* remained, for well over a thousand years, the most systematic attempt to grasp the dynamics of Rome's remarkable rise. In it, Polybius also made some effort to grasp the relations between the basis of this extraordinary ascent and the internal vulnerabilities to which, many centuries later, it, like any other human community, was eventually bound to succumb.

Polybius saw Rome from a singularly instructive angle. Born and raised in a leading political family in Megalopolis, the effective capital of the Achaean League, he was brought back to Italy as a hostage in his youth, following the Roman conquest of Greece in 168BC by the Consul Aemilius Paullus, and lived for decades in close contact with his conqueror's household, for at least part of the time as tutor to one of his sons. That son, Scipio Aemilianus, more than twenty years later, was to be the Roman general who finally defeated and sacked the city of Carthage, Rome's leading rival for Mediterranean domination for a full century beforehand, and half a century earlier, under its own great general Hannibal, very close indeed to being its final destroyer. Amongst other qualities, Polybius had a fine sense of historical occasion and records with some éclat the tearful response of his distinguished pupil, looking down over Carthage in flames, to the recognition that one day (as it happened over five hundred years later), Rome too would fall for ever.[102]

In some ways the picture which Polybius painted of Rome's political order is now hard to read. Large parts of his text have not come down to us. His book was composed over an extended period of time and, like Aristotle's *Politics*, it probably changed significantly in its central subject matter from the author's point of view in the course of composition. As far as we can judge today, it is also reasonable to conclude that some aspects of his thinking never became entirely clear or coherent. But what is unmistakable is that it seems never to have occurred to him that Rome in the period after it ceased to be a monarchy, several centuries earlier, had at any point become a democracy. Viewed from one of the city's principal political families, suppliers of Consuls for generation after generation, this was not surprising. Like Aristotle, if a trifle less clear-headedly, Polybius fully acknowledged the practical value of a democratic element in the organization of a political community, and in his case more particularly in the organization of Rome's Republic. But, again like Aristotle, he was at pains to insist that this value depended strictly upon its firm restraint by two further elements, aristocratic and monarchical, which restricted power of initiative over many issues, in the Roman case above all to the Senate and Consuls.[103] It would have been extremely odd for a client of Scipio's family to see Rome as a democracy, even if the prospects for its male members to win high political office continued to depend on their capacity to get elected by citizen assemblies.[104]

A simple comparison between the composition, authorization and practical powers of the Athenian Council (*Boule*) and Rome's Senate shows just how implausible any such equation is,[105] as it plainly was to Polybius himself. What is striking, however, was Polybius's judgement, not that Rome already was (or could readily be conceived by anyone as being) a democracy, but that in the long run, and disastrously, it might in due course become one. If and when it did, Polybius warned, that condition could not last long, and must inevitably destroy the city itself.[106] If the flames of Carthage were the portent of a final foreign conquest, a sack of Rome, like Alaric the Goth's, Polybius himself also contemplated the possibility of a purely domestic end to Rome's great journey: the coming of democracy.

At this point in his analysis, Polybius's vocabulary muddied somewhat, and democracy was retitled, following a Platonic precedent, *ochlocracy*[107] (the very worst sort of democracy, the rule of the lowest and most disorderly component of the *demos* or, as the English later put it, the mob). But this was more the deepening of an insult than a refinement in diagnosis. The political structures (*politeia*) which had enabled Rome to conquer most of the world it knew, with its deft, if wholly unplanned,[108] balance of contending elements, might all too readily end in the unrestricted exercise of power by just one of these elements, with a loss not merely of all external restraints upon that power, but also of every internal inhibition amongst those who then exerted it.

Polybius's portrait of Rome disappeared from view completely for a millennium and a half. But before it did so, and when it came back into view in the aftermath of the Renaissance, it could hardly have done less to recommend democracy as a promising regime form to the world at large. Seen through his eyes, democracy was the worst nightmare or the final ruin of by far the most imposing historical model of which any European was even aware: both a symbol and a potential mechanism for the doom of an entire civilization. Who would have thought that this word, of all words, was due to conquer the world?

The word *demokratia* entered the Latin language, as far as we know, in the 1260s, in the translation by the Dominican Friar William of Moerbeke of Aristotle's *Politics*,[109] the most systematic analysis of politics as a practical activity which survived from the ancient world. (It is important for the intellectual history of Islam and the political history of the modern Middle East that it had not already entered the Arabic language, with the very elaborate and substantially earlier reception of Aristotle's thought in the great centres of Islamic civilization.)[110] Once duly latinized, it became available, and has remained so ever since, as an aid in assessing political practices and possibilities. In this guise, it soon proved its utility, less because there was a throng of sovereign democracies to hand to consider, than because, as Aristotle had carefully noted, very different sorts of political regimes may each have some democratic aspects. The self-governing city states of a thirteenth-century Italy had their own conceptions of the purpose of their internal organization and used the Roman language of republican liberty extensively to explain and commend it in all its turbulent variety.[111] Some cities combined relatively broad citizen bodies with elective magistrates and a clear legal framework for the exercise of power. But none of these chose to adopt the new-fangled Greek vocabulary of Moerbeke to vindicate the merits of its own regime. Ptolemy of Lucca, the continuator of St Thomas Aquinas's book *The Rule of Princes*,[112] recognized the second-century BC creation of the office of Tribune at Rome as adding an element of democratic primacy (*democraticus principatus*) to the unmistakably aristocratic primacy in its republican regime, epitomized by the Senate and Consuls.[113] Bartolus of Sassoferrato, a leading civil lawyer writing at much the same time about city regimes (*De Regimine Civium*) and with his eye very much upon contemporary Italy, distinguished, as Aristotle enjoined, between good and bad versions of the rule of a few (*aristocratia* and *oligarchia*) and good and bad versions of the rule of the many (*politia* or *democratia*).[114] But no medieval or early modern

Italian writer bluntly described any Italian city government of which we know as a democracy; and anyone deploying Aristotle's vocabulary in Latin (or any other language into which it came to be imported) could only have been insulting the city in question, by doing so.

It took a good three centuries for the term to recapture some of its Greek descriptive neutrality and simplicity, and shake off the stigmatizing company of its more respectable Aristotelian twin *politeia*. Even once it had begun to do so, *politeia* (polity) at least retained its strong positive connotations: not merely a mixed form of government, which somehow combined the best of monarchy, aristocracy and democracy, but a structure which contrived to constrain democracy in ways which could reasonably hope to keep it on its best behaviour.

Only in the seventeenth century does the term at last begin to shake off these negative connotations and be used, slowly and with much hesitation, to defend and justify existing political arrangements or insist on the urgent need for new ones. It does so in several different settings. The opportunity was clearly there for a Catalan early in the seventeenth century. The Perpignan lawyer Andreu Bosch firmly insisted that Catalonia under its existing constitution with the two core institutions, the Cortes and the Generalitet, was in fact governed on a democratic basis, as, according 'to common law, in all republics and towns, the government simply is the people' (*es lo govern lo poble*).[115] On this occasion the opportunity to describe the regime itself roundly as a democracy does not seem to have been taken up. But, as the century went by, it at last began to be so, most strikingly in the powerful, commercially dynamic and quasi-republican regime of the United Netherlands, in stray places in the tough, disabused writings of Johan and Pieter de la Court,[116] in Franciscus Van den Enden's *The Free Political Propositions and Considerations of State in 1665*,[117] and above all in the deep but obscure reflections of the dissident Jew Benedict de Spinoza.[118]

Even at this point the term *democracy* was far from serving as a rallying cry. In the great seventeenth-century struggles which it is natural for us to see as blazing a trail for democracy, and most of all in the Leveller drive to use a greatly broadened franchise to hold England's government to the active consent of its subjects,[119] the term democracy plays no public role. Where it does begin to appear, more and more insistently, is in anxious conservative responses to the great seething mass of rebellion which shook England's state to its foundations. Thomas Hobbes himself placed the blame for the Great Rebellion and the regicide itself on many different factors, not least the translation of the Christian Bible into the vernacular,[120] the development of Protestant theology and the endless proliferation of priestly ambitions. But pride of place amongst his villains falls to the 'democratical gentlemen' of the House of Commons, puffed up with the cheap and silly learning of the Universities,[121] and giddy with the republican indiscretions of the ancient world.[122]

When Hobbes described the Members of the Long Parliament as 'democratical', he was certainly not using their word, and scarcely providing a fair description of any beliefs which they actually held. But in the long run he was perhaps right to be so confident that he could see more clearly than they did, not merely into the sources of the beliefs and attitudes which they held, but also into the political implications which ultimately followed from them. Perhaps by the time of the English Civil War, and certainly by the time that it became available for recollection in anything but tranquillity, the potential of this pejorative analytical term to pick out potent sources of allegiance was at last in clear view. From then on, its rise to world mastery, at least at a verbal level,[123] was to be just a matter of time. In the centuries since the printing of Hobbes's *Behemoth* (1676), allegiances have come and gone and regimes have risen and fallen. But all the time, and ever more insistently, one word has worked its way forward. It has shaken off its esoteric and shame-ridden past and claimed an open and proud future. This is much more than its due, and a very poor description of the real basis of its triumph. But it is a striking and consequential enough shift in human experience to require recognition in its own right.

By the beginning of the next century this shift in its apparent powers of attraction becomes easier to pick up. It appears first very much in private self-description. We find, for example, the still relatively youthful Irish Deist John Toland, illegitimate son of a Catholic priest and already author of the widely execrated *Christianity not Mysterious* (1696), boasting in 1705 of his exploits in publicizing the lives and editing the works of James Harrington, John Milton and other advocates of 'democratical schemes of government'.[124] But this was firmly in the context of a private letter, and far from frank even in its own terms. Toland was a figure of disorientating charm and legendary indiscretion, who maddened everyone who had to deal with him, from the loftiest aristocratic patrons to the grubbiest fellow hacks. He was also indefatigable in his own self-advancement and notably unfastidious in the techniques which he was willing to deploy in promoting it. Yet even Toland would have hesitated to proclaim his political allegiances in public with such unflinching clarity.

To see what made the shift possible, we need steadier and franker views. For these, it is hard to do better than turn back to two of the seventeenth century's greatest political thinkers, Hobbes and Spinoza. Hobbes wrote at some length against democracy and did his pungent best to pin down its principal demerits once and for all. He saw it, as his ancient sources encouraged him to do, as disorderly, unstable and intensely dangerous. But he also saw it very much in his own way, as combining much of the insecurity of the state of nature (a condition of comprehensive and standing peril) with a level of mutual offence only conceivable in a setting in which human beings were expected to listen to one another patiently and at undue length. It was a paradise, especially, for orators (or those who fancied themselves as such), and also in effect a form of tyranny by orators: of subjection against one's will to the force for others, not of the better argument, but of the more potent speech.[125] Hobbes captured better than anyone before or since the pain of oratorical defeat, and the centrality of these feelings within democratic participation for anyone who cares about what is at stake but has no particular oratorical flair:

some will say, That a Popular State *is much to be preferr'd before a* Monarchicall; *because that, where all men have a hand in publique businesses, there all have an opportunity to shew their wisedome, knowledge, and eloquence, in deliberating matters of the greatest difficulty and moment; which by reason of that desire of praise which is bred in humane nature, is to them who excell in such like faculties, and seeme to themselves to exceed others, the most delightfull of all things. But in a Monarchy, this same way to obtain praise, and honour, is shut up to the greatest part of Subjects; and what is a grievance, if this be none? Ile tell you: To see his opinion whom we scorne, preferr'd before ours; to have our wisedome undervalued before our own faces; by an uncertain tryall of a little vaine glory, to undergoe most certaine enmities (for this cannot be avoided, whether we have the better, or the worse); to hate, and to be hated, by reason of the disagreement of opinions; to lay open our secret Counsells, and advises to all, to no purpose, and without any benefit; to neglect the affaires of our own Family: These, I say, are grievances. But to be absent from a triall of wits, although those trialls are pleasant to the Eloquent is not therefore a grievance to them, unless we will say, that it is a grievance to valiant men to be restrained from fighting, because they delight in it.*[126]

The key egalitarian prerogative of the Athenian *demos*, the equal right to address one's fellow citizens as they take their sovereign decisions (*isegoria*), has always been offset by the less agreeable (but accompanying) duty to hear out the persuasions of every fellow citizen who chooses to exercise it, and by the still more painful duty to accept whatever these fellow citizens together then proceed to decide. Under the conditions of a modern commercial society, the rewards of this egalitarian prerogative were not merely offset but effortlessly outweighed by its evident inconsequentiality for the great majority and by the ever more prohibitive opportunity costs of exercising it. Modern liberty (as Benjamin Constant assured the audience at the Athénée Royale in 1817 in the wake of Napoleon's fall and the Bourbon Restoration), the liberty to do what you like for at least a substantial proportion of your life, now made almost everyone an offer it was all but impossible to refuse. Ancient liberty, the opportunity to do your best to bend the sovereign judgement of your fellows to your own will by pressing your views upon them in public, promised almost nothing in practice. But in the nightmare months of the Terror, the ghost of that ancient promise had raised the temperature of politics to fever pitch.[127] Better a quiet and enjoyable life, even under a monarchy of some absurdity. To pursue ancient liberty under the conditions of modern commerce was to clutch at a mirage, to suffer in return a penal weight of irritation and ineffectuality, and to run in addition a considerable and pointless risk of extreme danger.

As Constant pressed the point in the wake of the Jacobin Terror, it came out as a demonstration of the superiority of modern representative democracy over ancient participatory democracy. In Hobbes's hands, however, the main thrust of the case was still against the dispersion of political power across the adult membership of a political community and in favour, by contrast, of the superiority of monarchy over every other form of regime. Even Hobbes, though, conceded not merely that democracy was a plausible basis on which for political society to have begun, but also that it was in a sense equivalent to the establishment of a political order in the first place. Since a political order can only be created through the choices of individual human beings, it must at its inception simply be their own personal agreement to accept a common structure of authority over themselves. It was that agreement which made them into a People, a single entity, capable of ruling and exerting authority, and not a mere multitude of quarrelsome individuals.[128]

Once converted into a People and rendered capable of ruling, any People could choose to rule itself,[129] through a 'Councell' of all the citizens with equal rights to vote (a *Democraty*), or to have its rule done for it by 'Councells', where the right to vote was more narrowly restricted (an *Aristocraty*), or by a single person (a *Monarch*). In each of these, Hobbes strikingly insists, the People and the Multitude remain quite distinct.

> *The* People *rules in all Governments, for even in* Monarchies *the* People *Commands; for the* People *wills by the will of* one man; *but the Multitude are Citizens, that is to say, Subjects. In a* Democraty, *and* Aristocraty, *the Citizens are the* Multitude, *but the* Court *is the* People. *And in a* Monarchy, *the Subjects are the* Multitude *and (however it seeme a Paradox) the King is the People.*

For his contemporaries it certainly was a paradox to equate King with People, and a paradox viewed either way round. The equation incensed Charles I well before the People (or those who claimed to act in its name) placed him on trial for his life and took it on the scaffold.[130]

Hobbes was too eccentric a thinker and too independent a person to find tact easy; but he viewed the turmoil of mid-seventeenth-century England from a highly privileged angle, as tutor briefly to the young Charles II at his exiled court in Paris, on tour with a miscellany of young aristocrats of varying educational susceptibility, and as long-term tutor and secretary to the Cavendish family.[131] No one could have mistaken him for an advocate of 'democratical schemes of government'. Spinoza was distinctly less well connected (except with other intellectual luminaries),[132] but, as even Hobbes noticed, if anything was even less disposed to tact.[133] Born as the second son of a prosperous Portuguese Jewish family in a fine merchant house in the centre of Amsterdam,[134] his worldly prospects were transformed for the worse by the destruction of its extensive foreign business by English maritime predators and Barbary pirates, and ensuing bankruptcy[135] and his own vituperative excommunication from the Sephardic community at the age of twenty-three, for his evil opinions and acts, his abominable heresies and his monstrous deeds.[136] The philosophical basis for these heterodoxies seems to have been laid remarkably early; and it gave him a considerable underground reputation for intellectual originality and incisiveness, which lasted from his late twenties until his death and well beyond. He appears from that time onwards to have lived principally on earnings from grinding optical lenses, with some pecuniary help from his friends,[137] and to have devoted the bulk of his energies to developing a remarkable intellectual system, which set the life of human beings as a whole within the order of nature with unique steadiness and resolution.

The political implications of this system were summarized in two works, the scandalous *Tractatus Theologico-Politicus*, published surreptitiously in 1670 (which cemented his reputation as an atheist by offending every extant religious confession within range), and the *Tractatus Politicus*, left unfinished at his death and published only posthumously.[138] Both texts say many appreciative things about democracy (as well as some less appreciative things). The *Tractatus Politicus* breaks off with a brief (and notably perfunctory) defence of the view that there is no pressing occasion to treat women as political equals. (They have less physical strength; and treating them as equals will aggravate men's already dismaying tendency to inane sexual competition.) But before it does so,[139] it certainly appears on the point of settling down to defend an egalitarian and participatory democracy as the ideal political order. It is not clear quite how this defence would have run, nor how it would have fitted with his earlier acknowledgement that no states have proved less lasting than popular or democratic ones, and none as apt to be disrupted by sedition.[140] What is clear, however, is that Spinoza abhorred political disorder and fought hard and consistently throughout his life for the primacy of the human need for freedom of thought and expression. This commitment was clearly central to both his major political works; and he was at pains to insist that the need could be satisfied as readily and securely under a sound monarchy or aristocracy as in a democracy, and would pose no more threat to the viability of the former than to that of the latter. Human beings need to think freely and express their thoughts without fear. They also need a clear and effective framework of authority to protect the lives which they live together. Neither need necessarily encroaches on the other, and neither has any clear priority over the other.

Democracy is a state in which sovereignty (the authority to make and repeal laws and decide on war or peace, the key prerequisite for every commonwealth) is exercised by a Council composed of the common multitude.[141] A commonwealth holds and exerts the power of a multitude led as though by a single mind,[142] a union of minds (*animorum unio*) which does not make sense unless the commonwealth itself (*civitas*) aims to the highest degree at what seems, to sound reason, useful for all men.[143] If democratic commonwealths are shorter lived and more disrupted than their aristocratic or monarchical counterparts, the overwhelming verdict of the tradition on which Spinoza drew, this union of minds was scarcely more likely to persist in a democracy. Nor was there any obvious reason why Spinoza should have seen democracies as wedded any more dependably to freedom of thought or expression. All he clearly believed in this respect, like Hobbes and virtually all other natural law thinkers, was that democracy was closest in structure to the basis of all political authority, the universal agreement, whether historical or presumptively rational, of the human beings over whom it was to be exercised. In this sense democracy was, as Spinoza insists in several places, the ultimate source of all political regimes,[144] and in just the same sense the most natural of all regimes. Democracy, the *Tractatus Politicus* concludes, is the third and completely absolute type of state.[145] In it all children of citizens, all native born inhabitants, and anyone else whom the laws choose to recognize, have a natural right to vote in the supreme council of the state and hold public office, a right which they can lose only through personal crime or infamy.[146] Democracy in this sense is[147] the most natural of regimes. It comes closest to preserving the freedom which nature allows to each human being. No one transfers their natural rights to anyone else so completely that they are never consulted again; but each transfers these rights to a majority of the community to which they belong. 'And so all remain, as they previously were in the state of nature, equal.'[148] In both works the potential disadvantages of transferring these rights to smaller numbers of people or to a single individual are explored in a variety of ways.

Spinoza at no point played a public role in the politics of the Netherlands. The exiguousness of his means and the notoriety of his opinions would scarcely have permitted him to do so even had he wished to. But he was for a time a clear partisan and may even have been a personal acquaintance and potential client of Holland's greatest seventeenth-century statesman, the Grand Pensionary Johan de Witt. On the day when the two de Witt brothers were dragged from prison and lynched by their fellow citizens, an *ochlocratic* moment if ever there was one,[149] Spinoza himself was living just across the town in the Hague. Four years later, he confided in person to the philosopher Leibniz that only his Lutheran landlord's understandable insistence on locking the house up had prevented him from sallying forth the same day to put up a placard denouncing the murderers as utter barbarians, and being promptly torn to pieces himself.[150] Some intellectuals can stretch a point in retrospective accounts of their own heroism on such occasions; but everything we know about Spinoza suggests that, if he said this at all, he can only have been telling the simple truth.

What exactly was he trying to tell his contemporaries about democracy? He was not, quite certainly, seeking to assure them that liberty of thought and expression, for him the most urgent of all distinctively human needs,[151] was any safer in a democracy than anywhere else.[152] He cannot have been telling them that democracy gave them any more solid guarantee of their individual physical security than its more potent rivals. He was scarcely telling them that democracy was a particularly effective form of state in face of armed threats from foreign enemies,[153] let alone boasting, like the English republican Algernon Sidney,[154] of the superior capacity of any form of republic, democratic or otherwise, to level armed threats of its own at everyone else. The clearest practical merits which he ascribed to it were in direct comparison with the competing state forms which had supplanted it throughout the civilized world: aristocracy and monarchy. While no inhabitant of the Netherlands during Spinoza's lifetime as an adult could have seen his judgement that democracy was more at home in peacetime as a practical advantage,[155] they could perhaps have seen some connection between the military advantages of its more successful competitors and their uglier domestic political consequences. Spinoza was no rhapsodist of democracy's edifiying spiritual impact on the ruling *demos*; but he was an acute and forthright critic of the corrupting effects of personal power upon aristocrats and monarchs, a subject matter on which there was then considerably more extensive and recent evidence. It is hard to see in his ultimate verdict, broken off abruptly,[156] any clear claim for the superiority of democracy on grounds of security or liberty (then, as now, the most evocative bases on which to vindicate a political regime). What there is, and what can only have disconcerted as cool a political judge as Johan de Witt,[157] was a consistently disabused view of the limitations of every form of government and a sharp assertion of the special tie between democracy and equality.

The significance of that tie is still as hard to judge after over three centuries of practical exploration. But the tie itself goes back to the beginning and lay at the heart of the vision and practices which the Athenians evolved to realise and secure democracy.[158] The relation of freedom or liberty to any state form can be specious (at the mercy of persuasive definition, or brazen mendacity). In every state, freedom and liberty by necessity must be defined in the end, however intricately and courteously, on the state's terms and by the state itself.[159] But equality, whatever equality lurks in nature itself (the way we simply are, irrespective of what subsequently happens to us) does sound like an external limit to the state's claims, and perhaps even ultimately to its powers. If democracy expresses human equality (whatever equality comes with simply being human) better than any other regime could, then that might well prove, sooner or later, a comparative advantage of some weight. Perhaps in the end it might come to seem a *decisive* advantage?

But can a state really express equality? Is not a state the most decisive and, at least in aspiration, the most permanent erasure of equality? And one backed, too, by an effective monopoly of the means of legitimate violence? How can whatever equality lurks in nature itself survive within a structure of uniform and relatively effective subjection, in which some in the end will always be deciding who is to be coerced by whom, and others in due course carrying out the coercion required? How can equality be more than a cruel dream in a world in which some own and control and consume vastly more resources than others? How can it be so when they own and control these resources on a basis which, unless ceaselessly and skilfully overridden, ensures that the inequality re-creates and magnifies itself into an indefinite future?

What we affirm today, when we align ourselves with democracy, is hesitant, confused and often in bad faith. It becomes less convincing, almost always, the more clearly we bring out the premises which lie beneath our own values and the more openly we acknowledge the realities which make up the institutions which we take them to commend. Where we have become clearer, more frank and more confident as time has gone by is in what we deny when we take our stand on democracy. Above all what we deny is that any set of human beings, because of who or what they simply are, deserve and can be trusted with political authority. We reject, in the great Leveller formula, redolent of England's seventeenth-century Civil War, the claim (or judgement) that any human being comes into the world with a saddle on their back, or any other booted and spurred to ride them.[160]

C h a p t e r   T w o

DEMOCRACY'S SECOND COMING

As it entered the eighteenth century, democracy was still very much a pariah word. Only the most insouciant and incorrigible dissidents, like John Toland or Alberto Radicati di Passerano,[1] could take their political stand upon it, even clandestinely or amongst intimates. Anyone who chose to do so placed themselves far beyond the borders of political life, at the outer fringes of the intellectual lives of virtually all their contemporaries. Yet, within a century, something had changed decisively. We can pin down with some confidence where the change first became apparent. What is harder to judge is what caused it to occur.

What brought democracy back to political life, late in the eighteenth century, was two great political crises on either side of the North Atlantic. The first arose in the mid-1760s amongst the set of British colonies in North America which had never fallen under French rule; the second, some two decades later, in metropolitan France itself. The two settings could scarcely have been more different. The thirteen British colonies which chose to revolt formed as fluid a society and as dynamic an economic milieu as any in the world, opening out on to a vast and still largely unknown (if far from uninhabited) landscape.[2] *Ancien régime* France (as it soon came to be called) was the proudest and most self-consciously civilized state in continental Europe, locked in a century-long struggle with England for world mastery. It was the epitome of absolute monarchy, the formidable heritage of the Sun King Louis XIV; but its haughty rulers found themselves challenged increasingly by an assertive society, ever more suspicious of their political intentions and ever less reconciled to their own effective exclusion from political choice. In America's War of Independence, France threw its military and diplomatic weight behind the revolting colonies. For a time these two arenas meshed, leaving by its close a new nation and a high water mark for France's naval and military triumph, but also a burden of governmental debt which neither the organization of France's economy nor the structure of its state was equipped to handle. Six years after the war ended, France too found itself in revolution, a domestic struggle so drastic that it gave the world a new and uniquely disruptive political conception – the modern idea of revolution itself – that spilled irresistibly across the continent of Europe and beyond.

The two crises differed in their causes, their rhythms and their outcomes; but each has marked the history of democracy ever since in indelible ways. The term democracy played no role at all in initiating the crisis of the North American colonies, and no positive role in defining the political structures that brought it to its strikingly durable close. Where it featured at all in the language of America's political leaders in the course of their great struggle, it did so most consistently and prominently as the familiar name for a negative model, drawn from the experience of Athens, of an outcome which they must at all costs avoid. Only in retrospect, as America's new constitution was put to work and the new nation went on its way, did the perspective alter sharply. When it did so, the familiar practices of England's own representative government, above all the election of a key body of its legislators (in North America, usually on a far broader franchise than in most English parliamentary constituencies), found themselves rechristened in the language of the ancient world. Once they had been so, Americans began to see themselves, in the mirror of their protracted colonial past, as having long been democrats already without knowing it. The classic rendering of that picture was given not by an American author but by a young French aristocrat, Alexis de Tocqueville, writing some half a century after America's independence, and explaining the Americans not merely to his fellow countrymen and European contemporaries but also to themselves, more insinuatingly than anyone else has ever done before or since.[3] The key to America's experience as Tocqueville saw it was also the source of its exemplary force in due course for every other future human society across the globe, the pervasiveness throughout its ways of life and forms of awareness of the brooding presence of democracy itself. In Tocqueville's book *Democracy in America*,[4] we find for the first time the recognition that democracy is the key to the distinctiveness of modern political experience and that anyone who hopes to grasp the character of that experience must focus on and take in just what it is that democracy implies.

America's Revolution was an anxious response to a widely perceived threat to liberties long enjoyed, the very liberties which, as time went by, were to form the evidence for its protracted democratic past.[5] Once those liberties had been successfully defended, or won back by force of arms, the constitutional order which the Americans constructed to secure them in future came in retrospect to seem a uniquely clear-sighted exercise in thinking through the requirements for political liberty and implementing the conclusions of this remarkably public process of deliberation. Nothing quite like it had ever occurred before; and no subsequent episode in constitution making has fully matched the acumen in diagnosis shown by the new nation's political leaders, still less the remarkable longevity of the remedies on which they settled. Ninety years later William Ewart Gladstone, Queen Victoria's great and infuriating Prime Minister, described the product of their efforts as 'the most wonderful work ever struck off at a given time by the brain and purpose of man'.[6] In the aftermath of America's savage Civil War, the grimmest evidence of the limits to diagnosis and to remedy, this was a generous assessment. But it scarcely conveyed the levels of effort, the range of participants, or the fluster and animosity of the process of decision-making which had made it possible.

The Constitution was initially drafted in a secret Convention held in the city of Philadelphia between May and September 1787, through an elaborate process of manoeuvre and bargaining.[7] The resulting draft was first made public on 17 September 1787, and put to the twelve State ratifying Conventions, for their approval or subsequent emendation. For the next ten months it was debated publicly State by State. By July of the following year, all but North Carolina and Rhode Island had duly chosen to ratify it. During the opening session of the First Congress which met under its auspices, between March and September 1789, as Revolution accelerated in France, two funda-mental elements were added to it. A Bill of Rights, the first ten Amendments to the Constitution, drafted by James Madison on the basis of scores of recommendations from the individual State Conventions, was sent back to the States for their approval; and a Judiciary Act, creating the Federal court system, and endowing it with the requisite powers, was passed by the Senate.[8]

The most intense phase in this process followed the initial publica-tion of the Constitution. It involved not merely the 1,500 delegates to the State ratifying Conventions, who worked over its entire text, but a volume of public and private discussion, in pulpit, newspaper press and personal correspondence, which reached across the entire nation.[9] Through this hubbub of assessment and argument, one text in partic-ular now looms with extraordinary authority. It appeared at the time as a series of anonymous newspaper articles by three already promi-nent political figures, James Madison, Alexander Hamilton and John Jay. Hastily written week by week, and barely co-ordinated between the three authors, whose views differed appreciably from one another, it intervened boldly and effectively in the ratification debate. The case which the *Federalist* made for the merits of the new system of government, while it failed to convince a great many amongst its immediate audience,[10] rapidly became the barely disputed rationale for the basis of America's Republic ever since. It was a case for the need for, but also for the safety of, a strong central government, which could raise revenues, control naval and military forces, and sign treaties with foreign powers like any other state, but do so in a way which posed no threat to the personal liberties which the Americans had won back at such peril from their former colonial masters.

The case for America's Revolution had been exaggeratedly simple: that unrestricted power was a mortal threat to personal liberty, and that Britain's imperial government was moving deliberately and with some energy to dismantle all restrictions upon its power. More than half of the *Federalist* was written by Alexander Hamilton,[11] one of the most economically sophisticated of America's leaders and uniquely sensitive to the commercial and strategic threats and opportunities which it was sure to face in the centuries to come. But the essays which have given the *Federalist* its unique authority were not written by Hamilton. Their author was the shy, diligent, unabrasive elder son of a Virginia planter, thirty-six years of age as the Constitutional Convention opened in Philadelphia, James Madison. By May 1787[12] Madison had played an active part in America's struggle against Britain and in the tangled politics of the new nation for over eleven years. He brought to the Federal Convention an elaborate set of proposals on how the American Confederation, with its single-chamber Congress, could be reconstructed as three independent branches of government, with a two-House legislature with distinct responsibilities, elected on contrasting bases of representation.[13] The first delegate to reach Philadelphia from out of State[14] and one of the very few present on the day when the Convention was due to begin, Madison, together with his colleagues from the Virginia delegation, seized the opportunity of this forced interlude to draft a fifteen-point Plan of Government around which all subsequent debate revolved. Characteristically, he also set himself, once the Convention formally opened, to the enduring gratitude of historians, to take a full record of its debates.[15] His main purpose in doing so was to ensure his own grasp of an extraordinarily complicated and consequential agenda. The Plan of Government was not the work of Madison alone; and the constitutional draft which emerged from the Convention's deliberations clashed in places with some of his strong convictions. But in his steady, patient, unhistrionic and wonderfully thoughtful way he did more than anyone to give it its ultimate shape.

The central purpose of that shape he set out and defended with exemplary clarity in the most celebrated of all the *Federalist Papers*, number 10, echoing the arguments of a letter composed a month earlier to his fellow Virginian and close friend, Thomas Jefferson, drafter of the Declaration of Independence. The tenth *Federalist* sets out a remedy for the violence of faction, the key weakness of popular governments[16] and source of the 'instability, injustice and confusion' which plague their public councils, 'the mortal diseases under which popular governments have everywhere perished' and 'the favourite and fruitful topics' of the adversaries to liberty. Faction cannot be eliminated except by eliminating liberty itself. Its latent causes are 'sown in the nature of man', in the variations in human faculties, the contrasts in the ownership of property, and the consequent divisions of society into different interests and parties. The sources of party identification are endlessly variable; but the most potent and consistent of them is the 'various and unequal division of property'.[17] The propertied and those without property 'have ever formed distinct interests in society'. (The immediate back-cloth to this perception in 1787 was the issue of whether to honour or repudiate the vast debts, always to individual creditors, which every American State had run up in the course of winning its independence.) How were these sharply opposed interests to be balanced justly against one another?

The causes of faction, Madison was very sure, cannot be removed. All that could reasonably be hoped for was to control its effects.[18] A minority faction could provoke endless trouble; but within a republican government it ought never to find an opportunity to impose itself through the law. Where a faction forms a majority, however, popular governments give it every opportunity to sacrifice both the rights of minorities and the public good to its own passions and interests.[19] The key challenge to popular government was to secure both public good and private rights against the threat of a factious majority, without at the same time sacrificing the spirit and form of popular government. (A 'pure Democracy', Madison insisted,

> *a Society, consisting of a small number of citizens, who assemble and administer the Government in person, can admit of no cure for the mischiefs of faction. A common passion or interest will, in almost every case, be felt by a majority of the whole; a communication and concert results from the form of Government itself; and there is nothing to check the inducements to sacrifice the weaker party, or an obnoxious individual.*[20]

That is why such democracies have always been so turbulent and contentious, have always proved incompatible with personal security or property rights, and 'have in general been as short in their lives, as they have been violent in their deaths'. Theoretical partisans of democracy, accordingly, have had to presume, in Madison's view absurdly, that reducing men to perfect political equality would at the same time render them perfectly equal in their possessions and uniform and harmonious in their opinions and passions.

In place of that perilous project of levelling and homogenization, Madison offered a different model which promised to provide a cure for the ills of democracy: 'a Republic, by which I mean a Government in which the scheme of representation takes place'. A Republic in

Madison's sense differed from a pure Democracy in several ways. 'The two great points of difference between a Democracy and a Republic are, first, the delegation of the Government, in the latter, to a small number of citizens: secondly, the greater number of citizens, and greater sphere of country, over which the latter may be extended.' The Union of American States covered a vast territory and took in a very substantial population. It required a scheme of government which could encompass both in a way that 'Democratic Government' plainly could not. It was compelled to choose, therefore, a relatively small number of representatives to act on behalf of a very large number of citizens; and this very selectivity, Madison optimistically assumed, would ensure the quality of the representative so chosen. The scale of its territory and the size of its citizen body would create a wider variety of parties and interests, and lessen the risk of majority coalitions intent on encroaching on the rights of other citizens. Even where such coalitions did arise, the need to operate politically on a far larger stage would itself impede the co-ordination of surreptitious and plainly disreputable policies. Religious bigotry, 'a rage for paper money, for an abolition of debts, for an equal division of property, or for any other improper or wicked project' are far less likely 'to pervade the whole body of the Union' than they are to infect a particular State, just as they are more likely to taint a particular county or district than an entire State.[21]

The extent and structure of the Union, therefore, could and would provide 'a Republican remedy for the diseases most incident to Republican Government.'[22]

Three and half months later, in *Federalist* 63, Madison returned to this judgement, qualified one aspect of it but reaffirmed its central element. The principle of Representation formed the pivot of the American Republic.[23] There were elements of representation even in the purest of Greek democracies, in the election of public officials who held executive power.[24] 'The true distinction between these communities and the American Government' was '*the total exclusion of the people in their collective capacity* from any share' in it,[25] not the comprehensive exclusion of popular representatives from the administration of the *polis*. Successful representative government would have been impracticable in these small and all too intimate communities. But on the scale of the American Union, the evident need for it could and would provide it with enough political support for it to operate with sufficient calm and for long enough to make its solid advantages very clearly apparent.

Even though we use the term democracy so differently today, the force of Madison's insistence on the total exclusion of the people in their collective capacity from any share in the American Government still comes as something of a shock. For Madison himself, however, it was the clearest evidence how unlike the democratic city states of classical Greece the new state which he was struggling to defend really was, and the proof that it, unlike them, was not a democracy at all. In his vocabulary, as in Plato's or Aristotle's, a people totally excluded in their collective capacity from the government of their community could not conceivably be thought to rule it directly themselves. What controlled it in the end was the will of the majority of its citizens. But immediate control over it rested somewhere quite different. Whatever else the new American state might or might not be called, it could not properly be termed a democracy.

A representative government differed decisively from a democracy not in the fundamental structure of authority which underlay it, but in the institutional mechanisms which directed its course and helped to keep it in being over time. These depended for their effect not solely on the legal precision with which they had been defined ('parchment barriers against the encroaching spirit of power'),[26] but also and more decisively on the practical relations between them and the political energies on which they could hope to draw. In a democracy, 'where a multitude of people exercise in person the legislative functions, and are continually exposed by their incapacity for regular deliberation and concerted measures to the ambitious intrigues of the executive magistrates', the threat of tyranny might come principally from the executive. But in America, the principal threat came from the legislature, the threat, as Jefferson had put it in his *Notes on the State of Virginia* three years earlier, of 'elective despotism'.[27]

As the Americans moved towards Revolution in 1774, John Jay, a young New York aristocrat, and in due course co-author of the *Federalist* and future Secretary of State, described them with pardonable exaggeration as 'the first people whom heaven has favoured with an opportunity of deliberating upon and choosing forms of government under which they should live'.[28] At this stage the opportunity seemed exhilarating, and the risks associated with it (in stark contrast to those of defying the British) relatively negligible. If the term *democracy* carried no particular inspiration, it held little or no immediate menace. Even such a hardened political sceptic as John Adams felt confident that 'a democratic despotism is a contradiction in terms'.[29] The new State constitutions redrew the boundaries of electoral districts to make them more equal, insisted on annual elections, widened the suffrage, imposed residential requirements on electors and representatives alike, and empowered constituents to instruct their representatives.[30] In doing so, they reinforced and sharpened a key contrast between American and British experiences of political representation, with the Old World emphasis on historical continuity, the sovereign unity of a single community, and the symbolic and virtual character of the links between represented and representer discarded firmly for an insistence on actuality, choice, consent, and an ever fuller and more equal participation.[31]

In the immediate aftermath of the Constitutional Convention this process of deliberation and choice was still very much in train; and there were no surviving public advocates of a less participatory or egalitarian basis on which to approach it. What had become drastically more salient were the risks of failing to reach a firm conclusion, and the substantial contribution which democracy itself could and almost certainly would make to aggravating those risks.

At this stage the Americans had in essence four options. They might have chosen to repudiate the most democratic elements in their new state, the uniquely prominent place which it gave its free male population for wide popular participation in conditions of near political equality in framing and taking public decisions. In continental Europe, even a century later, there were still many prominent (and sometimes powerful) defenders of this response; and between the two World Wars, in Europe and also in Japan, Fascist governments sought to implement some aspects of it, with devastating consequences at home and abroad. But in America, with the defeated Loyalists fled to Canada or across the Atlantic, it had no surviving public advocates.

They might also, as Madison noted, have chosen instead to press the principle of political equality (still confined to males, and still juxtaposed with little apology to a very substantial slave population) boldly forward, so that it clashed with and overrode the claims of property, abolished debt, redistributed large land holdings and remade a society to be equal all through. Here too, at this point, there seem to have been no advocates amongst the Americans for this more drastic, and potentially equally destructive, alternative.

More realistically perhaps, they might also very readily have failed to choose at all, recoiling from any strengthening of the central power of America's new state for fear that this must re-create the alien and always potentially tyrannical structure from which they had just escaped at such a high cost. In effect this would have been the immediate practical upshot of the victory of the Antifederalists, a passive acceptance of the existing forms of government, as these had already emerged under the Articles of Confederation, with no effective overarching structure between the individual State governments.

The option they chose, in broad outline the option which Madison and his fellow authors pressed upon them, was embodied in the new Constitution, as this survived the ordeal of ratification and amendment, and then of implementation in Washington's first Presidency. That option gave the Americans, and in due course the world, a great deal. It failed to reconcile a regime of political liberty (at least for men) with the widespread ownership of slaves, a reconciliation effected only partially even three-quarters of a century later in the convulsions of Civil War. Even today there is as little agreement as ever over how far that reconciliation has since been carried, or what hope remains that it will ever be completed. What is certain is that the option taken in 1787 has conspicuously failed to eliminate the egalitarian impulse from America's continuing political imagination. But it has given that impulse a distinctive cast, rendering it far less vital, insistent or prominent an element within the American imagination than it has proved in most other societies across the globe over the following two centuries. It secured the new Republic extremely effectively, and, as we now know, for a very long time. In doing so, it turned the United States into the most politically definite, the best consolidated and the most politically self-confident society on earth. It also, over time and to the vast prospective gratification of its raffish and impatient Secretary of the Treasury, Alexander Hamilton, opened the way for it to become overwhelmingly the most powerful state in human history.

When Madison looked back on the making of the Constitution in his old age,[32] evoking 'the distracted condition of affairs at home, and the utter want of respect abroad' which surrounded its birth, he still saw every reason for pride in 'a constitution which has brought such a happy order out of so gloomy a chaos'. No human government could eliminate the risk of the abuse of power. But America's federal republic, on the evidence of over a third of a century, had cut those risks to a bare minimum.[33] It had not done so by embracing the claims of democracy without reservation; and Madison himself shows little sign of warming to the term in later life. But he did recognize how deep the inroads of the new conception of democracy now were, and how futile it was to resist them openly. By the early

1820s, property qualifications for the suffrage, which had seemed so obviously benign at the time of the Convention, had become a pointless anachronism.[34] A more obdurate conservative like Chancellor James Kent of New York might still not hesitate to argue overtly for their key role in taming 'the evil genius of democracy'.[35] But for Madison by this point, where a propertyless majority threatened a propertied minority, this was not a danger which could appropriately be handled by excluding that majority from the franchise. To exclude a majority from the suffrage 'violates the vital principle of free government, that those who are to be bound by laws ought to have a voice in making them'.[36] It also establishes a basis for governing which was certain in practice to destroy any free government: 'it would engage the numerical and physical force in a constant struggle against the public authority, unless kept down by a standing army, fatal to all parties'.[37] Instead, Madison placed his hopes, over and above the internal restraints of the Constitution he had done so much to create, on the ameliorative impact of education. In its sobriety, his conclusion had much in common with the verdict, delivered fifteen years earlier by the prominent architect Benjamin Latrobe, in a letter to Jefferson's Italian friend Philip Mazzei: 'After the adoption of the federal constitution, the extension of the right of Suffrage in all the states to the majority of the adult male citizens, planted a germ which has gradually evolved, and has spread actual and practical democracy and political equality over the whole union.'[38] The results were undoubtedly impressive: 'the greatest sum of happiness that perhaps any nation ever enjoyed'. But they did have their costs: 'our state legislature does not have one individual of superior talents. The fact is, that superior talents actually excite distrust.' This general erosion of deference and social distinction had 'solid and general advantages'; but 'to a cultivated mind, to a man of letters, to a lover of the arts', he noted frankly to his equally fastidious correspondent, 'it presents a very unpleasant picture'.[39] Henry James was waiting in the wings.

What presented this distasteful picture was a democratic politics become wholly routine, an entire way of political life, with its own logic and its own all too pervasive culture. Once become in this way a matter of routine, democracy might still be threatened by the bitter struggle between South and North over slavery, or perhaps even by the depths of the Great Depression almost seventy years later, seismic pressures on the foundations of the social order or the economy which sustained it. But, within politics itself, democracy had come to dominate the landscape. It faced no surviving rivals and was seldom under much pressure to reflect on its own nature, let alone defend itself against a real challenge to its ascendancy. For Americans, from then on, it filled the horizon of politics; and anyone who chose to reject it publicly simply rendered themselves politically impotent. In America, the battle for democracy, as Americans had come to understand it, was won effectively by default, even if much of its substance had been won much earlier and with much effort under very different names.

It was in Europe, late in the eighteenth century, that the term first figures in the speech of political actors, struggling to transform a state, and seeking to explain the basis on which they were planning their strategies and coming to understand the implications of their goals. In this guise it made its initial entry, sporadically and very much on the margins, in the Patriot Revolt which revitalized the faded political life of the Dutch Republic in the 1780s. At the outset this revolt was diffuse in its goals and more than a little confused in its political strategies.[40] But between 1785 and 1787 a number of the Patriot leaders at times shook themselves free of the hallowed squabbles between the wealthy urban oligarchs and the House of Orange, which reached back to the origins of the United Netherlands, and set out a novel and consciously egalitarian political platform.

The institutional key to the most radical aspects of their challenge lay in the urban popular militias of the Dutch Provinces, the

Free Corps,[41] which met in regular assemblies from December 1784 onwards, usually in Utrecht.[42] As the far from egalitarian Patriot leader, Baron Joan Derk van der Capellen tot den Pol, noted: 'Liberty and unarmed people stand in direct contradiction';[43] and by December 1784 the Patriot movement had taken up arms. At the peak of the movement, a delegate of the Delft Free Corps proclaimed ringingly:

> *The Burgher, dear comrades, no longer wanders in the shadows. He can show himself fearlessly in the light of our fiercely breaking dawn. The Sun of his freedom and Happiness shines more strongly from hour to hour, and we can assure you on the most powerful grounds that before she reaches her zenith there will be no more Tyrants of the People to be found in this land. The Armed Freedom will blot out their very name.*[44]

The Provinces of the Dutch Republic split bitterly between Patriot and Orange parties. By 1787, suppressing the Patriot movement required the intervention of a Prussian army, despatched to rescue Princess Wilhelmina of Orange, a Hohenzollern princess who had had the temerity to set out to travel to the Hague to raise the Orange flag and the misfortune to be apprehended en route by the Gouda Free Corps, and treated brusquely and with some indelicacy by her irritated captors.[45] By September 1787, the Prussian forces, under the command of the Duke of Brunswick, had restored the rule of the Stadholder at the Hague; and by 10 October, the last bastion of Patriot resistance, the city of Amsterdam, surrendered to him.

The Patriot movement did not at any point define itself as a movement for democracy. Its goal, in so far as it had a coherent and common one, was to establish a constitutional order for the Dutch Provinces which represented their inhabitants at large, and freed them from the control of a potentially oppressive Orange monarchy, or a wealthy and entrenched urban oligarchy, equally intent on usurping the people's powers.

In seeking to define a less oppressive and more appropriate form of representation for the Dutch nation, the Free Corps leadership found themselves on at least two occasions adopting a position which it was entirely natural to describe as democratic. The third Free Corps assembly, held in June 1785 in Utrecht, drew up an act of Association,[46] pledging its participants to defend a true Republican constitution to the last drop of their blood, to restore the lost rights of the burghers and to strive for a 'People's government by representation [*Volksregierung bij representatie*]'. A few weeks later, a Free Corps assembly in the Province of Holland adopted a still more revolutionary manifesto, the Leiden Draft. Its preamble stated boldly that: 'The citizens of a State, above all of a Republic founded on Liberty, confer this on each of them, head for head… Liberty is an inalienable right, adhering to all burghers of the Netherlands commonwealth. No power on earth, much less any power derived truly from the people… can challenge or obstruct the enjoyment of this liberty.' Its Articles affirmed the sovereignty of the People, the responsibility of elected representatives to their electors, the absolute right of free speech as foundation for a free constitution, and the denominationally impartial admission of all citizens to the militia (the effective coercive guarantee of their continuing freedom). Taken together, they formed a compelling expression of 'the ideas of a Republican popular sovereignty'.[47]

In the aftermath of its military suppression, the Patriot movement was soon caught up inextricably in the international political and military maelstrom of France's great Revolution. As it disappeared into this swirling chaos, its presumptive heir, the Batavian Republic of 1795–1805, shed any trace of national autonomy and came to seem a mere puppet of the French state in the latter's rapid metamorphoses. At its nadir, the Emperor Napoleon was rude enough to describe the Netherlands as an alluvium washed down by 'the principal rivers of my empire'.[48] But the Dutch themselves naturally retained a keener interest in their domestic disagreements. As they strove to define these more clearly, they found themselves increasingly attracted to a vocabulary drawn largely from Paris. In the course of these efforts, *democracy* and *democrat* won an unprecedented prominence in Dutch political programmes and identities. By 1795 Amsterdam boasted a leading newspaper *De Democraten*, and a political club whose goal was the winning of a '*democratisch systema*'. By 1797 France's own Directory was assuring its Holland agent that what the Dutch wished for was a 'free and democratic constitution'. In January of the next year, a third of the members of the Dutch Constituent Assembly duly signed a petition for 'a democratic representative constitution'; and in the succeeding month a committee of the same assembly unwisely boasted to the French agent that the Dutch were 'capable of a greater measure of democracy than would be suitable to the French'.[49] By this point, aristocrats had long surrendered the centre of the stage. But in Holland, as in France itself, it had been *Aristocrats* who first served to define a political grouping, well before *Democrats* could come to do so. In 1786 Gijsbert Karel van Hogendorp, a long-term partisan of the House of Orange, described his country in French to a correspondent as troubled by a cabal, which people say 'is divided into aristocrats and democrats'.[50] Van Hogendorp himself was certainly by Dutch standards very much an aristocrat, even before he became Pensionary of Rotterdam in 1787. He moved in elevated circles; and it was his son who provided the immediate stimulus to Princess Wilhelmina's ill-judged escapade.[51] He was also a practised caballer in his own right, and was still intriguing vigorously on behalf of the Orange cause at the time of the Orange restoration a quarter of a century later.[52] But in 1786 his perspective on Dutch factional squabbles still aspired to be external, detached, cosmopolitan and sophisticated: a painstaking exercise in political judgement. It was not itself a political act; nor was it cast in terms intended as either domestic or distinctively Dutch.

The first setting in which the term democrat does appear incontestably as a pole of domestic political affiliation in Europe's (or the world's) modern history was not in one of the more advanced states, economies or societies of the continent (in Holland, France or Britain), but in what is now Belgium and was then the Austrian Netherlands. The provinces of the Austrian Netherlands, all subject to the Austrian Emperor, formed the southern half of the Low Countries which Spain contrived to reconquer after the sixteenth-century Revolt of the Netherlands. As a result of that reconquest, and in drastic contrast to the Provinces which got away, it was still solidly Catholic, and effectively excluded from international commerce by the closing of the river Scheldt to sea-going traffic, enforced by the terms of Dutch independence. Within it, the Church dominated political and economic life to a remarkable (and somewhat stifling) degree, making it a virtual 'museum of medieval corporate liberties'.[53] The Dutch Patriot refugees who fled across its borders in 1787, as the Duke of Brunswick reimposed order, found it 'backward, superstitious, priest-ridden and oligarchic'.[54] Belgium's awakening from its political slumbers came very much from the outside, and in response to the spirited reform initiatives of the Emperor Joseph II, the archetype of the Enlightened Despot. Joseph first set himself, with characteristic vigour, thoroughness and lack of tact, to reform the penal law by abolishing torture, to rationalize the activities of the Church (dissolving a number of religious houses, regulating pilgrimages and the timing of popular festivities), challenging the guild monopolies, deregulating the terms on which masters could employ labour, and opening up public offices to non-Catholics.[55] In 1787, he went on, more drastically, to reorganize the entire administrative and judicial system of the Provinces. This was seen across Belgium, accurately enough, as an assault on the old order, and duly resented as such. The nobles of Alost, unabashed aristocrats to a man, complained forcefully that: 'Our right to judge is our property, Lord Emperor. We do not hold it by grace, but have received it from our fathers and bought it with blood and gold. It should not be taken from us against our will.'[56] The lawyers of Brussels, less grandly but no less cogently, remonstrated that they had paid good money to secure the positions they held, and done so, and laboured to acquire the knowledge needed to discharge their responsibilities, in the confident expectation of supporting their wives and children on the proceeds.[57] Their rights to do so rested on the historical foundation stone of the Province's liberties, the celebrated *Joyeuse Entrée*, issued by the Duke of Brabant over four centuries earlier in 1355.

Late in 1788 the Estates of Brabant and Hainault refused to pay taxes to the Emperor, and Joseph II responded by repudiating, over four centuries since its initial proclamation, the *Joyeuse Entrée*.[58] The two main leaders of the revolt, Van der Noot and Vonck, were each Brussels lawyers. Van der Noot was wealthy and at least related to the aristocracy, Vonck the son of an appreciably poorer farmer. Van der Noot assailed the Austrians in an incendiary pamphlet, but promptly fled abroad and busied himself with unavailing efforts to persuade the House of Orange to intervene and reunite the Netherlands. Vonck drew the moral of Brunswick's brisk suppression of the Dutch Patriots, and set himself instead, along with a group of Brussels friends, to organize a secret society *Pro Aris et Focis* (For Altars and Hearths), to co-ordinate groups of youthful volunteers to travel abroad for military training, and link these to a clandestine network of sympathizers within Belgium itself. Vonck attracted many followers across the entire range of Belgian society, from the abbots of the wealthiest monasteries to the grandest of the secular nobility.

On 18 June 1789 Joseph responded by dissolving the Estates of Brabant and annulling the *Joyeuse Entrée*. By this time France's own Revolution was well on its way and the Estates General had begun to meet in Versailles.[59] Only the day before, the representatives of the Third Estate proclaimed themselves the National Assembly.[60] In August, Revolution broke out too in the Prince-Bishopric of Liège,[61] and young Vonckists flooded across the frontier to prepare themselves for the armed struggle. In practice, little struggle was required, since the Austrian authorities gave up without a fight in one province after another. The network of urban revolutionary committees which Vonck had established set itself to reconstruct the patchwork of medieval liberties as a single sovereign national government. Vonck's allies in this task 'were called Vonckists by their enemies, but democrats by themselves'.[62] These enemies, unsurprisingly, included not only the earlier followers of Van der Noot, but also most of the major beneficiaries of the established order, with the great Abbot of Tongerloo now prominent within their ranks:[63] 'The abbots as a group represent the secular and regular clergy, and indeed they represent the whole rural country as well, being the largest landowners; and, finally, usage has always been this way, and should remain so, since it is constitutional, and the Constitution cannot be changed.'[64]

It was an unequal fight. The Vonckists found themselves tarred with the menace of France's Revolution, especially after March 1790, when many of their leaders were arrested, and the remainder, with numerous of their followers, found themselves forced to flee into exile in France itself. They also found themselves portrayed, not entirely erroneously, as catspaws of the new Austrian Emperor Leopold II, whose reform plans, if less draconic in style than those of Joseph II, were every bit as out of sympathy with the hallowed customs and whimsical privileges of Brabant. Neither alignment was reassuring to the foreign champions of the other; but the two together, however inconsistent the combination, were more than enough to unite a large majority of the Belgians against the Democrats. In June 1790, in a rehearsal for the bloodily suppressed counter-revolutionary rising in the Vendée three years later,[65] the parish priests of rural Brabant roused their devout peasant congregations by the thousands, and marched threateningly, week after week, into the centre of Brussels, carrying the insignia of their threatened faith, and brandishing an unnerving array of agricultural weaponry.[66] Vonck himself, who came from just such a parish, had never thought it wise to adopt a public programme for the democratic reconstruction of Belgium as a state. His followers did not see themselves as democrats, because they had chosen from the outset to pursue a clearer and more extreme version of France's national reconstruction. They did so because the immediate enemy they faced was a far denser and an even more arbitrary array of aristocratic privileges than those of France's first two Estates, and because this enemy was backed by much wider popular support than their French equivalents proved able to draw on. In Belgium, as in Algeria a little over two hundred years later,[67] a democratic outcome chosen by a majority of the adult inhabitants would certainly not have meant the establishment and consolidation of a secular and democratic republic. The *pays réel*, given the opportunity, would have voted any such democracy down without a moment's hesitation. No one thinking through the implications of the Vonckist movement and its fate in retrospect could possibly have inferred from it that the cause of democracy was destined to sweep the world.

To see why democracy faced that future, we certainly need to bear in mind its fate in North America over the next century, and the majestic rise of America's economy under its aegis. But, beyond the Americas, the impact of these experiences on the politics of other countries was still quite modest until the First World War, and did not really come into its own until the aftermath of the Second. Before then, democracy's unsteady dispersion across the world was no testimony to American power, and not much even to the force of American example. If anything, it testified, rather, to one of two things. It might be evidence of the intrinsic power of democracy itself as an idea (odd for a political term which had not even begun its life as a conception of the politically desirable, and which had long served to label the quite evidently politically undesirable). More plausibly, but still quite puzzlingly, it might instead be testimony to the force of another and far more obtrusively ambiguous historical example, the awesome Revolution which overwhelmed France.

What happened in France in the few short years between 1788 and 1794 changed the structure of political possibilities for human communities across the world almost beyond recognition. It did so, for reasons we still very vaguely comprehend, both radically and permanently. Even when it was over, with Robespierre's overthrow in Thermidor in 1794, or Napoleon's rise in Brumaire 1798, or on the plains of Waterloo, quite close to Brussels, in 1815 when Napoleon fell for the last time, it left a different conception of what politics meant, a new vision of how societies can or must organize themselves politically, and a transformed sense of the scale of threat which their own political life can pose to any society and all within their reach. It was within this new conception that democracy forced itself, slowly but inexorably, upon one community after another. It made these inroads, once again, not through its prominence in the speech of the Revolution's leading actors, or through the names adopted to pick out political groupings, factions or institutions. Those names – Jacobins, Girondins, the Mountain, the Left – all had their own history. Some, in due course, cast lengthy shadows over distant corners of the world. But none of them ever competed, even momentarily, for the role of world-wide basis for political legitimacy; and none ever offered a comparably firm standard for political authority to live up to. The democratic legacy of the Revolution was very much the product of its intense and often devastating political struggles. But it was no echo of its public symbols,[68] nor of the language in which those struggles were openly conducted. Only at a handful of points was the category of democracy deployed explicitly to define what was at stake within them, and even then only once at the storm centre of the struggle itself. Only in retrospect, as the most detached and analytical categories through which Europeans had striven for centuries to grasp what politics means and why it operates as it does were set to work to fathom just what the Revolution as a whole really had meant, did democracy slowly begin to emerge as its central issue, and do so in its own right and under its own name.

At this point, it linked back to one of the most intriguing visions of France's political predicament earlier in the century, the *Considérations sur le gouvernement ancien et présent de la France.*[69] The *Considérations* was the work of a prominent aristocrat, René-Louis de Voyer de Paulmy, Marquis d'Argenson. D'Argenson came from a long line of royal officials, and his father had been the Paris chief of police.[70] He served himself in several elevated positions, most notably as Minister of Foreign Affairs. But he was too brusque and too independent to be a practised courtier; and in many of his loyalties and much of his social imagination he was a traitor to his order. The *Considérations* was first published, anonymously and from a highly imperfect manuscript, in 1764.[71] It set out a plan for the political reconstruction of France which D'Argenson had already advanced as early as 1737, and which he for long hoped to persuade the King to permit him to carry out himself in the role of First Minister. In manuscript form, and subsequently in print, it had, as his son boasted in a Preface to the greatly augmented second edition twenty years later, left its mark on most of the great French political works from the middle of the century onwards: the Physiocrats, Quesnay, Mirabeau, Montesquieu, Turgot, Rousseau, Mably.[72]

D'Argenson's plan was a striking expression of the *thèse royale*, the perspective on French government, economy and society which saw in an enlightened monarchical reform the best hope for reshaping and rationalizing France as a state and society, and serving the interests of its people as a whole.[73] But D'Argenson approached the task of reform, as the title of his manuscript made clear,[74] not by seeking merely to restructure the royal administration, but by asking himself 'how far democracy could be admitted into monarchical government'. This was scarcely the sort of question calculated to win cheap popularity at the court of Versailles. In later decades, as the royal government clashed with its principal constitutional courts, the Parlements, D'Argenson at points modified the sharpness with which he sought to exclude the aristocracy from the strategic niches which enabled them to obstruct royal power.[75] But what marked him out throughout his political life was the extent to which he believed it essential to introduce democratic procedures and institutions into the way in which France was governed. What made these procedures indispensable, in his eyes, was less the difficulty of enforcing the common good through a purely monarchical structure of power, or any prospective divergence between the interests of the monarch and those of his people, than the sheer difficulty of locating what the common good was in the first place. For this latter task, democratic institutions and procedures enjoyed unique advantages. He put this point with particular clarity in his (equally unsuccessful) submission for the Academy of Dijon's 1754 prize competition which elicited Jean-Jacques Rousseau's *Discours sur les origines de l'inégalité parmi les hommes*. Nature

> *is divine and dictates to us only laws which are easy to execute. But you must listen to her to follow her; she makes herself heard only among equal citizens and friends. In these conditions, contradictory interests control and conciliate themselves, sharpness softens, difficulties are levelled* [s'aplanissent] *by what is evident, and the common good discovered. It is thus from equality alone that good laws come to us. It is through the assembly of men equal among themselves that their implementation* [manutention] *can be assured.*[76]

In the Plan of the New Administration which D'Argenson proposed for France,[77] the public good, the supreme law, was to guide a well-organized monarchy, with the aid of a well-understood democracy which in no way encroaches upon royal authority.[78] This left very little room (and no need whatever) for an intermediary power between king and people.[79] D'Argenson argued that the sole inconvenience of democratic authority was that it was too divided to make itself obeyed. It must therefore be regulated and directed by a single spirit which bears upon the entire body of the state but has no interest aside from the general interest. Such was the role of royal authority.

The role of democracy was to enlighten the sovereign, who, as all French monarchists stoutly maintained, had no interest of his own apart from those of his people, and so no motive for betraying them,[80] but who could all too readily fail to ascertain what their interests were. Any sovereign therefore needed the help of his subjects to identify which of their interests were truly common, just as urgently as the people in their turn needed to be aware of one another's judgements to distinguish particular interests from the general good. Nowhere did the monarch need this aid more urgently than in the assessment of the level and distribution of taxation, an ever more contentious issue as the costs of global military and naval conflict mounted inexorably, and the government's debts rose precipitously along with them.[81] Under D'Argenson's Plan, the administrators who set the tax levels in every district of France must be chosen from then on from men who resided and owned property within the district, by majority vote and through secret ballot.[82] They were to be subject annually to renewal or replacement at elected Assemblies of the district. Besides offering a belated political basis on which to meet France's spiralling fiscal crisis, this democratic choice of administrators would also help to intensify French agriculture, ensuring that all land was cultivated by its owners.[83]

In itself, D'Argenson's conception of democracy was conventional enough: 'Democracy is popular Government, in which the whole people shares equally, with no distinction between nobles and commoners.'[84] He distinguished in the classic fashion between true and false democracy:

False Democracy rapidly falls into Anarchy. It is the Government of the multitude, as when a People revolts. Then the insolent People scorns the Laws and reason. Its tyrannical

> *Despotism shows itself in the violence of its movements, and by the uncertainty of its Deliberations.*
>
> *True Democracy acts through Deputies, and these Deputies are authorized by the election of the People. The mission of those chosen by the People and the authority which supports them constitute the public power. Their duty is to insist on the interests of the greatest number of citizens to protect them from the greatest evils and secure them the greatest goods.*[85]

On the first appearance of his book in 1764, D'Argenson notes at this point that a democracy of this kind was, or should have been, the Government of the United Provinces. By 1784 he (or more probably his son) felt free to replace this assessment by the bold claim that the only true Democratic States in Europe at the time were the popular cantons of Switzerland.[86]

D'Argenson was an unabashed monarchist. He fully accepted the French monarchy's exclusive commitment to the Catholic Church, whatever his reservations may have been over the manner and timing of Louis XIV's Revocation of the Edict of Nantes and subsequent persecution of the Huguenots. For him democracy was a valuable adjunct to the monarchy, not its rival or potential replacement. But he differed sharply for most of his life from theorists of mixed government, then or earlier, who saw the political aftermath of European feudalism as a system of government uniting monarchical, aristocratic and democratic elements in careful balance against one another, and savoured, to varying degrees, the restraining influence on royal wilfulness of the intermediary powers of the aristocracy. In France this meant above all the *noblesse de robe*, who staffed the French constitutional courts and saw themselves as the dedicated custodians of the laws.[87] For D'Argenson the crying need of the French monarchy was not restraint but guidance; and neither aristocracy nor Church had the least capacity to provide that guidance in a dependable form.

D'Argenson was a frustrated monarchical reformer, who feared that a French monarchy left unreformed must collapse in chaos in the relatively near future. Although he had been dead for many years by the time that it did, his picture of its fundamental flaws was notably acute, and his sense of what was likeliest to hasten its end uncommonly prescient:[88]

> *If ever the nation were to recover its will and its rights, it would not fail to establish a universal national assembly [*une Assemblée nationale universelle*], dangerous to royal authority in quite a different way. It would make it necessary and always in being. It would compose it of great lords, deputies of each province and of the towns. It would imitate in every respect the Parliament of England. The nation would reserve legislation to it and would give the king only a provisional* (provisoire) *right to implement it.*

What broke the monarchy in the end was its own political clumsiness and bad luck, a wholly unpredictable succession of maladroit Ministers, failures of nerve, vagaries of judgement, and sheer mishaps. But what placed it within reach of catastrophe was less any special infirmity in the person of the reigning monarch, or even the acute unpopularity of his Austrian wife, than the obstinacy, conceit and ruthlessness of D'Argenson's key adversary, the French nobility, the order from which he came. France's Revolution was a revolution against aristocracy well before it turned against the incumbent monarch. As far as we know, none of its prominent native actors[89] was a convinced democrat (either in their own vocabulary or in ours) until well after it had unmistakably broken out. Even those who did most to foment it, like the Abbé Sieyes himself,[90] for long championed its democratic elements solely as complements to the continuing and effective authority of its monarchical government.

As with the making of America's Constitution, what drove the reconstruction of the French state was the crippling burden of war debt, and the political challenge of finding a basis on which to discharge it without openly repudiating it. In America what this principally required was the design of a system of government safe from capture by irresponsible enemies of property, a firm barrier to democracy's most notorious weakness, or to what D'Argenson called 'False Democracy'.[91] But in France the immediate obstacle to handling the debt effectively was the very partial and obstructed fiscal reach of the royal government and the elaborate tissue of exemptions, province by province and order by order, which served to limit it. All these exemptions were a matter of law, in most cases law of many centuries' standing. As they faced a government forced to live ever more desperately beyond its means, every one of them was a kind of privilege, a special form of legal immunity, or private legal right to elude the law as it bore on other French men or women. France was not a single kingdom, with one law for all its subjects. It was a vast archipelago of overlapping jurisdictions and endlessly differentiated statuses, all fiercely defended, and all at least pretending to centuries of antiquity. It defied systematic comprehension, let alone coherent excuse, every bit as obdurately as the customs of Brabant had defied Austria's reforming Emperors.

The two most prominent blocs of privilege belonged to the Church and the nobility, the First and Second of the three Estates, who, in the understanding of virtually all France's population who interested themselves in such questions, made up the French Nation. Neither Church nor nobility was ranged solidly against the interests of the royal government, let alone the French Nation. Between the year of America's Independence and 1789, each provided leading Ministers who struggled to persuade their recalcitrant fellows to surrender at least some of their tax privileges in order to bring the debt back under control. But Church and nobility both firmly refused, in one setting after another, to comply with these proposals.

The Ministers, noble or ecclesiastical (or in one case both), soon fell; and by August 1788, France's increasingly anxious King, Louis XVI, found himself forced to turn once more to a Minister who was neither a noble nor a Prince of the Church, indeed not even a French subject, the Genevan Protestant banker Jacques Necker.[92] More disconcertingly still, and even before his hapless Minister Loménie de Brienne had handed in his resignation, Louis found himself compelled to agree to summon the Estates General of France, for the first time for a full century and three-quarters. Brienne himself epitomized the political limitations of the *ancien régime* at the end of its tether. Archbishop of Toulouse at the time of his appointment, he had had the conspicuously poor taste to take advantage of his position to arrange for his own transfer to the considerably more remunerative Archbishopric of Sens; and his tactless and indecisive handling of the Provincial Estates greatly aggravated suspicion of the royal government throughout France.

Because it had not met for such an immense span of time, no one knew quite how to summon the Estates General, even once the decision had been taken; and no one could be certain quite how its members were to be selected, let alone what they would be commissioned to concede or demand. No one even knew what forms it would meet in once its members did duly assemble. Brienne himself belatedly recognized the need to fix the procedures for the election of its members, invited evidence and opinions on how it had last been, or should now be, constituted, and lifted the censorship, so that the answers could be properly considered. The result was overwhelming.

Throughout France, in the months from July onwards, busy archival research in one place after another probed into the question of how things had been done back in the distant days of 1614, with varying and confusing results. Every rank in French society was to be invited to take part in one forum or another, whether, like the grander aristocracy or the bishops, in the select company of their peers and with some hope of commanding attention for their views, or in the local rural assemblies in which even those of the peasantry with the nerve to take it were to be given their brief say, and permitted to cast their votes, before the outcome was filtered upwards. In each setting, lists of grievances (*cahiers de doléances*) were drawn up, as preconditions to the acceptance of any fresh taxes needed to refloat the French Treasury, or bargaining counters in the allocation of the new tax burden amongst different groups of the population.[93]

Amidst all this excitement, and the spontaneous optimism which it both prompted and reinforced, one particular public decision sharpened the inchoate contours of social and political interest and redefined suddenly the muddled struggle between nation and royal government as an open confrontation between the Third Estate and its two privileged counterparts. One of Necker's opening acts as First Minister was to reconvene in September 1788 the Parlement of Paris, the principal institutional challenger to royal authority in recent decades, summarily evicted only four months earlier from its ancient role of registering the public law of France and all royal edicts which covered the whole kingdom, in favour of a judicial body appointed by the King himself. Only two days after its triumphant return to Paris, the Parlement gave its decisive verdict on how the Estates General must meet: in the forms of 1614, as three distinct Orders, and with the Third Estate having no more and no fewer representatives than each of the other two. Two months later Necker reconvened the Assembly of Notables to see if they could be persuaded to reverse this outcome, with equally little success, and was able to secure a doubling in the number of Third Estate representatives only by a decree of the Royal Council at the end of December.

By this time the damage was well and truly done.

The Parlement's decision ensured that the population of France would be forced, as never before, to choose between the accumulated routines of its long past and a vital attempt to redefine itself, through political choice, as a single national community fully equipped to assume responsibility for its own security and destiny. Many able and well-placed figures throughout France held huge stakes in that past. Like the monarch himself, every French subject was deeply inured to seeing in it the source and basis of much of what made life worth living, and the ground of every practically serviceable right which they were fortunate enough to enjoy. But very many of them had also come to have at least a shadowy awareness that this way of viewing their lives over time made imperfect sense, and that it had a certain obvious shabbiness and absurdity to it. The crushing burden of the debt, the manoeuvres of the old regime's beneficiaries to shirk responsibility for meeting it and the debilitating squabbles over who was most to blame for the steady worsening in the predicament of both government and nation focused on the nobility, the Church and eventually on the Monarch himself, an unprecedented weight of ideological odium. In the end all three buckled beneath it. For the next five years, through turbulent political exploration and struggles, intense legislative deliberation and enactment, and bitter civil and international warfare, the French nation set out to endow itself with a new legal identity. It also set itself to design and implement a fresh set of institutions through which to live together without either ignominy or absurdity, and on a basis which guaranteed liberty and security to all its citizens. It remains almost as hard to see that convulsive effort clearly and calmly today as contemporaries found it at the time. The attempt to reconstitute France as a society and a state through political action was often nightmarish in its consequences, and as cruel, hypocritical, muddled and disorientating as the very worst abysses of the *ancien régime*. It ended, on its own terms, in failure: military dictatorship, a *parvenu* empire, and, a quarter of a century later, in the reluctant restoration of the dynastic monarchy. Before it had done so, it devastated the continent of Europe and ruined the lives of countless millions of its inhabitants. (Think of the imagery of Goya's *Disasters of War*.)[94]

But the same attempt to reconstitute France through political action also in due course defined a new universe of political and legal practices for every other human society across the globe, with the single and glaring exception of the United States of America. Many of those societies have yet to be forced to submit to its requirements. But none of them, not even Britain, France's global military, political and economic rival, which did most of all to bring the Revolution to its exhausted close, has since been able consistently to ignore it.

Given the depth of the nightmare, and the awesome impact of the Revolution's blood-stained wars, some of the models drawn from it, inevitably, were negative rather than positive – precedents to avoid or catastrophes to insure against at virtually any expense. Revolution and counter-revolution were born together, and have proved, as Edmund Burke promptly warned,[95] practically inseparable ever since. It is hard to tell whether the unintended consequences of the attempt to reorganize a society rationally for the benefit of its members have had any shallower an impact than the more edifying of the political goals which its leaders adopted and pursued in their uniquely conspicuous setting. The harms which it perpetrated over time did not stem solely from excess of audacity on the part of its partisans. They issued just as forcibly from the galvanizing effects of that audacity on its more obdurate enemies, and on the political entrepreneurs who traded in their fears. If Robespierre and the Terror looked forward to Stalin and Mao Tse-Tung and the vast famines which each unleashed, they also gave the cue for the extremities of struggles to arrest or reverse the threat of revolution for more than two centuries to come, to Fascism, the Third Reich, and perhaps even truly Islamic revolution.

One figure did more than anyone else to draw the battle lines and unleash the Revolution. Emmanuel Joseph Sieyes was a surprising candidate for the role, and in many ways ill-equipped to finish what he had started.[96] He was not one of the Revolution's great orators like Mirabeau or Danton, who could hold sway over the Assembly for a time by the sheer power of their words; nor did he have Robespierre's gift of assurance in arranging to have his political enemies killed. Forty years old when the Estates General was summoned, Sieyes had earned his living from within three years of his ordination by serving as secretary, first to the Bishop of Tréguier in Brittany, and then, following his patron's fortunate posting in 1780, to the far wealthier and less secluded see of Chartres, with its majestic cathedral and ready access to Parisian intellectual and political circles.[97] Once in Chartres, Sieyes became in turn vicar-general of the diocese, a canon of the Cathedral and in 1788 Chancellor of the Chapter. He also began to make his mark in a variety of the Church's representative bodies.

In 1788, under the pressure of events, he wrote in quick succession three striking pamphlets. The first to be composed (though last to be published) was a relatively cool and systematic analysis of how the Estates General could now best set about rescuing France from the deep quagmire of its political past: *Views of the Executive Means Available to the Representatives of France in 1789*. It drew extensively on the many years of careful reading and hard thinking which Sieyes had devoted to working out the political needs and opportunities of the highly commercialized society which France, like Britain, had long been. Behind it lay close study of what he called 'social mechanics':[98] the contribution of some of the most powerful economic, social and political thinkers of eighteenth-century Europe, and most decisively of all of Adam Smith. Sieyes's key insight was the shaping influence throughout this novel kind of society of a radical division of labour, guided above all by the single criterion of effectiveness.

This was not in itself an evidently democratic line of thought. Indeed, for Plato, over two thousand years earlier, it had served as the central ground for rejecting democracy en bloc for its brazen indifference to the demands of justice: 'distributing a certain equality to equals and unequals alike'.[99] But for Sieyes, far from flouting these demands, a political order could be dependably just or effective, if and only if it viewed and treated the human beings who made it up as equal bearers of rights, and organized itself to protect and benefit every one of them. Sieyes was as alert as Adam Smith[100] to the need for authority in any human community; but, like Smith, he believed that a state could hold its authority legitimately only by dint of meeting the needs of its own subjects. This did not make him a democrat, any more than it made Smith one. For Sieyes, democracy was neither a rhetorical rallying cry, nor a favoured political paradigm. (Neither, given its long history, could it have been one of his characteristic neologisms, deployed, like the interminable coinages of Jeremy Bentham, to pin down the shadowy worlds of politics and law with new clarity and precision, if seldom widely taken up by anyone else.) But, if Sieyes was no democrat, he was no simple enemy of democracy. Even in *Views of the Executive Means* he insisted robustly, as D'Argenson had done before him, on the need for every legislature to be refreshed by the democratic spirit,[101] and on the consequent need to minimize the number of levels which separated the inhabitants of the local communities who made up the nation from the successively elected representatives who would in due course legislate on their behalf. It was the scale of France as a society which necessitated an elaborate structure of representation: 'In a community made up of a small number of citizens, they themselves will be able to form the legislative assembly. Here there will be no representation, but the thing itself.'[102] Representation serves efficiency; but it also carries great dangers:

> *every human association has to have a common aim and public functions. To carry out these functions it is necessary to detach a certain number of members of the association from the great mass of citizens. The more a society advances in the arts of trade and production, the more we see that the work connected to public functions should, like private employments, be carried out less expensively and more effectively by men who make it their exclusive occupation.*[103]

Sieyes plainly viewed public administration as a thoroughly worthy employment for the talented; but it is less obvious that he had any clear conception of what a career in electoral politics was likely to involve. One point which he certainly did grasp, however, was that those who carry out this work, in whatever form, readily develop an interest of their own, which may be sharply at odds with those of their fellows. They come to see their role as a right and an item of property, and no longer as a duty to others. When they do, they dissolve the bonds of political community and establish a form of political servitude.[104] France as it was in 1788 was less 'a nation organized as a political body' than 'an immense flock of people scattered over a surface of twenty-five thousand square leagues'. To turn it into a politically organized nation, what it needed was not to probe into its murky and benighted past.[105] It was to heed the lessons of reason, draw boldly on the recent findings of social mechanics, and endow itself, all too belatedly, with a sound constitution, the sole means which could guarantee citizens the enjoyment of their natural and social rights, consolidate the elements in their common life which worked for the better, and 'progressively extinguish all that has been done for the bad'.[106] In the remainder of his pamphlet Sieyes set out carefully just how the Estates General must view and organize itself to provide France at long last with that constitution, and do so without allowing itself to be sucked back into the political whirlpool of the debt which had prompted its summons in the first place.

Unlike the *Views of the Executive Means*, the first of Sieyes's pamphlets to reach the public, in November 1788, the *Essay on Privileges*, was an immediate response to the Parlement of Paris's fateful September decision and an open call to arms. In his bitter tirade against the claims of privilege,[107] Sieyes broke openly with the nobility of France as an order and set himself to demolish the entire edifice of conceit and pretension which held its world together. The very idea of privilege (the basis on which the first two Estates held their formidable powers of political obstruction) was lethal to any good or happy society. The essence of privilege is to place its possessor 'beyond the boundaries of common right',[108] either an exemption from the prohibitions on wrong action which face every other citizen,[109] or the gift of an exclusive right to do what the laws would otherwise leave open to anyone. 'All privileges... from the very nature of things, are unjust, odious, and contrary to the supreme end of every political society.' Not only was privilege deeply wrong in itself, it was also profoundly corrupting of all who benefited from it. Privilege was not an honourable quest to earn the admiration of fellow members of society; it was a constant spur to insolence and vanity: 'You ask less to be distinguished *by* your fellow citizens, than you seek to be distinguished *from* your fellow citizens.'[110] It was a secret sentiment and an unnatural appetite, 'so full of vanity, and yet so mean in itself', that all who feel it seek to cloak it in feigned concern for public interest. The idea of country, in the heart of the privileged, 'shrinks to the caste to which they belong'. They come to seem to themselves 'another species of beings'.[111] This apparently exaggerated opinion, while in no way implied in the idea of privilege itself, 'insensibly becomes its natural consequence, and in the end establishes itself in all minds'. The effects were ludicrous, turning the imaginations of the nobility endlessly back towards a distant and ever more practically irrelevant past. They were also intensely pernicious, fomenting an *esprit de corps* and a relentless party spirit within their ranks.[112] The inheritance of privilege broke any possible link to desert,[113] and left its presumed beneficiaries to a life of intrigue and mendicity, of 'privileged beggary', at the expense of their fellow citizens.[114] It nurtured also in the scions of the nobility formidable skills in this ignominious competition for self-advancement. The inevitable result was to spread the corrupting example – 'the *honourable* and *virtuous* desire of living in idleness and at the expense of the public'[115] – throughout society.

The third, and far the most famous, of Sieyes's trio of pamphlets appeared next, in January 1789, turning this tirade into an open programme of revolution, and handing on to the young Karl Marx half a century later the classic formula for revolutionary consciousness.[116] We do not really know quite what gave this forty-year-old cleric his visceral hatred of aristocratic pretension. It may have reached back to his childhood as son of a minor royal official in the modest Provence township of Fréjus. It may have been nurtured later, in the course of his reluctant training for the priesthood in the Parisian seminary of Saint Sulpice, a career for which many besides Sieyes himself subsequently noticed his drastic lack of vocation. (As a boy he strongly preferred the prospect of life as an artillery officer or mining engineer.) What we do know is that, when he came to express it definitively in public early in 1789, the resulting text lit a fuse which raced across France. A year earlier, no one would have been likely to find 'What is the Third Estate?' evocative as a title, or even especially stimulating as a question. By January 1789 the summoning of the Estates General had made it the political question of the hour.

It was Sieyes's answer to that question which turned political crisis into Revolution. As they entered 1789 the first two Estates were still very much the fair sisters, pride and glory of a long and singularly self-assured history.[117] The Third Estate was at most their drabber and more nebulous adjunct, the Cinderella of France, with its claim even to belong to the same family eminently in doubt.[118] Both the first two Estates had a conscious solidarity, a sense of collective identity, a commitment to that identity and a confidence in its own power, dignity and worth. To enquire 'What is the First Estate?' was to ask how to see and understand Christianity itself, and the Church which embodied and interpreted it on earth. In France at least, that Church was well organized to answer the question on its own behalf, and free to draw on the resources of a long history of self-consciously continuous thought and devotion and a practised fluency in political self-assertion. To enquire what the Second Estate was was to ask how to view Nobility, again a question with many centuries of rhetorical effort devoted to working up flattering answers, if for the most part on the basis of distinctly less strenuous intellectual exertion. In his *Essay on Privileges*, already, Sieyes had highlighted the imaginative fragility of this carefully cultivated tradition of self-regard. In *What is the Third Estate?*, he turned the tables decisively on his smug and overbearing antagonists, and set out a quite new basis for political authority in what was already a very old state. He began, notoriously, by giving an astonishing answer to his title question. The Third Estate, he proclaimed brashly, is 'Everything'.[119] Up to then, in the existing political order of France, it had been 'Nothing'. It had carried no political weight, and received no formal recognition. The King's Ministers and the Privileged Orders had acted in its name and on its behalf, if at least presumptively for its benefit. In doing so, they had not been, as they fondly imagined, displaying a generous and attentive paternalism. They had simply usurped powers which legitimately belonged to it, and robbed it of the place which was its rightful due.[120]

To survive and prosper, a nation requires private employments and public services.[121] It must work the land, manufacture everything which its inhabitants require, and distribute these products to their eventual consumers. It also requires a huge variety of personal services from the loftiest to the most menial.[122] At present all the most rewarding and honorific of these services are monopolized by the first two Estates. But there is not a single one of them which could not perfectly well be provided by the Third. Already the latter carries out all the really hard work, while receiving virtually none of the honour. The Third Estate contains 'everything needed to form a complete nation'.[123] It is 'Everything; but an everything that is fettered and oppressed. What would it be without the privileged order? Everything; but an everything that would be free and flourishing. Nothing can go well without the Third Estate, but everything would go a great deal better without the two others.' The exclusion of the Third Estate from every post which carries honour is 'a social crime' against it.[124] It reflects a 'state of servitude',[125] which, however long it may have lasted, can only have arisen in the first place from conquest and can no longer be sustained against a people which 'is strong enough today not to let itself be conquered'.[126]

> *They may try in vain to shut their eyes to the revolution which time and the force of things has brought about: it is real for all that. There was once a time when the Third Estate were serfs and the nobility was everything. Now the Third Estate is every-thing and nobility is only a word. But beneath this word, a new and intolerable aristocracy has slid in, and the People has every reason not to want any aristocrats.*[127]

The political consequences are clear. The nobility has separated itself from the rest of the nation and made itself a people apart.[128] Its insistence on exercising its political rights on its own has made it 'foreign to the Nation by virtue of its principle, because its mandate did not come from the people, and second, by virtue of its object, since this consists in defending, not the general interest, but particular interest'.[129] The aristocracy monopolize high office in army, Church and magistracy. They form a caste which dominates every branch of the executive power. They side instinctively with one another against the entire remainder of the nation. Their usurpation is total. Truly they reign.[130]

The battle lines are sharply defined and already foreshadow civil war: 'the Privileged show themselves no less enemies of the common order than the English are of the French in times of war.'[131] By excluding themselves from the common ranks of citizens and insisting on their privileges, they have forfeited the political rights which only citizenship can carry, and made themselves 'enemies by estate of the common order'.[132] They form a caste which clings to the real nation like the vegetable parasites 'which can live only on the sap of the plants that they impoverish and blight'.[133]

'No aristocracy', therefore, must be the rallying cry for all true friends of the nation.[134] But the enemies of aristocracy are in no sense democrats. We 'will repeat "No democracy" with them and *against* them... representatives are not democrats;... since real democracy is impossible amongst such a large population, it is foolish to presume it or to appear to fear it.' What is all too possible is a 'false democracy' in which a caste of birth, independently of any popular mandate, claims the powers which the body of citizens would exercise in a real democracy. 'This false democracy, with all the ills which it trails in its wake, exists in the country which is said and believed to be monarchical, but where a privileged caste has assigned to itself the monopoly of government, power and place.' For Sieyes, his immediate political antagonist, the Second Estate, fighting tooth and nail as a single agent to preserve their privileges, forms a 'feudal democracy'.[135]

For Sieyes, democracy as such could pose no real threat in France, however deep its crisis, since it was simply impracticable. In a country as large as France, the *demos* could never assemble together to shape itself into an effective political agent. To act at all, it must be represented. A select and separate group, small enough to co-operate effectively and be capable of action, must act on its behalf. But, to act with its authority, that group must first be chosen by it.

As 1789 dawned, the aristocracy of France still had the presumption to claim the authority of the French people, and the coherence and solidarity to abuse that claim to press their own private interests. Sieyes was very sure that their time was gone: 'During the long night of feudal barbarism, it was possible to destroy the true relations between men, to turn all concepts upside down, and to corrupt all justice; but as day dawns, so gothic absurdities must fly and the remnants of ancient ferocity collapse and disappear. This is quite certain.'

Even in *What is the Third Estate?*, however, he was sometimes less confident of what exactly would replace it: Shall

we merely be substituting one evil for another, or will social order, in all its beauty, take the place of former chaos? Will the changes we are about to experience be the bitter fruit of a civil war, disastrous in all respects for the three orders and profitable only to ministerial power; or will they be the natural, antici- pated and well-controlled consequence of a simple and just outlook, of a happy co-operation favoured by the weight of circumstances, and sincerely promoted by all the classes concerned?[136]

History's answer was not the one for which he hoped, though not until Napoleon seized power did the profits in any sense accrue to those who currently wielded executive power.

From the opening months of 1789 France entered a state of barely suppressed civil war, setting the monarchy and its agents ever more intractably at odds with the people at large, and aligning it ever more fatally with the residues of the long night of feudal barbarism. The result was a cauldron of fears, threats and counter-threats in which any prospect of the simplest and justest of political conceptions achieving clearly intended and well-controlled consequences vanished without trace. When democracy re-emerged from those years of blood and confusion it had gained nothing in plausibility as a practical model of how France could hope to govern itself in peace, prosperity and good order. What it lost definitively was its reassuring air of practical irrelevance. As it won fresh friends across a Europe ravaged by decades of war, even those most troubled by its new prominence came to see in it a potently destructive ghost that must be laid to rest, not a simple phantasm which could safely be ignored.

In most settings beyond France itself (in Belgium, Holland, Italy, even Germany or Poland), '*Democracy*' served simply to label contending political factions.[137] Even in France it was seldom employed to define the terms of political struggle with much precision, let alone clarify the goals of competing parties or the strategy of key political actors. But three figures of some importance did, at one point or another, do their best to show just why the momentum of the

Revolution carried it insistently towards democracy, and why some version of democracy was an appropriate destination, and not an inevitable disaster or a clear disgrace. Two of them are familiar heroes of the Democratic Revolution: the flamboyant English artisan (and former staymaker) Tom Paine, whose pamphlet *Common Sense* had come close to launching America's open struggle for independence, and Maximilien Robespierre, the formidably self-righteous Arras lawyer who became the Svengali of the Jacobin Terror. The third was more surprising: the central Italian Bishop of Imola, Cardinal Barnaba Chiaramonti, in his Christmas Eve homily in 1797, a mere two years before his elevation to the Papacy as Pius VII. The Bishop's message was far from a call to arms. What it affirmed, in effect, was an historically somewhat premature version of Christian Democracy. Democratic government 'among us' was in no way inconsistent with the Gospel. It required all the sublime virtues which only the school of Jesus could teach: 'The moral virtues, which are nothing other than the love of order, will make us democrats, partisans of a democracy in the true sense.' It would preserve 'equality in its rightful meaning', equality before the law, with all due recognition for the marked differences between the roles of different individuals in a society. Its goal was to join hearts together in gracious fraternity. No devout Catholic need fear a tension between democracy and their religious duties: 'Yes, my dear brethren, be good Christians, and you will be the best of democrats.'[138]

Paine's position was more forensic. It appeared in the second part of his very widely circulated defence of the Revolution's goals against the criticisms of Edmund Burke, *The Rights of Man*. Paine presented the Revolution's political outcome as a triumph, not for simple democracy, but for 'the representative system'. That system retained 'Democracy as the ground' and rejected the corrupt systems of Monarchy and Aristocracy.

Simple Democracy was society governing itself without the aid of secondary means. By ingrafting representation upon

Democracy, we arrive at a system of Government capable of embracing and confederating all the various interests and every extent of territory and population; and that also with advantages as much superior to hereditary Government, as the Republic of Letters is to hereditary literature.

For Paine, America's new government was best seen as 'representation ingrafted upon Democracy'. This novel creation united all the advantages of a simple democracy; but it also avoided most, if not all, of its notorious disadvantages. 'What Athens was in miniature, America will be in magnitude. The one was the wonder of the ancient world; the other is becoming the admiration, the model of the present.' It was the simplest, most intelligible and most practically attractive form of government, avoiding Monarchy's ineliminable exposure to the risks of ignorance and insecurity in every heir to the throne, and simple Democracy's all too obvious inconvenience. It could be applied over any scale of territory, and across the most profound divisions of interest; and it can be applied at once. 'France, great and populous as it is, is but a spot in the capaciousness of the system. It is preferable to simple Democracy even in small territories.'[139]

The Rights of Man was Paine's attempt to defend France's Revolution, not only through its own informing political values, the *Droits de l'Homme*, but also through the reassuring precedent of America's relative domestic peace as an independent state. It saw in representation, as Sieyes and Madison had each done before it, an effective system for designing and organizing a form of government accountable over time to the governed and dependably committed to serving their interests. It firmly refused to see in the representative system the slightest element of regrettable concession to political, economic or geographical realities at democracy's expense.

In the Bishop of Imola's homily, democracy scarcely features as a load-bearing element in any serious attempt to understand politics.

Even in Paine's writings or speeches its appearance signals more a relaxation than a tautening in intellectual attention. But with Maximilien Robespierre, for the first time in modern history, democracy at last appears not merely as a passing expression of political taste but as an organizing conception of an entire vision of politics. In due course Robespierre was to become an unnerving figure even to the man who did most to launch the Revolution. ('If M. Robespierre asks for me',' Sieyes warned his Brussels housekeeper forty years later from the depths of flu, in muddled geriatric reminiscence of the year of Terror, 'tell him, I'm out.')[140] By that time Robespierre himself had been dead for well over three decades; but in the five short years between 1789 and 1794 he set his intensely personal stamp permanently upon the entire Revolution, defining its main goals with unique authority, and identifying himself ineffaceably with some of its greatest achievements and many of its most odious political techniques.

At the core of Robespierre's conception of politics lay a fiercely egalitarian and activist understanding of the rights of man, which set him at odds from the outset with even the remarkably broad franchise (all twenty-five-year-old male inhabitants, native born or naturalized, who appeared on the tax rolls) under which the Third Estate deputies were elected to the Estates General.[141] In October 1789, after the Third Estate deputies had transformed themselves boldly into the National Assembly and passed the Declaration of the Rights of Man and the Citizen, the Assembly turned to consider the September recommendations of its Constitutional Committee on the future bounds of the franchise. The Committee, largely on Sieyes's prompting, had already distinguished sharply between two types of citizen: active citizens who pay taxes and 'are the only real stakeholders in the great social enterprise', and the sole full members of the association, and passive citizens ('women, at least under current circumstances, children, foreigners, and those who make no fiscal contribution to the state').[142] Passive citizens are fully entitled to the protection of their person, property and freedom. But only active citizens have the right to take an active part in the election of public officials. The Committee's proposals restricted the franchise to adult male residents of twenty-five or older, duly qualified by birth or naturalization, who paid taxes of at least three days' local wages.[143] The resulting restriction was criticized by one or two speakers in the Assembly itself (the Abbé Grégoire and the Physiocrat Dupont de Nemours), and assailed in Camille Desmoulins's crusading newspaper *Les Révolutions de France et de Brabant*. But it was left to Robespierre to mount a full-scale attack upon it in the Assembly. The proposal to confine the franchise in this way, he claimed in his opening speech on the matter, clashed directly with three separate Articles in the Declaration of the Rights of Man.

> *All citizens, no matter who they are, have the right to aspire to every degree of representation. Anything less would be out of keeping with your declaration of rights, to which every privilege, every distinction and every exception must yield. The constitution has established that sovereignty resides in the People, in every member of the populace. Each individual therefore has the right to a say in the laws by which he is governed and in the choice of the administration which belongs to him. Otherwise it is not true to say that all men are equal in rights, that all men are citizens.*[144]

'A man is by definition a citizen,' he went on the next day. 'No one can take away this right which is inseparable from his existence here on earth.'[145] Two years later, in the final debate on the Constitution, he rejected the very idea of passive citizenship, 'an insidious and barbarous expression, which defiles both our laws and our language'.[146]

In February 1794, a few months before his death and at the height of the Terror, he linked this view finally with democracy itself, in the Report which he drafted to the Convention on behalf of the

Committee of Public Safety on the 'Principles of Political Morality which must guide the National Convention in the Internal Administration of the Republic'. His ambitions were characteristically lofty, and expressed with more than a touch of bombast.

'We wish in a word, to fulfil the will [*les voeux*] of nature, to accomplish the destiny of humanity, to keep the promises of philosophy, to absolve providence of the long reign of crime and tyranny.' Let France, for so long a country of slaves, eclipse 'the glory of all previous free peoples, and become a model for all nations, the terror of oppressors, the consolation for the oppressed, the ornament of the universe, and, sealing our work with our blood, may we see at least the dawn of universal felicity.'[147]

The sole form of government which could realize these prodigies was

democratic or republican: these two words are synonymous, despite the vulgar abuse of language, for aristocracy is no more the republic than monarchy is. Democracy is not a state in which the people, continuously assembled, regulates by itself all public affairs, still less one in which a hundred thousand fractions of the people, by isolated, precipitate and contradictory measures, would decide the destiny of the entire society. Such a government has never existed and if it ever did, all it could do would be to return the people to despotism.

Democracy is a state in which the sovereign people, guided by laws which are its own work, does by itself all it can do well, and by delegates all that it could not.

It is therefore in the principle of democratic government that you must look for the rules of your political conduct.

To found and consolidate democracy amongst us, to reach the peaceful reign of constitutional laws, we must end the war of liberty against tyranny and pass happily through the storms of the Revolution.

This is the goal of the revolutionary system.

*The fundamental principle of democratic or popular govern-
ment, the essential* ressort *which sustains it and makes it move,
is virtue, the public virtue which worked such miracles in Greece
and Rome and which would produce even more startling ones in
republican France – the love of country and its laws.*

*Since the essence of the Republic or democracy is equality,
the love of country necessarily embraces the love of equality.*[148]
It therefore presupposes or produces all virtues, [NB Two possibilities with sharply diverging practical implications] *since all
are simply expressions of the force of soul which enables a
person to prefer the public interest to all particular interests.*

Not only is virtue the soul of democracy, it can only exist inside
this form of government. In a monarchy the sole individual who can
truly love his country (*patrie*), and hence has no need for virtue, is the
monarch himself, since only he truly has a country or is the sovereign,
at least in fact. In effect he occupies the place of the people, and so
supplants it. To have a country one must be a citizen, and share in its
sovereignty. Only in a democracy is the state truly the country of all who
form it, and can it rely on as many interested defenders of its cause as it
numbers citizens. This is what makes free peoples superior to others.[149]

The French are the first people in the world who have established
true democracy, summoning all men to equality and the full rights of
citizenship. This is the real reason why all the tyrants leagued against
the Republic will be conquered in the end.

'Republican virtue is as necessary in the government as in the
people at large. If it fails in the government alone, there is still the
people to appeal to. Only when the latter is corrupted, is liberty truly
lost. Happily the people is naturally virtuous. A nation becomes truly
corrupt only when it passes from democracy to aristocracy or
monarchy.'[150]

In peacetime, popular government relies upon virtue. In revolution, it must 'rely simultaneously on virtue and terror: virtue, without which terror is deadly, terror without which virtue is impotent'.[151] Terror 'is merely prompt, severe and inflexible justice. Hence it is itself an emanation of justice, less a particular principle than a consequence of the general principle of democracy applied to the country's most pressing need.'[152]

The revolutionary government (Robespierre and his associates) was the 'despotism of liberty against tyranny': a grim indivisible war,[153] in which any faltering or holding back must simply increase the strength of the Republic's enemies and divide and weaken its friends.[154]

In this nightmarish struggle, the sole remedy was the *ressort général* (the panacea) of the Republic, virtue.

'Democracy perishes by two excesses, the aristocracy of those who govern, or the contempt of the people for the authorities which it has itself established, a contempt in which each faction or individual reaches out for the public power, and reduces the people, through the resulting chaos, to nullity, or the power of a single man.'[155]

In this great and terrible address the Revolution comes into clear view, rending itself to pieces. But already, mere months before it completed the task of self-destruction, it had inscribed this old, battle-scarred, but for so long also oddly scholastic, term ineffaceably upon its standard, handing it on without apology to fellow humans across the world and far into the future. It was Robespierre above all who brought democracy back to life as a focus of political allegiance: no longer merely an elusive or blatantly implausible form of government, but a glowing and perhaps in the long run all but irresistible pole of attraction and source of power.

Chapter   Three

THE LONG SHADOW
OF THERMIDOR

Robespierre is still a figure of reptilian fascination. But what matters for us is not the man himself, nor the role he played within the Revolution's lurid political intrigues. It is the words and ideas which blew through him. In that awesome speech, he saw something which has proved overwhelmingly important, and he expressed a judgement which most of us now in some form confidently presume to be valid. Just as certainly, however, he failed utterly throughout his life to bring whatever he did see into sharp and steady focus, let alone communicate it dependably to anyone else; and we, in our turn, are still straining to capture just where the valid element in the judgement that democracy is the mandatory form for legitimate rule really lies. It is quite possible that we are still at such a loss because there simply is no clear form in which the judgement is valid,[1] just a hurricane of abusive or seductive verbiage, and a blind shapeless human struggle which those words serve to shroud more than illuminate.

We do not need to decide whether in democracy Robespierre himself saw clearly something which was and remains genuinely politically compelling (how a state must be to fully earn the devotion of its citizens, the Form of the Modern Political Good), or whether what he saw, through a haze of blood, was no better than a shimmering mirage. You can read his speech even now as a conscious projection of Jean-Jacques Rousseau's answer to the central question of the *Contrat Social*: what can render legitimate the bonds of political authority (those bonds which everywhere bind humans each of whom was born free)?[2] You can also hear it, every bit as plausibly, as a desperate plea to his fellow citizens, in face of all the evidence, to feel and act as though the demands of their temporary and shaky rulers were fully legitimate – less a claim to truth than a bid for loyalty very much in extremis.

The democracy which Robespierre affirms is synonymous with the republic as a form of state. By 1794 it made some sense to insist that a republic, the reluctant political product of France's turmoil, could no more be an aristocracy than it could a monarchy. That was a lesson which no one could have drawn solely from the record of history, in which very many republics, from the grandest of all (ancient Rome) to the longest lived and most politically effective of its modern successors (Venice) had been ostentatiously aristocratic. France had begun its Revolution by declaring war on aristocracy; and its efforts to re-educate its monarch into dependable enmity towards its own aristocracy had been a conspicuous failure. The quest to combine democracy with monarchy in varying proportions persisted in France itself at intervals for almost a century, with at least one notable triumph along the way in the person of Napoleon. It was emulated widely elsewhere for quite some time, and is still not wholly discredited in some settings (Morocco, Thailand, Holland, Sweden, Britain, and in future perhaps even Saudi Arabia). But even today the very term republic (*respublica* – the public thing in contrast to the private thing)[3] is more a claim to enjoy the quality of legitimacy than an explanation of what that legitimacy might consist in, or an account of what could validly confer it. Heard clearly, it is far closer to a flat, indistinct, ideological boast, than an effective structure of ideological justification. By 1794 a republic claiming legitimacy could hope to vindicate its claim by setting itself against aristocracy, and could use democracy, without further explanation, to express and authenticate its categorical opposition to aristocracy.

What it could not do was to use the same category to settle the questions of how exactly its own rule should be organized, what if anything should limit its powers in practice, or who should acquire the opportunity to exercise that rule for how long and by just what means. Ancient democracy was the name of a set of relatively definite political arrangements, worked out to preclude the continuing rule of aristocrats, or self-appointed and permanent monarchs (tyrants, as the Greeks called them). It was also, however, the name of the goal of avoiding either type of subjection, a goal which could be, and was, adopted as a shared purpose by a very active community of citizens. Robespierre was clearly appealing to this aspect of the term's history when he invoked it on behalf of himself and his political collaborators. In doing so, he faced the immediate political inconvenience that the practical arrangements to which it had referred in the ancient world differed so starkly from the unnerving routines of the Committee of Public Safety.

When he assured the Convention, in that Committee's name, that 'democracy was not a state in which the people continuously assembled regulates by itself all public affairs',[4] he was underlining something salient and evidently important about the term's history. A 'state in which the people continuously assembled regulates by itself all public affairs' was an excellent, if selective, description of what ancient democracy had aimed at with some determination and at times largely achieved.[5] It was a wholly implausible description of France's Revolution at any point along its turbulent way. Even the people of Paris, the *menu peuple* who formed the angry crowds which drove the Revolution forwards, storming the Bastille or the Tuileries Palace, or even surging into the Assembly itself, were in no position to assemble continuously, and never entertained the fantasy that they might truly be ruling France.[6] They intervened, in the great revolutionary *journées*, not as rulers themselves, but as citizens deeply affronted by the actions or inaction of those who genuinely were ruling France (or at least should have been), to force them into bolder courses, sharply restrict their future freedom of action, or change the cast drastically. To acknowledge that, even in Revolution, France was no democracy in that clear and serviceable sense was merely to acknowledge, as Sieyes and Madison had done before him, that a territorial state on the scale of France, if it was to be democratic at all, would have to be made and kept so by a system of representation. It would have to be, in a phrase casually coined over a decade earlier by Alexander Hamilton, a *representative democracy*.[7]

A representative democracy was no system of direct citizen self-rule. Instead, what it offered was a system of highly indirect rule by representatives chosen for the purpose by the people. To acknowledge this indirection was merely to recognize the obvious. In insisting on applying the category of democracy to France's revolutionary state in this way, Robespierre was not arguing against committed enemies so much as deploying the term in a mildly eccentric manner of his own. What was less obvious was the basis of his urgent repudiation of the second possible interpretation of what democracy might still now mean: 'one in which a hundred thousand fractions of the people, by isolated, precipitate and contradictory measures, would decide the destiny of the entire society'.[8] In this guise, democracy was no unreal dream of political community somewhere else very long ago. It was an all too real nightmare of the chaos into which France had often threatened to descend in the course of the previous five years. The hundred thousand fractions, although a numerical exaggeration, were the local sites and units of revolutionary agitation, the *Section* meetings of Paris itself, the political clubs across the nation, the *Sans-culottes* gatherings which endlessly frustrated every attempt to cool the Revolution down and bring it to a steady and reassuring close. In the opening years of the Revolution, while Robespierre was establishing his reputation and forging the structures of identification and political support which for a time gave him such power, these sites and their occupants formed his main political resource. With the Terror, the strains of war and the worsening challenge of provisioning Paris with food which most of its inhabitants could afford to eat, his erstwhile friends turned increasingly against him. Their multiplicity, disorganization and practical indiscretion no longer afforded an endless array of opportunities to disrupt the governmental strategies of his ruling enemies. Instead, they became an increasingly perturbing and infuriating obstacle to his own attempts to rule France coherently and effectively in face of its deadly peril.

In February 1794, if ever, France desperately needed a government. The alternative of dissolving into anarchy had no open champions. But at each setting throughout France, the 'hundred thousand' fractions of the people naturally viewed their own purposes very differently; and, even in retrospect, they and their self-conscious descendants saw the closing down of this seething disorder less as a belated recognition of the requirements of political reality than as a crushing defeat in conditions of overwhelming external menace. Two years after Robespierre's death a handful of these former friends plotted clumsily to overthrow the new rulers who had taken power from Robespierre on the Ninth of Thermidor and unleash the second and greater Revolution, which was also to be the last of all Revolutions.[9] The plot itself may have been largely a confused and defiant dream; and most of its participants (real or supposed) were picked up effortlessly by the police.[10] But one of the few who certainly did belong to it, a spoiled and intemperate Tuscan aristocrat, Filippo Michele Buonarroti,[11] lived long enough to immortalize them over thirty years later by publishing in Brussels exile his own stirring account of the Conspiracy, a text from which Karl Marx later drew much of his sense of the Revolution's political and social dynamics.[12]

It was the leading figure in the Conspiracy of the Equals, Gracchus Babeuf, who provided it in retrospect with its name. In his defence before the tribunal of Vendôme he gave it an outline far sharper than the muddled reality of the conspiracy itself, and led promptly to his own execution. The main motif in Buonarroti's account was his insistence on equality as the Revolution's deepest and most transformative goal, and on the profound gulf between the true defenders of equality and their sly and all too politically effective adversaries, the partisans of the order of egoism, or 'the english doctrine of the economists',[13] who had struggled against them throughout its course, and ended by triumphing over them. The Revolution had marked an ever-growing discord between the partisans of opulence and distinctions, and those of equality or of the numerous class of workers.[14] The partisans of egoism saw national prosperity as lying in the multiplicity of needs, the ever-growing diversity of material enjoyments, in an immense industry, a limitless commerce, a rapid circulation of coined money, and, in the last instance, in the anxious and insatiable cupidity of the citizens.[15] Once the happiness and strength of a society is placed in riches, the exercise of political rights must necessarily be denied to those whose fortune provides no guarantee of their attachment to the creation and defence of wealth. In any such social system, the great majority of citizens is constantly subjected to painful labour, and condemned in practice to languish in poverty, ignorance and slavery.[16]

The fundamental struggle on which the Revolution had turned, in the eyes of both Babeuf and Buonarroti, was the struggle between the order of egoism and the order of equality. In the order of egoism, the sole *ressort* of the feelings and actions of the citizens was purely personal interest, independent of any relation to the general good.[17] For its partisans, Rousseau's party, equality formed the basis of sociability and furnished the consolation of the wretched. For their opponents, depraved by the love of wealth and power, it was merely a chimera.

The order of egoism was aristocratic in substance because it inevitably generated inequality, and because it both required and ensured the exercise of sovereign power by one part of the nation over the rest. The freedom of a nation is the product of two elements: the equality which its laws create in the conditions and enjoyments of the citizens, and the fullest extension of their political rights.[18] The second is no substitute for the first; and the friends of equality clearly recognized the destructiveness of concentrating on constitutional reconstruction at the expense of real equality of condition. They saw their more constitutionally preoccupied opponents, the Girondins, as a branch of the vast conspiracy against the natural rights of man.

Throughout Buonarroti's story, '*Democrat*' appears as a party label, the political form of the partisans of the order of equality. It was the expression of *democratic* ideas which shows the partisans of the order of equality re-entering politics after the crushing blow of Robespierre's fall, *democrats* who carried their campaign forward over the next year, *democrats* whom the conspiracy's Secret Directory must ensure were elected to the new national government by the people of Paris, one for each *département*, once tyranny was over-thrown.[19] What had lost France both democracy and liberty even before Thermidor was the diversity of views, the conflict of interests, the lack of virtue, unity and perseverance in the National Convention.[20] The new, and carefully vetted, National Assembly at which the conspirators aimed, *democrats* to a man, would display none of these vices and weaknesses. The point of the vetting, and the grounds for operating not merely in secret but as a tightly organized body bound together in shared conviction, was precisely to eliminate them.

One reason why democracy remained such a fiercely divisive political category in Europe for the next fifty years was that Buonarroti's conception of what it meant continued to strike a deeper chord than the very different view worked out in practice at the same time in the United States. In America, once the Constitution was firmly in place, democracy soon became the undisputed political framework and expression of the order of egoism. It also developed, in retrospect quite rapidly, a rich understanding of its own character, centring, as Tocqueville in due course showed,[21] on the idea of equality, interpreted in terms fundamentally different from those of Babeuf or Buonarroti. American equality was above all an equality of standing, and a comprehensive rejection of all overt forms of political condescension. It arose from and endorsed a society both self-consciously and actually in rapid motion, expanding in territory, growing in wealth, and looking forward to a future of permanent and all but limitless change. Even aside from the long and ineffectively repressed trauma of slavery, it was sometimes a society ill at ease with many aspects of itself; and throughout the nineteenth and twentieth centuries it continued to harbour its own partisans of the order of equality, understood in much the *Babouviste* manner. But no American partisan of equality who wished to deny its compatibility with the order of egoism could afford to offer their followers or potential supporters a political access less open than the rowdy rituals of electoral competition already provided. They might fight long and hard on other terrain, for a time win many battles, and accumulate, as at points with the labour unions, a considerable amount of local defensive power. But in the long run, and on the terrain where they must secure their victory in the end, in elections to Congress and to the Presidency, they were always to find themselves heavily out-spent and out-voted.

In America, therefore, the story of democracy has blended indistinguishably into the political history of the country as a whole. It has remained a potent political counter within the ideological struggles which defined that history, as a goal and as an instrument for hastening (or impeding) movement towards that goal. At points too, often courtesy of the most purposefully anti-democratic element of the Constitution, the well-protected autonomy of the Supreme Court, it helped to break through dense barriers to equality: slavery, segregation, dismally effective political exclusion. In the long run it has ensured that the great majority of America's adult citizens now enjoy political rights which they can exercise, if they choose to.[22] (A growing number in practice, no doubt for their own good reasons, now often choose not to.)

You can see that outcome at least two ways, as a comprehensive practical refutation of Babeuf's and Buonarroti's somewhat rudimentary understanding of political and economic possibilities, or a crushing historical defeat for the ideals to which they clung. But it is still far from evident that there is anything wrong or confused in seeing the same outcome both ways at once. The order of egoism always had ample reason to rely upon the adequacy of its motivational support.[23] In democracy in America it discovered how to combine the abandonment of distinction as an organizing principle in politics or social form with its uninhibited efflorescence in economic and social reality. America today remains a society uncomfortable with every surviving vestige of explicit privilege, but remarkably blithe in face of the most vertiginous of economic gulfs, and comprehensively reconciled to the most obtrusive privileges of wealth as such. Behind this outcome lies the continuing vitality of its economy, the real source of the victory of the partisans of 'distinction, or the english doctrine of the economists'. Not all the economists, of course, did promise America or anywhere else permanent prosperity, let alone ever-growing prosperity. But the context in which American democracy has developed as it has was given, above all, by the extent to which those who assured their readers that long-term growth in the wealth of nations was to be expected have so far proved to be right, at least in the case of America itself. It has also been shored up quite effectively by the extent to which other economists, who cast varying degrees of doubt on that prospect, and insisted instead that equal or greater prosperity, and on more prepossessing terms, could be provided there or elsewhere on some wholly different basis, have proved more or less catastrophically wrong.

James Madison, as we have seen, provides no explanation of why the form of state which now dominates the world should have come to call itself a *democracy*. For him, as for most of his American contemporaries who were even acquainted with the word, democracy was something altogether different and distinctly unenticing. What his brilliant analysis in the *Federalist* papers does offer, alongside Alexander Hamilton, is a sound explanation of why a state of broadly this form should have proved so successful. It is above all that this form of state alone can hope to represent its own people effectively over time. It, and perhaps in the very long run, only it, can unite immediate practical viability with a convincing claim to act on behalf of and by courtesy of the body of its own citizens. To delegate government to relatively small numbers of citizens but also insist that they be chosen by most, if not all, of their fellows was a cunning mixture of equality and inequality. It could not guarantee sustained victory in practice to the partisans of opulence and distinction. But it could and did open up an arena in which that victory could be sought and won time and time again, and won through the judgements and by the choices of the citizens themselves. By doing so, and by leaving their victory apparently permanently at the mercy of reconsideration, in the long run, it also won them the war.

Unsurprisingly, this has proved a very considerable service to the patrons of opulence and distinctions. But it has done so over time, of course, only because opulence and distinctions (the combination offered) have struck more citizens on balance as collectively beneficial than as simply malign.[24] What gives the formula such strength over time is its elasticity in settings where opulence has duly grown. It could scarcely work for long anywhere where distinction must be sustained through stagnant or diminishing wealth, and has been widely and understandably abandoned, often with very little hesitation, in circumstances of this kind: in Europe of the 1920s and 1930s, in Latin America sometimes for decade after decade, in East or South East Asia, in Sub-Saharan Africa, sooner or later, almost everywhere but in the post-Apartheid Republic of South Africa itself.

The elasticity never provides a perfect shield. The balance of benefit and revulsion shifts everywhere all the time. But it is hard to exaggerate the political advantage of the protection it does provide. You can see why that advantage is so huge by setting Madison's misgivings about democracy side by side with Babeuf's and Buonarroti's picture of what democracy requires. For Madison what made democracy clearly impracticable was above all its scale. The United States simply could not be governed as a democracy. But its blatant impracticality did not render democracy any less alarming as a political idea. In that guise even Madison had no difficulty in recognizing its disruptive appeal. It was the appeal, above all, of immediacy and directness, with its deliberate openness to the most erratic of judgement, to unrestricted factional passion and to swirling intrigue. At the limit, he noted, it suggested irresistibly to its admirers a remaking of society and a reconstitution of property relations, to render the citizens as equal in other aspects of their lives as they strove to be in the activity of governing themselves.

For Babeuf and Buonarroti the point of democracy was to attain just such a comprehensive equality, the only undelusive and uncorrupting condition in which human beings could live together with one another on any substantial scale. The appeal of that goal has naturally varied dramatically across time and space, at its most acute whenever, as in the aftermath of Thermidor, the partisans of distinction and opulence are unmistakably in the saddle, and very many must live alongside them in misery. What in the long run has blunted equality's appeal as a goal is the unpromising instruments for realizing it and the rigidities inherent in its pursuit. (Had it been reached, the goal would no doubt have proved to harbour further repulsions of its very own; but these, thus far, remain a matter of theoretical speculation, not a truth of experience.) These rigidities come in effect from the goal itself. Conspiracy, of course, was not an instantly plausible political form for democrats to adopt. Still less so was its successor form, fine-tuned for the next three decades by Buonarroti himself, the closed conspiratorial secret society, of which in some cases he appears to have been the sole member.[25] But anyone in political adversity may have to choose between stealth and surrender; and Babeuf and Buonarroti hoped to conspire briefly, in order to live and act freely and more or less openly, into an indefinite future. The outcome of the conspiracy, such as it was,[26] certainly showed they had every reason for stealth. Under less dangerous and flustered conditions, the goal of equality proved less alluring to most citizens than either had hoped, easily set aside in favour of modest material gains and a quieter life. Wherever the opportunity to vote freely has been extended across an entire adult population, the majority has found it unattractive to vote explicitly for the establishment of equality. (The closest to a counter-example has been the remarkable governmental dominance of Swedish Social Democracy, which has made Sweden a very different country to live in from any of its European counterparts, but even today is clearly widening the room for distinctions as well as opulence.) What Babeuf and Buonarroti hoped for in democracy's triumph has been as far from coming true as what Madison feared from the same outcome. Democracy's real triumph has been a triumph for their word, as much as for Pericles's; but its practical political and economic consequences have proved far more a triumph for Madison's idea.

As soon as it became a word, democracy very clearly implied a form of government. For us it has come to name not merely a form of government, but also, and every bit as much, a political value. In retrospect this extension of meaning must have been quite rapid. By the time that the Old Oligarch set himself to diagnose its political appeals, or Pericles spoke so glowingly in praise of it, it had come to be just as much a political value for the Greeks themselves, as admired or even loved by some, as it was despised and detested by others. For most of its history as a word, as we have seen, far more of those to whom it meant anything at all viewed it with scorn or suspicion than felt any trace of admiration for it. Today, things could scarcely be more different. In practice, such scorn and hatred are still often every bit as intense as they ever were. But in most settings at most times they now find it prudent to express themselves considerably more surreptitiously. Democracy does still retain principled opponents in some quarters. Iran's Guardianship Council, for example, seldom hesitates to express its contempt for the liberal reformers voted in with President Khatami, and still does all it can to place them beyond reach of popular election in the future. But even in Iran, the advantages of staging elections are implicitly accepted by those who most fear to lose them; and the principled rejection of elections has become very much a minority taste.

The historical momentum of the term *democracy* from 1796 up to today leaves us two very different elements which we plainly need to understand. One is a matter of the fate of political institutions: the diffusion of a variety of forms of state increasingly eager to describe themselves as democracies, and the relatively sudden and widespread victory of one type of claimant to the title over all its extant competitors. The second may at first sight seem simply verbal, the ever more pervasive diffusion of the term *democracy* as a ground of political commendation, a way of capturing the supposed or real merits not just of one set of political institutions against another, but of almost any features in the organization of our lives together, organized as we would like them to be, and not as we would emphatically wish they were not.

If we keep these two targets for potential understanding firmly apart, we would expect to find very different ingredients to their explanations. The fate of forms of government must turn on the capacity to create and defend wealth and enforce compliance, all of which can be assessed with some confidence, at least in retrospect. But it also turns on the sustained capacity to persuade, which is far harder to judge with any accuracy, before, during or after its exercise.

The creation and defence of wealth, too, and even the capacity to enforce compliance, under scrutiny, turn out to require a sustained capacity to persuade (what David Hume called 'opinion').[27] Over the last century and more, the commendatory force of the idea of democracy has proved a key element within the intensely competitive process of sustained persuasion which makes up so much of the political life of every human community. If we try to follow the historical vicissitudes of the state forms and verbal commendations which have implicated the term *democracy* from 1796 to the present day, we shall certainly find the two stories merging inextricably with one another over much of the time and distance which we need to cover. We shall also find, whenever we can keep them apart for a moment or two, each affecting the other quite brusquely and almost at once.

The distinction between being persuaded and being coerced, as every child, spouse or colleague knows, is not necessarily a sharp one within human experience. But there is scarcely another contrast to which most human beings attach greater importance. Undisguised coercion is frequently dismaying; and coercion ineffectually disguised as persuasion can be acutely offensive. A large part of the story which leads from 1796 up to today (the story of modern politics),[28] has been the record of a continuing rise in the practical importance of persuasion in shaping the terms on which human beings live with one another, and the forms within which they seek to do so. As a modern political term, *democracy* is above all the name for political authority exercised solely through the persuasion of the greater number, or for other sorts of authority in other spheres supposedly exercised solely on a basis acceptable to those subjected to it.

Persuasion, of course, had been central to the practice of democracy in Athens itself.[29] It was by the direct force of persuasion, exercised on innumerable and overwhelmingly public occasions, that the political leaders of Athens held or lost control over the city's political decisions. It was by persuasion, exercised in the last instance in the Assembly itself and against all comers, that Pericles for a time, in

Thucydides's eyes, turned Athens effectively into a monarchy, the rule of a single man by continuing consent of the people.[30] *Democracy* is a far more insinuating name than *republic* for a politics openly centred on persuasion. It recognizes the people not merely as notional bearers of ultimate authority, but also as a site of power in themselves, with a capacity to act and exert force on their own behalf. There may be a large element of unreality in that recognition, a stilted and insincere courtesy which veils a sometimes all too authentic contempt. If democracy today, as the Austrian expatriate Joseph Schumpeter bluntly assured his Harvard audiences and in due course the world, is 'the rule of the politician',[31] it is at least the rule of politicians under real pressure to address their subjects politely and solicit their endorsement, and refrain from reconstituting their rule as an informal aristocracy or monarchy of their own. Even in the hands of the shiftiest of career politicians, democracy has not proved a compelling name for styles of government which are openly autocratic, authoritarian or tyrannical. The Big Lie can succeed remarkably as a short-term political tactic; but it has failed to show itself in the long run a potent formula for securing political authority.

As the title of a form of government, in the key ideological outcome of the last two centuries of an ever more global politics, the partisans of the order of egoism have captured the word of the Equals. The Equals, in the meantime, have largely been driven from the political field. But neither their scattered remnants, nor even their more sophisticated intellectual admirers,[32] have felt inclined to surrender a word they still find irresistibly compelling. To them, the capture, even now, seems not a conquest in a just war, but an unabashed theft, secured by expedients they still do not really understand. Even fifty years ago the outcome of that war was very far from obvious to anyone; and the failure to anticipate it no more surprising in the case of those who loathed it than it was in the case of those who longed for little else. By now, however, the incomprehension of the losers is no testimony to their political intelligence. Once a war is well and truly lost, it is seldom hard to see quite why it has come out as it has.

What is far harder to understand is why the partisans of the order of egoism should have bothered to capture the Equals' word. It was not a word commended to them by their wisest intellectual advisers, by Madison, or Sieyes, or even Adam Smith. It was not a word which appealed to the ruling authorities or military commanders who, for more than the next century, ensured across Europe that the partisans of equality were defeated time and time again: in the revolutions of 1848, in 1871, in 1918. Today, by contrast, no serious partisan of the order of egoism would deny themselves the political advantages of democratic authorization, as anything more than a temporary expedient, an enforced and mildly humiliating departure from the demands of political decorum. In embracing the term democracy so steadily and so purposefully, the political leaders of capitalism's overwhelming advance have not been juggling idly with empty symbols. They have recognized, and done their best to appropriate and tap, a deep reservoir of political power.

This is the vital judgement. If it was wrong, then politics would have no special place in the story of democracy's triumph, and that triumph might well have no real political significance. The sources and mechanisms of the triumph would have had to come from somewhere quite different, above all, no doubt, from the laws of economics and the crushing weight of weapons of ever more massive destruction. The real stories which we needed to follow would be stories of economic organization and technical change, and of armaments and their deployment. Those stories would be insulated and self-contained. They would carry within them the prerequisites for their own passage through time and space, and owe nothing of consequence to the efforts, whether on their behalf or against them, of rulers or politicians. Or, if they owed anything at all, they would owe it solely to the decisions which rulers or politicians make, for better or worse, over the shaping of economies and the acquisition or use of the tools of war.

There have been striking attempts to see human history in these terms, of which Karl Marx's was much the most inspiring, and for a time had by far the greatest historical impact: not least on the development of economies and the deployment of weapons systems. But in the end these pictures are not merely misleading; they are simply incoherent. The ideas which give them their shape and their air of force, seen clearly, do not even make sense. Economies are permanently at the mercy of rulers. Private property, the foundation on which a capitalist economy operates, is sustained or cancelled at political will. Money, the medium through which it operates, must be nurtured by political prudence, and can be jeopardized or even dissolved by the clumsiness or dishonesty of rulers or public officials. Currencies rise and fall, and economies thrive or disintegrate, through the good sense and scruple, or the cynicism and folly, of those who govern. No government can make a country prosper; but any government can ruin one; and most today are in a position to do so very rapidly and extremely thoroughly.[33] Democracy's real triumph, its victory over the last three-quarters of a century, has come in an epoch where the powers of rulers to damage an economy and harm the lives of entire populations have shown themselves greater than they have ever proved before.

Once we recognize democracy's triumph as a political outcome, many things fall into place. We can grasp that it was not, and could never have been, an automatic concomitant of something quite different, beneath, above or beyond politics. We can see at once both how recent and how extraordinary that triumph really is, everywhere beyond the United States itself. We can see that what has triumphed is not merely an exceedingly vague word, and a form of state associated, perhaps somewhat speciously, with that word, but above and beyond both, a pressing and engaging political agenda. An agenda is a summary listing of what is to be done; and every government requires such a list sooner or later. What is special to democracy's agenda is its assertion that in the end it must be the people that decides what is to be done. This is never a good description of what determines what is done, still less of who takes the decision. What it is is a permanent reminder of the terms in which governmental decisions must now be vindicated, and the breadth of the audience that is entitled to assess whether or not they have been vindicated. Until democracy's triumph, the rightful scale of that audience was always seen as pretty narrow. It was defined by a layering of exclusions: those without the standing, those without the knowledge or ability, those without a stake in the country, the dependent, foreigners, the unfree or even enslaved, the blatantly untrustworthy or menacing, the criminal, the insane, women, children. Democracy's triumph has been the collapse of one exclusion after another, in ever-greater indignity, with the collapse of the exclusion of women, the most recent, hastiest and most abashed of all. Today only the child remains excluded everywhere, openly and without much embarrassment; and even for them, the age at which childhood ends is creeping steadily down.

For most of human history it has been above all dependence and exclusion which have given structure to human societies. With the coming of literacy, and the formalization of many aspects of the relations between human beings over most of the world's inhabited surface,[34] both dependence and exclusion were converted increasingly into self-conscious principles of social order. Democracy's triumph has been above all the backwash from this great movement of subordination. It signals and reinforces the steadily rising pressure to break the sway of these two principles and refashion the relations between human beings on softer and less offensive lines. Democratization is the working through of their prospective successors, the imposition of the apparent requirements of equality on the endlessly resistant material of human lives. No one today could mistake it, as Babeuf and Buonarroti each plainly did, for movement towards a known and clearly defined destination. But for all its open-endedness and untransparency, it shows unmistakably the continuing force of the

Equals' word, even buried deep inside the order of egoism itself.

The market economy is the most powerful mechanism for dismantling equality that humans have ever fashioned. But it is not simply equality's enemy, as Babeuf and Buonarroti confidently supposed. Instead, two centuries later and after much considered thought and many confused struggles, that economy has settled with growing resolution on a single political form and a particular image of society. Each grounds itself directly on the claim to recognize the ways in which humans are equal and to protect them equally in living as they choose. You do not need to accept the validity of that claim (or even its sincerity) to see what a momentous shift the claim represents.

This great choice has been a single story. In all its complexity and opacity, it has also been very much democracy's story. As stories go, it lacks a clear narrative line and conspicuously fails to carry its own meaning clearly on the surface. Its massive silences weigh just as heavily as its loudest choruses. Most prominent on its surface has been the spectacular diffusion of a word, but a word which, on examination, carries no clear or fixed meaning. Almost as obtrusive has been the staccato passage of several competing forms of government, each claiming to embody that word, from one geographical setting to another. The story of the word's diffusion has also been the story of an endless enquiry into what it does or should mean (how it may or may not justifiably be employed). The passage of forms of government has been at the same time an uninterrupted struggle over who exactly is entitled to act in the people's name, and on what grounds, over which forms of inequality, dependence or exclusion are to survive, be suppressed or re-created, and over who is to be subject to whom over what.

If we view the story fastidiously and from a great distance, we can see it above all as the quest for a secular grail: a clear sight of the Form of Equality, which must also be the Form of the Good and the Just[35] In this guise it is as unclear as ever whether what has made the quest so forlorn has been the overwhelming imaginative inroads of the order of egoism,[36] or the deeper blindness of gender, reaching back far further in the past, or whether the quest itself has been throughout a hunt for a chimera: a treasure which was never there to find, the Form of something which from the outset simply never had a form.

If we view it more companionably, however, it must surely look very different, and in many settings altogether more encouraging. Not a quest for anything at all, but a stumbling, myopic blend of quarrelling and shared exploration of the inescapable issue of how to sustain everyday lives together as agreeably as possible. This is an eminently democratic perspective on the story, a view not from above, before or after, but simply from within. You could see it as a democratic practical enquiry into what democracy as a political value turns out to mean, as one people after another explores it together in the space that history and their enemies leave open to them.

We have followed the story of democracy as word over the two thousand years and more that separates its departure from the country of its birth from the point when it comes back to life in the fashioning and defence of political arrangements at the centre of a great state. There is no clear reason why it should have survived that lengthy passage. All we know is that, sometimes by the narrowest of margins, it somehow just did. No one knows what, if anything, will come after democracy. What we can hope to grasp, if we concentrate our minds on the issue, is four things about democracy as it now is. We can see why the word has changed so sharply in meaning between the days of Babeuf and those of Tony Blair or George W. Bush. We can see why the form of government to which it now principally applies should be so different both from its distant Greek originals and from any political practices which Robespierre or Babeuf can have had in mind. We can also see why the form of government which now comes so close to monopolising its application should have won such astonishing power across the world so rapidly and so recently. More intriguingly, if perhaps a shade less clearly, we can see, too, why this victorious regime should have picked this old Greek word of all words for its political banner. The contours of the history of a word, the fashioning of a novel form of state, the outcome of a global struggle for power, are all well-defined targets for understanding. Only the last question – the choice of a label by a type of state – may seem at first sight both elusive and relatively trivial.

This is a reasonable intellectual suspicion; but it is also deeply undemocratic. If we see these two hundred years and more as a single sequence of political choice, taking in an ever-widening cast list, the adoption of democracy as preferred label for the winning form of state must emerge as anything but an arbitrary quirk of taste. The history of the word will simply express that political choice as legibly as the clarity of the choice permitted in the first place. The state form can be seen to have won, not through its exquisite adjustment to something altogether different (the requirements for the competitive flourishing across the world of vast corporations of dubious local allegiance), but principally through the changing balance of preference, and in many settings and more directly, the allegiance through the harshest of ordeals, of that ever-widening cast list.

The history of democracy's triumph since Babeuf's head fell from the guillotine has been above all a history of political choice. That one vast overarching choice has been composed in turn of myriads and myriads of other choices, swelling in number, surging out across the continents of the world, but each in the end made by a single partially self-aware living human actor. To make sense out of that story, we need to grasp the contexts in which those myriads of choices were made and register the fierce external pressures which drove huge numbers of persons in one direction rather than another – in the great stampedes into and out of communist rule, or the vast convulsions of the two World Wars. To grasp those contexts and recognize those pressures will to some degree safeguard us against the temptation to romanticize our sense of what has been in play, or draw it too ingenuously from our own parochial horizon of experience. It will not exempt us from the responsibility to take a political attitude of our own to what the story means. Here democracy imposes an odd and austere requirement. On a democratic view, everywhere's political history must be equally valuable and equally significant (also, equally likely to prove silly, ludicrous or disgraceful). Its ordinary everyday squabbles and bemusements must carry just the same weight whenever and wherever they occur. None of it has any claim to privileged attention; and none can justifiably be discounted or ignored. There can be no elect nations, or continents, or even civilizations.

With democracy's triumph, this is a most disconcerting demand. It dissolves the pretensions of intellectuals and corrodes the claims to authority of all who happen at the time to exercise political authority anywhere in particular. It also decisively undermines any assumption that historical priority in the story could give privileged insight into its meaning (as though the Greeks, or the French, or the Americans, or for that matter the Belgians or the Swiss, might have understood democracy better than those who came later and so be in a position to determine whether or not their successors, or even imitators, have met or fallen short of standards already set once and for all).[37]

When America's President, George W. Bush, assured the world that 'The global expansion of democracy is the ultimate force in rolling back terrorism and tyranny',[38] he was drawing on deep convictions as well as expressing a devout hope for his own short-term political prospects. He was also expressing a political judgement on the record of America's role in the world over the last three-quarters of a century, in which its victories over Germany and Japan, and its triumph with the fall of the Soviet empire and the disintegration of the USSR, were alike testimony to its own political excellence, and the ever more irresistible recognition of that excellence across the world. More edgily, he was announcing too, the shape, if not the timing, of a local political strategy for the use of American military and economic power inside a still imperfectly subdued Iraq. The core of the strategy was to install in due course new institutions of government in Iraq, with at least some family resemblance to those of countries which the United States views as democracies, manned with dependable enemies of terrorism and tyranny as the United States elects to define them. This is not a process, rather evidently, which has ever been under firm control. Perhaps more importantly, it is also one which could remain under firm control for any length of time only by continuing miracle, or careful repudiation of its own core pretensions. Under democracy, it must be the people of Iraq who decide whom or what they wish to befriend or oppose. They prove to differ bitterly with one another over the question; and very few of them seem drawn to American views on the matter. If democracy does in the end triumph in Iraq, even in the limited sense of establishing a continuing electoral basis for acquiring new governments, it will do so by a sequence of Iraqi choices, and with abundant mutual odium. It will also do so less by spontaneous imitation of the admired practices of an exemplary model, graciously offered by the present occupying powers, than through grudging acceptance of imposed terms of peace. Terrorism and tyranny lie in the eye of the beholder; and under democracy each beholder not only will perceive them for themselves, but is explicitly entitled to do so.

In its own terms, and by its own standards, the story of democracy's triumph is a story that cannot be told. To tell it as a single story, you must stand outside it, and claim to stand above it, define terms and apply standards to it, which can be vindicated in their own right, and independently of its bemusing struggles. This is a very bold claim; and there is no reason whatever for anyone else to accept its validity. But if none of us can hope to tell the story itself with any adequacy, we can readily recognize that it has occurred, and try to answer some of the more salient questions which it raises.

Democracy's triumph, in the first place, has been the triumph of a word. What triumphs along with that word is a particular way of thinking (and refusing to think) about the authority to govern, and a range of institutions for selecting and restraining governments which claim to fit with that way of thinking. The way of thinking is never wholly convincing, since it equates ruler with ruled, while everywhere, as Joseph de Maistre noted, ruler and ruled remain stubbornly apart: 'the people who command are different from the people who obey.'[39] But for all its insubstantiality (and often its gross implausibility), it serves admirably to define the central challenge to rulers in the world which capitalism has refashioned. That challenge is to show the ruled that the authority which confronts them simply is their own: that it is their will which stands behind it, and their interests which it is compelled in the end to serve. To close that gap is a forlorn task, in logic, in psychology, in politics. But the acknowledgement that the gap should not be there, that no government has the right to rule anyone simply against their own will, is a vast concession. It marks a whole new world from the days when King Charles I of England on the scaffold, with stubborn confidence, assured his people in his dying address that 'a subject and a sovereign are clear different things'.[40] Only two months earlier Charles himself had picked out a term for that world, accusing his parliamentary enemies and the armies which they had unleashed of labouring 'to bring in democracy'.[41] It was not a word which attracted most of his enemies; and it made remarkably little political headway for at least the next century and a half. But, in the long run, it is the word which has stuck.

What makes it so adhesive is the posture of involuntary self-abasement which it imposes on any ruler who uses it. Self-abasement is neither a natural nor an agreeable posture for most rulers. Many, inevitably, continue to refuse it with some asperity. But it has proved a far more insinuating ground from which to claim authority than every other less dutiful expression of humility (let alone all the open expressions of arrogance or contempt).

For much of the time between 1796 and today there was little agreement over what sorts of institutions of government best met the term's demands. The task of differentiating true democracy from the many impostors which competed with it proved difficult as well as contentious. Today, the outcome of that competition looks suspiciously clear cut: more natural, or even inevitable, than it very probably should. It is not that the losers did not richly deserve to lose: just that it is still far from clear how far or why the present winner deserved to win and, if it did, quite what enabled it to do so. The Democratic and Popular Republic of Korea, the regime of Kim Jong Il, now seems as exotic as the world of Kubla Khan.[42] As almost the last surviving relic of a lengthy and potent challenger for the term's monopoly, it dramatizes in a particularly extreme way both the arbitrariness with which it can be invoked, and the implausibility of using it at all to describe the institutions of any modern state. Here the people rules twice over for good measure, and is ruled in response with as little apology or recourse as anywhere else on earth.

On a grim but plausible view, the Democratic and Popular Republic of Korea is the *terminus ad quem* of the Conspiracy of the Equals: not what Babeuf and Buonarroti wanted, but what in the end they were always going to get. It is not, of course, the sole candidate for that destination. Others with equally little enduring appeal have been the period of War Communism, which succeeded the Bolshevik Revolution, Mao's Cultural Revolution and the killing fields of the Khmer Rouge.[43] In these later episodes, in all their desolation, the rage for equality becomes for a time something very close to a rage against the reality of other human beings or the very idea of a society. Each made a certain kind of sense for a small group of overweeningly ambitious politicians, and a very different kind of sense for varying numbers of other groups to whom these politicians could appeal, and on whose support they relied. Each was made possible at all by extreme and mercifully unusual circumstances. No one is less equal, at the point of death, than murderer and victim. But what these episodes show is how far the principle of equality can carry, if left without impediment from any other principles, left to structure the lives of human beings all on its own. By equality's own standard, they may seem no more than a brutal caricature. But they show something far more instructive than the openness to abuse of a beguiling idea. They show that that idea is bound to prove self-contradictory if it ever comes to be treated as the unique structuring principle for the relations between human beings. Elevated to this lonely eminence, it both foments and licenses a deep impatience with the tastes, loyalties and commitments of the existing inhabitants of every real society. Between 1789 and 1796 a great many of the French population were made to ask themselves, sooner or later, whether they were in the end friend or enemy to the *ancien régime*. By 1796, a more select handful had come to recognize that they must side for or against the order of egoism, the global commercial civilization, founded on an ever-deepening division of labour and an endless proliferation of novel tastes. Some of this far smaller number were very clear that the answer to the second question followed from the answer to the first: that any enemy of the *ancien régime* must be an enemy, too, to the order of egoism. But in the long run this handful turned out to be wrong, if not indisputably in taste, at least unmistakably in expectation. Since 1789, throughout the world, the great majority of those who have had the chance have turned against the *ancien régime* in their own habitats. In ever more such habitats, sooner or later, it has proved impossible for their rulers to prevent them from doing so. Rule itself has certainly gone on virtually everywhere more or less throughout, very often on a far more intrusive basis, and sometimes with vastly greater brutality. But in ever more settings also, sooner or later, it has had to make terms with the principle of equality. What it has stalwartly refused to do is to make at all the kinds of terms which the Equals expected. It has chosen their word (perhaps even stolen it). But the subjects over whom it rules, and who permit it to rule them, have insisted for their own part, ever more pervasively, on embracing alongside it, and with at least equal passion and conviction, the order of egoism.

Placed within the order of egoism, equality faces more impediments, with greater powers of resistance, than it could have faced in any earlier form of human association. To Babeuf or Buonarroti, in this deeply inhospitable setting, equality would seem not so much confined, as tamed, or even neutered. But they may not be the best judges. Equality has not simply struck its colours, or abandoned its appeals to the passion and intelligence of its human audience. What permits the rulers to rule, in ever more settings and in the long run, is the response of that audience: the terms which it will accept. The key element in those terms has come to be the offer of a certain degree of equality, extended, as Plato long ago complained, to equals and unequals alike.[44]

This may sound a trifle fanciful. If inequality persists, and still more if it is regenerated ceaselessly by the central dynamic of the order of egoism, why should the proffered equality matter at all? Why should anyone even think it worth insisting on? There are three elements to the answer. In the first place, it matters because some recognition is better than none. Other things being equal, more recognition would plainly be better than less. But other things are far from equal. The Conspirators of 1796, in so far as they assumed anything definite, assumed that only full recognition could be either just or worth having. Only untrammelled and complete equality could bring the last Revolution, and reconcile human beings finally to one another over time. But untrammelled and complete equality is not even coherent as an idea; and the route towards it has always proved savagely divisive. It appeals to too few human emotions, for much too little of the time, and is swamped, rapidly and fatally, by the immediacy and impact of its incessant collisions with far too many other emotions. As a goal for rule it requires of any ruler who tries to implement it extreme and permanent coercion; and it guarantees to their subjects nothing but recognition (if indeed that). Certainly neither ease, nor comfort, nor amusement, and for the recalcitrant amongst them (those with opinions, tastes and wills of their own) not even much in the way of security. As Benjamin Constant saw it, early in the nineteenth century, it offers ancient liberty, the delusory rewards of a notional share in rule, in exchange for the surrender of modern liberty, the real rewards of living as they please, within the bounds of the criminal law and their own incomes.[45] It then turns this offer into a doctrinaire programme which suppresses the order of egoism en bloc.

In the long run, this last suppression proves simply unsustainable. Ease, comfort, amusement, and most of all security, attract too many too strongly for far too much of the time. Highly coercive rule seldom proves a plausible form of recognition. The order of egoism has no difficulty in generating overwhelming coercive power, and little difficulty in protecting itself, if not everywhere always, at least in more and more settings for more and more of the time, against the many enemies it ceaselessly evokes. The winning offer from rulers to ruled is not a fixed sum, but a highly plastic, and always partially opaque, formula. It blends minimal recognition with quite extensive protection of the institutional requirements of the order of egoism. It ensures property law, commercial regulation, and a due balance between taxing enough to provide the protection and protecting enough against all forms of expropriation (very much including taxation itself) for the order of egoism to proceed buoyantly on its way. The scope of recognition offered and the degree of protection provided are each renegotiated endlessly.

The offer matters in the first place because some degree of recognition (recognition as an equal, if necessary in the teeth of the evidence) carries a very deep appeal, enough appeal for huge masses of human beings to be prepared to fight for it long and hard, and fight with particular bitterness to retain or recapture it, when they are threatened with its withdrawal. It matters too, in the second place, just because the content of that recognition is always open to reinterpretation; and anyone can therefore hope at any point to deepen or consolidate what it has already given them. It offers a field of aspiration and an arena for struggle. It matters, lastly, because the recognition offered, while it may always threaten in practice the fluent operation of the order of egoism, is at least not openly contemptuous of, or hostile to, that order and its requirements. The equal citizens of a modern democracy may not listen very attentively or prove especially practically wise. But any of them can be importuned at any time, through their equal citizenship, to pay some heed to the requirements of the way of economic life on which they depend, and from which they draw the modern liberties they most prize. In this setting, it offers those who volunteer to rule them (and whom they then select for the purpose) at least a set of terms on which to address them on the requirements of collective prudence over time: above all, the need not to starve the goose that lays their golden eggs.

Chapter Four

WHY DEMOCRACY?

It is tempting to believe that democracy has won its present eminence for either or both of two reasons. Some prefer to attribute its victory to its evident political justice, its being plainly the best, and perhaps the sole clearly justifiable basis on which human beings can accept the apparent indignity of being ruled at all. Others find it easier to believe that it owes this eminence to the fact that it and it alone can ensure the well-protected and fluent operation of a modern capitalist economy. Neither cheery view, unfortunately, can possibly be right. Democracy in itself, as we have seen, does not specify any clear and definite structure of rule. Even as an idea (let alone as a practical expedient) it wholly fails to ensure any regular and reassuring relation to just outcomes over any issue at all. As a structure of rule, within any actual society at any time, it makes it overwhelmingly probable that many particular outcomes will turn out flagrantly unjust. The idea of justice and the idea of democracy fit very precariously together. They clash constantly in application. Any actual structure of rule will face incentives quite distinct from, and often sharply at odds with, the requirements for the fluent operation of a capitalist economy. But democracy, quite explicitly, thrusts upon its sovereign and notionally equal electors the right, and in some measure the opportunity, to insert their own preferences directly into the operating conditions of the economy, in the attempt to do themselves a favour. As a bargain, this has many great advantages. But no one could reasonably see it as a safe recipe for ensuring the dynamic efficiency of the economy at the receiving end.

If we want to understand how democracy has won this eminence, we must set aside these presumptions and think again and less ingenuously.

Let us take again the four questions which must have reasonably accessible answers. Why, in the first place, has the word democracy changed so sharply in meaning from the days of Babeuf to those of Tony Blair? Why, in the second place, is the form of government to which it now predominantly applies, through all its striking variation over time, culture and political economy, always so different, both from its Greek originals, and from Robespierre's or Babeuf's dreams? Why, in the third place, has that drastically different form of government won such extraordinary power across the world, so rapidly and so recently? Why, in the fourth place and somewhat more elusively, should this highly distinctive regime have picked this word of all words for its political banner? The first two questions are quite easy to answer, once you recognize that their answer depends on the answers to the last two. The third question today (now that the victory is in) is also relatively easy to answer, at least in outline. Once it has been answered, it also gives us the vital clue to the fourth question's answer. What is not possible is to answer that fourth question on its own, and solely through its own terms.

In retrospect Babeuf's Conspiracy was always a less than plausible embodiment of democracy. Free and open choice by all the citizens deliberating together can scarcely be mistaken in good faith for a secret conspiracy intent on seizing power and passing it promptly on to a government hand picked to exercise it acceptably.[1] But it was certainly important for Babeuf himself that this new government was to be only a temporary expedient, in face of the repressive power and will of the existing Thermidorian incumbents, with their shameless dedication to serving the interests of the wealthy. Babeuf himself did not accept the legitimacy of the Thermidorian regime. What he hoped would supplant it was less a clearly defined political structure (like the Assembly and Council of Athens) than a continuing practice of rule, not merely on behalf of the poorer majority of France's population, but with their active co-operation. This was still extremely close to Aristotle's or even Plato's conceptions of the least edifying variant of democracy (the rule of all by the poor majority for the poor majority), with the allegiance simply inverted. Babeuf's democrats might find themselves for a time forced to convert themselves, however nebulously, into a clandestine party. But there was nothing furtive about their political objectives. They saw no occasion for apology in a new regime in which most of the (adult male) population, in the modest circumstances in which they found themselves, would rule on their own behalf, or at least actively monitor and promptly correct any of those whom they chose to rule for them. By 1796 this was not a prospect which attracted the rich anywhere in the world. Today, by a long and winding route, in all the wealthiest countries in the world, the rich have learned to think better of the proposal and become quite thoroughly inured to it.

Democracy has changed its meaning so sharply between the days of Babeuf and those of Tony Blair, above all, because of and through a vast shift in political expectations. It is natural for us to see this shift predominantly as a movement from ingenuousness to sophistication, from the simple-minded delusions of Babeuf to the cool acuity of those who staff the re-election campaigns of George W. Bush (or even Tony Blair). But it is more illuminating to see it instead as a passage from one horizon of political experience to another, very different horizon. On the matter of democracy as each understood it, there was very little difference in expectation between Babeuf and his Thermidorian enemies. What each meant by democracy and imagined it would imply in practice was virtually the same. Where they differed intractably was in their evaluation of it and in the practical implications which they drew from that evaluation: in what they felt moved to try to bring about or avert.

A blithe view of the history of modern democracy would see this change in expectations as following docilely in the wake of a prior shift in moral and political conviction. It would see democracy's triumph as the victory of a compelling formula for just and legitimate rule, aptly rewarded after a discreet interval by the happy discovery that such rule holds few terrors for the rich, and promises at least some benefits to practically everyone. But with the partial but weighty exception of the United States, that was scarcely the history which in fact occurred.

Babeuf's own political venture was too ineffectual to shed any light on the realism of his political expectations. In the hands of more effective successors, most notably Lenin,[2] political expectations had already been recast purposefully before the bid for power was launched; and the tensions between egalitarian and democratic goals and authoritarian means and structures became and remained acute. It was not hard for those who detested the goals to highlight the gap between pretension and consequence, and present the continuing project of equality, through that yawning gap, as a deliberate fraud or a hideous and murderous confusion. After 1917 this ceased to be a simple debating point and became an extremely potent political accusation. The world of which Babeuf dreamed, a rich-free world at last made safe for the poor, never won widespread credibility. But the grander and far more intellectually self-congratulatory project of Communism, Equality on Stilts,[3] in due course secured very large numbers of overt adherents. For as long as it retained at least their titular allegiance, it clung on tight to Babeuf's political nostrum, interpreted with all the flexibility which he found natural himself. Democracy became in effect the regime name of the route towards equality, gracing whatever political institutions volunteered to shoulder the responsibility of pressing on towards that elusive goal. It was not until the change in expectations had run its course, and the defenders of equality had formally surrendered, that the claim to a special tie to democracy was surrendered along with it. This was not an internally generated change in belief or taste. It was a capitulation to the crushing weight of a wholly unwelcome experience.

The main battleground on which the struggle for democracy's mantle was initially fought out was the continent of Europe, and more particularly the western parts of Europe which Napoleon's armies controlled for longest and with least effort. The one key setting which those armies barely touched was the largest of the British Isles. (The record of Ireland was somewhat different.) But even in Britain, as throughout the European continent, until almost the end of the nineteenth century, democracy, under that name, remained the political goal of small groups of extreme dissidents, or movements which sought to challenge the existing order frontally and fundamentally.[4] Viewed from today, the practices which make up democracy, legislative elections based on widening franchises, greater freedom or even full secrecy at the ballot itself, executives at least partially accountable to those whom they ruled, were extended dramatically, sooner or later, across most of the continent. But their main forward movements, especially when these proved relatively durable, came not from the revolutionary collapse of the old order, or under the banner of democracy itself, but from deft defensive gambits by audacious conservative politicians, Count Cavour in Piedmont and in due course Italy, Otto von Bismarck in Prussia and later Germany, Benjamin Disraeli in Britain.[5] Even in France itself, under the revolutionary Second Republic, the new electors promptly ushered in the Second Empire of Bonaparte's unexhilarating descendant Louis Napoleon. Universal suffrage, as the anarchist Proudhon noted morosely at very considerable length, was a most uncertain political good and could readily in practice be hard to distinguish from counter-revolution.[6]

The extension of legislative representation and the widening of the franchise aroused bitter conflict sooner or later almost everywhere, often threatening the survival of the regime. With the Great Reform Bill, even Britain seemed for a time to many contemporaries, and at least some subsequent historians, very close to revolution. At least in peacetime, however, the cumulative experience of electoral representation proved remarkably reassuring. The prerogatives of ownership, and even the flourishing of commerce and industry, survived the extension of the franchise more or less intact, and with surprisingly little strain. By the early twentieth century the idea that even women might safely be permitted to vote no longer seemed an extravagance; and mass socialist parties with democracy on their banners could be left to compete with their rivals, if not in most settings yet on equal terms, at least without constant harassment. Madison's early-nineteenth-century discovery that universal male suffrage was no real threat to property was made independently, if appreciably later, in well over half the countries in Europe, not always by direct experience, but by ever more obvious inference. But virtually none of this, as yet, not even the first stirrings of the enfranchisement of women, had happened under the rubric of democracy itself. (The inclusion of women within the electorate was always an excellent proxy for the literal-mindedness of democracy as an idea. If everyone has to rule (or at least have a hand in rule) for rule to be legitimate or safe, what clearer evidence could there be for the idea being treated with reserve than the spontaneous and almost wholly unreflective omission of over half the adult population from the ranks of the rulers?)

What came out with ever greater clarity was the stark political logic of ever-widening representation: that it was obviously in practice quite unnecessary to confine electoral representation, and equally obviously on balance advantageous, both to ruling politicians and to those they ruled, to extend it more or less as far as it would go. This plainly is what we now call democracy, incomplete no doubt, and far from fully self-convinced, but unmistakably the thing itself. But why should we have come to call it democracy? Why indeed is it even distantly appropriate to describe this form of government as a democracy? Why is the term not an obvious and brazen misnomer?

It is still not clear how to answer this last question. Perhaps democracy simply is a misnomer for any of the regimes to which we now apply it, a flagrant, and at some level deliberate, misdescription. But misnomer or not, the term has clearly come to stay. It is no use wringing our hands at the semantic anomaly or moral effrontery. What we need to grasp is why it has come to stay. The key to this is to register when the term arrived. It made its entry in this essentially new guise, beyond the North American continent, as the christening of a new formula for civilized rule (rule of the civilized by the civilized), offered by the victors of two successive World Wars to a world in dire need of civilization. The first offer was made by Woodrow Wilson, an academic political scientist and former President of Princeton University, who became President of the United States and would-be architect of a new world order.[7] At this point, the offer was not a practical success. Wilson's recipe for world order foundered in the vindictive intrigues of the Versailles conference and was essentially repudiated back home in America (a repudiation which did little to give democracy a good name anywhere else). The Europe it left behind it remained in acute economic peril, riven by bitter social conflict and intense ideological and national rivalries, biding its time none too patiently to unleash world war all over again. Democracy was challenged savagely from the right by those who volunteered to defend Europe's populations against the continuing menace of equality, pressed home by an equally authoritarian political movement with its own primary allegiance to a very foreign power. It was defended principally, and with far greater conviction, by those who still hoped to press far closer to equality themselves. It was neither a natural name nor a compelling practical formula for the unruffled hegemony of the order of egoism.

For it to become so, a second vast war had to be fought and won, and another and far lengthier struggle, which at times menaced even greater destruction,[8] had to be endured and survived. It was in that second struggle, and in face of the horrors of the Third Reich and the brutalities of Japan's Asian conquests, that Europe's threatened and largely conquered peoples joined ranks with America beneath the banner of democracy. At first they did so very much alongside the Soviet ally whose immense sacrifices and sustained military heroism did so much more to check Germany's advance, break its huge tank armies and drive it relentlessly back home.[9] After Operation Barbarossa, the *blitzkrieg* in which Hitler destroyed more than a third of its airforce on the ground and broke through its forward defences for many hundred miles, it also had no residual difficulty in identifying the Third Reich as its primary enemy. On the matter of democracy the Soviet Union learned nothing and forgot nothing from the bitter ordeal of the Second World War. But further west the political leaders of the order of egoism did learn one great and enduring lesson from this overwhelming trauma. They learned that there could be circumstances in which that order, the basic operating principle of their economies and societies, needed this word and the ideas for which it stood very urgently indeed. In the last instance, and in face of intense suffering, they needed it above all to focus their citizens' allegiance, and to define a cause worth fighting to the death for in a way that the order of egoism could never hope to provide for a good many.

Neither the Third Reich or Italy's Fascists, nor imperial Japan in its own phase of fascist militarism, set any store by democracy. So the term served comfortably enough to define their enemies without further need to resolve its ambiguities. Only once the war was over, and the grip of the Soviet Union tightened over eastern Europe, did it become necessary to define democracy more resolutely, to explain the proper bases for political alliance or enmity both domestically and across the world. At that point a quarrel which had mattered intensely for Socialists ever since Lenin seized power became of far wider interest.[10] Before October 1917 virtually all twentieth-century western Socialists were democrats in their own eyes, however much they might differ in goals, political temperament or preferred institutional expedients. Within three years, socialists across the world were divided bitterly by the new Russian regime, rejecting it categorically for its tyranny and oppression, or insisting that it and it alone was the true bearer of the torch of the Equals.[11] For those who adopted the second point of view, anyone who disputed its title to democracy or censured its governmental style simply showed themselves partisans of the order of egoism: abject lackeys of the rich. The charge that they were lackeys of the rich stung Social Democrats everywhere. But for electoral politicians with other allegiances it carried no special stigma; and they found it relatively effortless to adopt the democratic element in the Social Democrats' denunciation, shorn of any associated egalitarian encumbrances. The ensuing quarrel was never a well-shaped political argument; and it is far from clear that in the end either side can be accurately said to have won it. What was quite unmistakable by 1991, however, was that one side had emphatically lost it.

It was not that the victors' pretension to embody democracy was vindicated by the collapse of the Soviet Union: simply that the claims of the vanquished Communist Party of the Soviet Union to rule as the people, along with their claims to deliver equality in any shape or form, dissolved into absurdity once they no longer retained the power to rule at all. By 1991, too, that absurdity was already a very open secret. The four decades of the Cold War provided something less than transparent collective self-education; but they did establish beyond reasonable doubt that it is a simple and ludicrous abuse of language to describe a wholly unaccountable ruling body, which denies its subjects the opportunity either to express themselves freely, or organize to defend their interests, or seek their own representation within government on their own terms, as a democracy (or indeed, for that matter, a People's Republic).

What made the term democracy so salient across the world was the long post-war struggle against the Soviet Union and its allies. From its outset, that quarrel was certainly between defenders of the order of egoism and those who openly wished it ill. But it came increasingly to be a quarrel, too, over the political ownership of the term democracy. Because of its intensity, scope and duration, the lines of battle within it were often confused and disconcerting. For decades at a time, in Indonesia, in South Korea, in Taiwan, in South Vietnam, in Chile, quite open and unabashed dictatorships were enrolled with little apology in the ranks of the western democrats. (The enemy of my enemy is my friend.) But this lack of fastidiousness attracted unfavourable comment at the time; and as the decades went by, it became increasingly clear that it was not merely politically unprepossessing but also costly to spread the democratic mantle quite so widely. American statecraft became, very slowly, a little more fastidious; and wealthier and better-educated populations in many different countries took sharper exception to authoritarian rule, whenever the latter faltered for a time, or the economic cycle turned sharply against it. Under this American provenance democracy was presented and welcomed as a well-established recipe both for nurturing the order of egoism and combining its flourishing with some real protection for the civil rights of most of the population. It threatened relatively few and held out modest hopes to a great many. Economic prudence (a due regard for the requirements for nurturing the order of egoism) was incorporated, sometimes with some pain,[12] into the professed political repertoires of most contending political parties within democratic regimes.

After 11 September 2001, abruptly and with strikingly little embarrassment, the spread of democracy across the globe shifted in meaning all over again, and acquired a wholly new urgency. From being the heraldic sign on America's banners, it became as well, at least for a time, a key political weapon. As President Bush himself acknowledged in November the following year, 'The global expansion of democracy is the ultimate force in rolling back terrorism and tyranny.'[13] The United States had found little difficulty in reconciling itself to tyranny in foreign countries for decades at a time, if the tyrants in question proved serviceable in other ways. It had viewed with studied indifference (or even limited sympathy) the practice of terrorism itself, sometimes over equally lengthy time-spans, in a variety of foreign countries, from the State of Kashmir to the Russian Republic, and perhaps even at some points Northern Ireland. What made it suddenly imperative to roll back tyranny was its presumed link to terrorism, and more pressingly to terrorism within the United States itself.

Tyranny, it now appeared, bred terrorism. To stamp out terrorism (or at least prevent it reaching as far as North America) it was now necessary to stamp out tyranny too. The modern name, and the uniquely efficacious modern practical recipe, for eliminating tyranny was now democracy. Only a globe united under the sway of democracy could be a world in which the United States felt wholly safe from terror. This particular strategic appraisal may not last very long. The globalization of democracy, even in this limited sense, is a costly political agenda with many immediate enemies. It is far from clear that achieving it would yield the desired outcome. There is no obvious reason why those who feel bitterly enough to sympathize with terrorism or succour its practitioners should feel more inhibited in acting on their feelings merely because they acquire somewhat more control over their own rulers. Democratizing the West Bank and Gaza would do little by itself to endear the citizens of the state of Israel to most of the existing inhabitants of either. In its present form this looks less like a reliable political talisman than a glaring instance of ideological overstretch.[14] But temporary though it will surely prove, it does represent the culmination of one particular ideological sequence. We may change our mind quite drastically (and even the American government may change its mind somewhat) over whether this is a good way in which to understand what democracy is or means. Succeeding American leaders will almost certainly modify their assessments of what it is reasonable to hope (or cease to fear) from democracy so understood. What can scarcely happen is that anyone raises substantially this estimate of the benefits which democracy, so understood, is likely to prove able to supply.

We can now see how to answer three of our four questions. Democracy has altered its meaning so sharply since Babeuf because it has passed definitively from the hands of the Equals to those of the political leaders of the order of egoism. These leaders apply it (with the active consent of most of us) to the form of government which selects them and enables them to rule. It is a form of government at least minimally adapted to the current requirements of the order of egoism, shaped within, and adjusted to, the continuing demands to keep that order in working condition. The Greek originals of democracy could scarcely have provided that service, either organizationally or politically; and the service itself cannot plausibly be claimed to have figured in the dreams of either Robespierre or Babeuf. The conjunction of representative democracy with the increasingly self-conscious and attentive service of the order of egoism has faced pressing challenges throughout these two centuries. But within the last fifteen years it has surmounted all these challenges and settled with unprecedented resolution on the conclusion that democracy, in this representative form, is both the source and to a large degree also the justification for the scale of its triumph. What has enabled it to surmount the challenges is still open to question. But much of the answer unmistakably lies in the sheer potency of the order of egoism.

Early in the last century, a determined Russian statesman, Pyotr Stolypin, made a last desperate effort to rescue the Tsarist regime by breaking up the egalitarian torpor of Russia's peasant communities and subjecting them to the stern demands of the order of egoism.[15] His name for this strategy was 'The Wager on the Strong'. It is a good general name for the political strategy of serving the requirements of the order of egoism, whether in one country or across the globe. In

contrast with Babeuf's or Buonarroti's disapproving vision of a political regime centred on defending the privileges of those who were
already rich (and always potentially somewhat effete), it captures
admirably the momentum of a strategy which aims at constant
change, and at harnessing the power to realize that change in whoever
proves to possess it. Robespierre's unnerving associate on the
Committee of Public Safety, Louis Antoine de Saint-Just, proclaimed
thrillingly at one point at the height of the Terror that it was the poor
(the *malheureux*) who were the real powers of the earth.[16] But he has
proved a most inferior prophet. The Wager on the Strong is a wager
on the rich, to some degree perforce on those with the good fortune
to be rich already, but above all on those with the skill, nerve and luck
to make themselves so. In the long run the Wager on the Strong has
paid off stunningly. But what of the fourth question? Why did the
Strong select this of all words to name the form of government which
has served them best of all in their titanic struggle to mould the world
to their purposes?

Even now I do not think we quite know the answer to that question.
But what is clear is that the key phase in their selection of it occurred
in the United States of America, and did so before the young Alexis
de Tocqueville took ship to appraise its implications. From then on it
is relatively easy to follow this word as it moves onwards with the
stream of history, sometimes hurtling through rapids, sometimes
drifting out in great slow eddies, or disappearing for lengthy intervals
into stagnant pools. It is easy too to see why it attracts or repels so
many different users, summoning up allegiances or fomenting
enmities. It is even easier to see why it constantly loses definition
along the way, stretched in one direction then another, and largely at
the mercy of anyone who chooses to take it up. What still remains
harder to see is just how it aids or impedes those who do choose to
use it, augmenting their political strength, exposing their deceit or
blurring their comprehension of their own goals. (Whatever its other
merits, it is hard to believe that this is a term which has greatly

assisted anyone to clarify their own political goals for any length of time.)

At this point democracy's ideological triumph seems bewilderingly complete. There is little immediate danger, of course, of its running out of enemies, or ceasing to be an object of real hate. But it no longer faces compelling rivals as a view of how political authority should be structured, or of who is entitled to assess whether or not that authority now rests in the right hands. Its practical sway, naturally, is very considerably narrower, crimped or disrupted almost everywhere. But the surviving doctrines which still contend with it at the same level, and without benefit of special supra-human validation, and which have also kept the nerve bluntly to deny its hegemony, are all faltering badly. None of them any longer dares to try to face it down in free and open encounter.

This odd outcome leaves many questions open. Is it still right, at this late stage, to think of democracy primarily as a form of government? If so, just what form of government, and quite why? Or is it equally or more appropriate to think of it instead as a political value, very imperfectly embodied in any actual form of government, and perhaps flatly incompatible with many obvious aspects of the form of government to which most of us now habitually apply it? If we see it primarily as a political value, a standard of public conduct or political choice to which forms of government should ideally measure up, should we also go on to recognize in it, as Tocqueville in effect did,[17] an entire way of life, social, cultural and even economic, just as much as narrowly political? Can there be truly democratic politics (for better or worse), without democratizing every other aspect of social, cultural and economic life?

No one, after the last century, can sanely doubt that forms of government matter greatly. It may be true that even the grandest of states are in some respects less powerful today than their predecessors of half a century ago.[18] But it is certainly also true that most states are vastly more powerful in a great many other readily specifiable respects than they have ever been before. Government may shift elusively between levels, moving upwards and downwards from the individual nation state; and governmental aspirations can shrink as well as expand. But the world in which we all now live is governed more extensively and more intimately than it has ever been before;[19] and few things matter more in practice to most of its inhabitants over time than what form that government takes.

The form of government to which most of us do now apply the term democracy is more than a little blurred in outline. What causes it to operate as it does in any particular setting and at any particular time remains exceedingly obscure.[20] But some aspects of it are more settled and less contentious than they have ever been before. Very few countries which entertain the idea of democratic rule at all any longer dispute that the sovereign ruling body, the citizens, should consist of virtually all the adults duly qualified by birth. There is more continuing dissension even today over the terms on which citizenship can be acquired from the outside, or non-citizens admitted equally to the vote. There is also continuing strife over the terms of personal exclusion, of derogating from the privileges of citizenship by sufficiently egregious breach of its responsibilities, or through crippling mental incapacity (crime, insanity, even the purposeful withholding of tax). But virtually nowhere on earth which stages voting at all as a means for forming a government still excludes women from the opportunity to participate in it on formally equal terms. (Saudi Arabia, which apparently at present still does, emphatically does not envisage democracy as a way of forming its government.) This vast change has come everywhere within less than a century. In most places it can scarcely yet be said to have had the effect of democratizing every other aspect of social, cultural or economic life. But the most jaundiced observer now can hardly miss its impact anywhere where it has obtained for any length of time.

The variations within this form of government, Presidential or Parliamentary rule, judicial review, contrasting party or electoral systems, even republics or monarchies, matter greatly for the politics of any individual country. In some cases, in practice, they leave little room for doubt that their main purpose is to insulate the rulers as radically as possible from the erratic sympathies and judgements of the citizens at large. What unites them is their common acceptance of a single compelling point, the expediency of deriving the authority to rule, in a minimally credible way, from the entire citizen body over whom it must apply. The claims made by these rulers on their own behalf, and in some measure endorsed by less partial champions of the form of government itself, naturally reach much further. They claim that the election of representative legislatures and executives, however structured, not only confers upon them the authority of the citizen electors, but also provides those electors with an effective control over the laws to which they are subject, and the persons who make, interpret or enforce those laws upon them. In itself this is an extremely far-fetched claim. It is also one which loses plausibility fairly steadily with experience. But it is not absurd. The predicament of being governed by those whom a clear majority can eventually dismiss is far less dire than the corresponding predicament of being governed indefinitely by those of whom you can hope to rid yourself only by rising up and overthrowing them by force of arms.

Is democracy a good name for a system of rule in which, in the end, a steady and substantial majority can be confident that it holds the power to dismiss rulers it has come to loathe? That is not what the term *democracy* originally meant; but it is also not a plainly illegitimate extension of that original meaning. The case against the extension of meaning, nevertheless, remains simple and weighty. In Athens it may have been the Laws, rather than the *demos* itself, who held final authority over the Athenians.[21] But the Laws could exercise that ultimate ascendancy only through the continuing interpretation and the active choice of the citizen Assembly and the Law Courts. Athenian democracy had very serious reservations about the division of political labour. Except under the special conditions of open warfare, where Generals were elected and often left to fend for themselves for as long as the annual campaign lasted, it simply refused to pick individuals to exercise power in its name, and without further recourse to it. It organized the daily tasks of government, quite largely, by rotating them across the citizen body; and it made every great decision of state, legislative, executive, or even judicial, by the majority choice of very large numbers, whether in the Assembly or the Courts. Under democracy the citizens of Athens, quite reasonably and accurately, supposed that they were ruling themselves. But the vastly less exclusive citizen bodies of modern democracies very obviously do nothing of the kind. Instead, they select from a menu which they can do little individually to modify, whichever they find least dismaying amongst the options on offer. Benjamin Constant, who wished to commend this arrangement, saw the goal of their choice as stewardship, the full management of their interests by suitable persons chosen for the purpose.[22] This, he underlined, was how the rich approached the allocation of their own time. There was nothing humiliating or necessarily alarming in having your interests managed for you. The rich at least were never in serious doubt that they could find many more rewarding things to do with their time.

But even for those who approved of it, this was never the only way in which to view the bargain. Constant was writing well before the professionalization of politics. By the time, over a century later, that the Austrian émigré economist Joseph Schumpeter[23] set out his own more elaborate picture of what democracy really is and means, the practical implications of governing on the basis of electoral representation had become far clearer. To Schumpeter, democracy was essentially a competition between teams of politicians for the people's vote and the power to govern which would follow from it. The victors in that competition won the opportunity to govern for a limited period. As a system, therefore, electoral democracy was 'the rule of the politician'.[24] What the electors picked their politicians for was still the prospective quality of their stewardship. But once the politicians in question had been picked, the terms of the relationship changed abruptly. For most citizens most of the time there was little room for doubt that they were still being ruled. The rich might find themselves cheated or even tormented by individual stewards whom they had been injudicious enough to select. But it was not a credible picture of the relationship between the two to describe the rich as being ruled by their stewards. The amalgam of rule with stewardship is a far more rigid and committing transfer of power and responsibility than any the citizens of democratic Athens were ever asked to make (except on those rare occasions when they were asked, or compelled, to abolish the democracy itself). It is easy for electors not merely to regret individual past choices (bargains that have gone seriously astray), but also to lose heart more generally in face of the options presented to them. It is not simply because modern liberty can take so many other forms (because it offers so many more amusing ways of spending one's time) that the percentage of those who bother to exercise their vote has fallen so relentlessly across the democratic world. Some of the fall in voting rates is best attributed less to a preference for private enjoyments[25] than to dismay at what electors have got for their votes. At its most dismaying, this can result in the desertion of the electoral forum by very large sections of the population. Career politicians can come to be seen as systematically corrupt manipulators, reliably intent on nothing but furthering their own interests[26] by using public authority ruthlessly in the service of the evidently sinister interests of small groups of independently powerful miscreants. 'Democracy', the French syndicalist Georges Sorel sneered almost a century ago, 'is the paradise of which unscrupulous financiers dream.'[27]

The ethos of democratic Athens evoked in Pericles's great speech could scarcely have been more different. But it is wrong to see the contrast between Periclean glory and the squalid financial scandals of the Third Republic as one which mirrors an essentially valid application of a clear term over against an obvious abuse of the same term. Some of the contrasts between the two unmistakably come out in the wrong direction. Even in Sorel's day, the franchise of the Third Republic was very considerably less exclusive than the citizenship of ancient Athens.[28] Even those contrasts which do clearly come out in the right direction often turn on something quite other than democracy itself. The citizen pride celebrated by Pericles certainly encompassed the freedom (for the citizens themselves) embodied in the political organization of the *polis*. But it turned more in the end on the splendour and dynamism of the life of the *polis* community, the former funded largely by resources drawn from other communities, and the latter also often exerted very much at other peoples' expense. Democracy probably meant more to some contemporaries of Pericles than it can have meant to any of France's population in the opening decade of the twentieth century. But it did not mean more because the Athenians understood democracy, and the French did not, but because the Athenians saw their city as being at the zenith of its greatness, and associated that greatness with the form of its rule, while the French, in the lengthy shadow cast by the Franco-Prussian War, were in no position to do so, and had correspondingly little occasion to congratulate themselves on the distinctiveness of their political arrangements.

If democracy is simply a way of organizing the relationships between communities and their governments, it can scarcely in itself be an occasion for intense pride. Where communities are self-confident and proud, some of that pride will rub off on their political institutions, however the latter are structured (a point familiar to tyrants across the ages). Under less ebullient circumstances, the attitudes of communities to their governments are likely to be moulded largely by how groups or individuals within them see their own interests as served or damaged by their government, a matter of skill and luck as much as good or ill will, sense of duty or culpable neglect. Political scientists and advertising agencies have each studied these shifts of sentiment and sympathy in great detail, and developed enough insight into what determines them to earn, at least in the latter case, considerable sums of money for passing their conclusions on to the competing teams of politicians. The formidable scale, cost and elaboration of a modern American Presidential campaign, already certain to be larger than ever in 2004, could rouse a sense of personal freedom in most individual citizens only through sheer delusion. But neither the remorselessness of the manipulation attempted, nor the lavishness of the resources squandered, are enough in themselves to invalidate its claims to embody democracy. To run against it, any coherent complaint must in the end once again be made on behalf of the order of equality, and against the order of egoism. However else we understand democracy today, we cannot safely or honourably brush aside the recognition that it has been the clear verdict of democracy that the struggle between these two orders is one which the order of egoism must win. It is above all democracy, in this thin but momentous sense, which has handed the order of egoism its ever more conclusive victory.

The big question raised by that victory is how much of the distant agenda of the order of equality can still be rescued from the ruins of its overwhelming defeat. That question can be seen in two very different ways, as one of institutional architecture and the meanings to ascribe to it, or as one of distributive outcomes (with the ascription of meanings left severely to the individual winners or losers). The first way of seeing the issue is bound to attach special weight to the sense that democracy can only be adequately seen not as a form in which individual states are or are not governed, but as a political value, or a standard for justifiable political choice, against which not merely state structures, but every other setting or milieu in which human beings live, can and should be measured.

Democracy, so viewed, promises (or threatens) the democratization of everything (work, sex, the family, dress, food, demeanour, choice by everyone over anything which affects any number of others). What it entails is the elimination of every vestige of privilege from the ordering of human life. It is a vision of how humans could live with one another, if they did so in a context from which injustice had been eradicated. Even thought through with limitless energy,[29] this remains quite an elusive idea. What is not elusive about it, however, is that it requires the systematic elimination of power (the capacity to make others act against their own firm inclinations) from human relations. At the very least it demands the removal of any form of power stable enough to disclose itself to others, and resistant enough to survive for any length of time once it has done so. The removal of all power (what thus far causes much of human life to go as it does) from the relations between human beings is most unlikely to prove coherent even as an idea. It is also spectacularly unlikely to occur, since it forswears in the first instance the principal medium through which human beings bring about consequences which they intend.[30] But incoherent and implausible though it almost certainly is, it is also unmistakably the full programme of the Equals, and in a clearer and more trenchant form than Babeuf ever took the trouble to elaborate it. What it is not, however, is a programme ever widely adopted by any groups in the real world, still less one even weakly reminiscent of a form of government. It is a value that might perhaps inspire a form of government, and which, at least in negative forms, often has inspired groups of men and women, sometimes on a very large scale. But it is not a coherent description of how power can be organized, or institutions constructed: not a causal model of anything at all.

The democratization of everything human is not a real possibility: as illusory as a promise as it is idle as a threat. But as a political programme it carries very considerable allure. In many places it has already made far greater progress than the Abbé Sieyes could have imagined. Within the richer countries of the world the back-breaking toil and casual brutality which dominated the lives of huge numbers of people even a century ago have been lifted from the shoulders of all but relatively small minorities. When the conditions of those minorities emerge sporadically into public view they cause as much shock as they arouse shame. Entire dimensions of social, cultural and economic life have been challenged irreversibly: most dramatically of all the relations between men and women. Usually slowly, often bemusedly, and almost always grudgingly, those relations have begun to recompose themselves comprehensively to fit the requirements of equality. The surrender of the vote was the merest beginning. None of us yet knows how far that transformation can go, or quite where it will end. If you view democracy solely as a value, you can be very sanguine about the extent of this progress. Gender may seem not merely a privileged and uniquely urgent domain for equality to conquer. It can serve as a proxy, too, for every other domain in which equality is still effectively obstructed: race, ethnicity, literacy, even class. The sole boundaries to its progress are the limits to human capacities to think clearly and imagine coherently.

But that gives far too little weight to democracy as a form of government. It misses entirely the significance of its diffusion across the world, as one very particular form of government, over the last two centuries. It simply suspends political causality (what causes politics to work the way it does). Almost certainly, on careful analysis, it must suspend along with it most forms of social, economic and even cultural causality too. If in this guise democracy has spread across the world, especially over the last half-century, by backing the order of egoism to the hilt, the order of egoism reciprocally has built itself ever more drastically at the same time by adopting and refashioning democracy in this particular sense. The world in which we all live is a world principally structured by the radicalization and intensification of inequalities. Between the inhabitants of much richer countries, these inequalities need not result in wider gaps in wealth, status or personal power than those which existed many centuries earlier, or still exist in far poorer countries today. But, by the principle of economic competition and its cumulative consequences, they work through, and have to work through, the sharpening and systematization of inequality in the lives of virtually everyone.

It is by its pervasiveness and its peremptory practical priority that the order of egoism precludes equality. It tolerates, and even welcomes, many particular impulses towards equalization. But what drives it, and in the end organizes the entire human world, is a relentless and all-conquering principle of division and contrast. That was what Babeuf saw and hated. It is still there to see (and, if we care to, to hate) to this day. What there can be, today and as far as we can see into the future, is not the democratization of human life in its entirety, either in one institution, or in one country, or in the globe as a whole. What there can be is the democratization of human life anywhere, as far as the order of egoism proves to permit. This is not a struggle which equality is going to win. The precise limits which the order of egoism sets to equality do not form a clear fixed structure which can be specified in advance of political experience. They are an endless and ever-shifting battleground. What is clear and fixed, however, is the strategic outcome of that long war, and the identity of its victor.

The outcome itself is not one which any of us cares to see very clearly, and perhaps not one which anyone who did see it clearly could unequivocally welcome. It makes no direct appeal to the moral sentiments,[31] let alone the moral sense.[32] To put the point less archaically, it is an outcome which must offend anyone with the nerve to recognize what it means.

The role of democracy as a political value within this remarkable form of life (the World Order of Egoism) is to probe constantly the tolerable limits of injustice, a permanent and sometimes very intense blend of cultural enquiry with social and political struggle. The key to the form of life as a whole is thus an endless tug of war between two instructive but very different senses of democracy. In that struggle, the second sense, democracy as a political value, constantly subverts the legitimacy of democracy as an already existing form of government. But the first, too, almost as constantly on its own behalf, explores, but then insists on and in the end imposes, its own priority over the second. The explorations of democracy as a value vary in pace, urgency and audacity across time and space. At times, as in the work of the American philosopher and educator John Dewey,[33] the imagery of a democratic way of life bites very deep and summons up intense imaginative energies. More often, the mobilizing force of the value is negative and far more specific – the demolition of spectacular and long-entrenched injustice in one domain after another of collective life. Everyone will have their own favourites among these stirring stories. Many, too, no doubt, their own especial aversions. What adult men or women may or may not do with their own or one another's bodies or their own embryonic fellows. How one (self- or other-defined) racial grouping may or may not treat another. How money may or may not be exchanged directly for office, power or honour, or office, power or honour in their turn be exchanged directly instead for money. The terms of trade, overt or covert, on which we live our lives together.

Most of modern politics is taken up by quarrels over what to revere or repudiate within these struggles. The true definition of democracy is merely one prize at stake in those quarrels. None of the stories ends in unalloyed triumph. What sets the limits to their triumph is often hard to ascertain; but almost always, sooner or later, it turns on definite decisions by powerful agents within the formal apparatus of democratic rule, career politicians or those whom they in the end license. The balance between cultural exploration, social struggle and public decision by ruling institutions of representative democracy is never fixed firmly or clearly. But there are denser barriers to how far it can go in one direction than in the other. The periods when, for a brief time, these barriers seem lifted, like the youth uprisings of 1968, can be times of fervent collective hope, as well as transitory personal transformation. But they offer no rival instruments with which to leave behind them solid institutional guarantees for any ground they may win. Grand victories are often largely undone by long strings of petty defeats.[34] Where they fail to carry through to the laws passed by representative legislatures, and to the political decisions to ensure that those laws are enforced, they can vanish as easily and rapidly as they came.

One important fact about this strange form of life we now share is that almost no one within it tries to take in the fate of democracy in both of these two key senses anywhere at all. This is neither surprising nor simply inappropriate. Only someone of great arrogance, and probably also someone in considerable intellectual confusion, would dream of attempting to grasp the fate of both across the entire globe. But the sharp bifurcation of attention for the vast majority of us between these two domains, however natural its sources or individually prudent its grounds, has extraordinarily malign consequences. It prompts us to split a preoccupation with the ethical and the desirable from any sustained attempt to grasp what is happening in the world and why it is happening. It sanctions the cultivation of normative fastidiousness, a connoisseurship of the prepossessing and the edifying. It also recognizes and applauds a cumulative knowledge and mastery of the practicalities of political competition. But it makes virtually no demand that these two should meet, and at least confront one another. Except opportunistically and by individual contingency, they therefore virtually never do.

The clearest setting of this disjunction in our social and political understanding is the organization of academic life, the modern intellectual division of labour at its most aspiring and self-regarding. What no competent modern student of politics can sanely attempt is to master both with equal resolution. Even to try to do so betokens either intellectual confusion or personal frivolity. But if the synthesis is beyond any possible professional, how are the huge amateur majorities of modern citizens to undertake it, as the sovereign choosers they presume themselves to be? (And what, if they prove to have neither the time, the nerve nor the inclination to do so, can they honourably do instead?)

There is something deep about the structure of this outcome. The condition of involuntary collective befuddlement which it unrelentingly guarantees is not what Plato held against democracy. But it is hard not to see it as a blemish within our own form of life. It is hard to see, too, how in the end it can fail to corrupt each sense of democracy pretty thoroughly, abandoning the form of government to the tender mercies of the professionals, and abandoning too the conduct of refined cultural and intellectual enquiry to ever more scholastic and narcissistic introspection.

The strongest pressures behind democratization are resentment at condescension, and the will of individuals or groups to find better ways to defend their own interests. The power of the first is admirably captured by Tocqueville.[35] It focuses essentially on form and appearance, and rightly presupposes that democracy, however obstructed it may prove in practice, must at least surrender privilege at the level of form. It must recognize all citizens as equals and give each at least some opportunity to insist on being treated equally in ways which especially concern them. What it cannot in practice give them is equal power to defend their own interests. What prevents it from doing so above all is the scale and pervasiveness of inequality dictated by the order of egoism. In the Assembly at Athens any fully adult male with the good fortune to have been born a citizen, if they happened also to be present on the occasion and wished to do so,[36] had an equal right to address the people on what was to be done. They could, if only they had the courage, defend their own interests in person with their own judgement and in their own voice. In the law-making (and still more the war-making) decisions of a modern democracy, nothing vaguely similar is ever now true. Ordinary citizens are never present in their personal capacity within a legislative assembly. Still less do they ever hold executive authority as ordinary citizens within a modern state. In most modern democracies, most of the time and on most issues, ordinary citizens are almost certainly freer to speak or think than the Athenians ever were. The penalties they face for voicing views which most of their contemporaries dislike or find scandalous are far less harsh and altogether less public. But most also have little chance to make themselves at all widely audible; and no one at all, except by resolute, strenuous and extremely successful competitive effort, has an effective right of direct access to legislative deliberation. The newspaper press, which John Stuart Mill offered to mid-nineteenth-century Britain as an effective substitute for the political immediacy of the Athens Assembly,[37] still does something to offset the lobbying power of great economic interests. But most of it, in many different parts of the world, belongs to a relatively small number of private individuals; and the ways in which it operates cannot be said seriously to modify the evident political impotence of the great majority of citizens at most times and over almost all issues. This effect is even more pronounced in the cases of television and radio, the most insistent of contemporary media of public communication. In Italy, in a scandalous but deeply symbolic conjunction, a single man at present owns several of the national television channels (as well as the biggest publishing company), controls most of the other television channels in his capacity as Prime Minister and heads the government as leader of a party which is effectively a personal fief.[38] What furnishes most of us with almost all the effective representation we receive for most of our interests is not our own access to any public forum or site of binding political choice. It is an enormously elaborate structure of divided labour, most of which operates wholly outside public view, and can be dragged into the light of day only sporadically, with great exertion, and as a result of some wholly undeniable political disaster. It is not, of course, part of the meaning of the term *democracy* that the political institutions which govern our lives should be so far beyond the reach of most of us almost all the time. But it remains clearly true that this is what democracy as a form of government now amounts to. How far could it still really amount to anything fundamentally different?

Because this complex of institutions and practices was never designed or chosen by anyone, it must be true that every aspect of it could perfectly well be quite different. Because it has spread so widely now, however, and spread principally by imitation and competition, it can scarcely also be true that the complex as a whole could readily or rapidly alter into something drastically different. Still less could it hope to do so in ways which relied on winning general applause or even on gratifying most of those who were consciously aware of them. The key issue for this modern variant of democracy is how far it necessitates a level of alienation of will, judgement and choice which any ancient partisan of democracy could only see as its complete negation: at most a partially elective aristocracy,[39] and at worst a corrupt and heavily mystified oligarchy.

If ancient democracy was the citizens choosing freely and immediately for themselves, modern democracy, it seems, is principally the citizens very intermittently, choosing under highly constrained circumstances, the relatively small number of their fellows who will from then on choose for them. There are many obvious ways in which modern citizens have no need whatever to accept this bargain. They could insist on taking particular state decisions personally for themselves: putting them out to referenda, in which every adult citizen is just as eligible to vote as they are in a legislative election. Referenda do indeed play a role in the national politics of some states, both over key issues of inclusion or exclusion, and over especially contentious decisions, sometimes including constitutional amendments.[40] In the case of Taiwan, for example, early in 2004, an incumbent President even used the threat of a referendum asserting the right of the citizens to choose for themselves whether or not to reunite with China, to strengthen his hand against local opponents who favoured a more diplomatic approach to the People's Republic. (This came very close to putting the central issue of state security out to direct popular decision.) What referenda today have in common is that the terms of the choices offered are always decided by a ruling group of career politicians. It is more reasonable to see them as manoeuvres open to career politicians who expect them to work to their own advantage than as real surrenders of power back to the citizens from whom it supposedly came. Where their expectation is disappointed, or the sway of the ruling group is successfully disrupted by their opponents, the consequences of adopting the expedient may dismay its initial sponsors. But the role of the electors who vote in the referendum will still be principally to hand the victory to one team of career politicians at the expense of another.

A more substantial democratic opportunity would go beyond the right to vote on issues which it suits the incumbent government to put to a referendum (on terms they can largely control for themselves). It would demand as well the opportunity to put to a referendum whatever issues the citizens themselves happen to wish, and permit them to define the terms of the resulting referendum on their own behalf. The first element in this opportunity is quite substantial, and not hard to supply. A right of citizen initiative in placing issues on the ballot has existed for some time, both in the State of California and in the Swiss Cantons.[41] In each setting it has naturally had many critics; and some of its consequences have proved extremely damaging. The right to take such decisions can readily extend as wide as the citizen body, or the openness of the Athenian Assembly to any citizen who wished to speak in it. What cannot be distributed so widely is the opportunity to focus the terms of the choice offered. There the division of labour which rationalizes, and in some degree causes, the professionalization of modern politics enforces an effective alienation of the task of formulation from a constituency as wide as the citizen body to a relatively small group entrusted to think, choose and write on its behalf. To draft a coherent text of any length requires in the end a single process of consecutive thought: if not the mind and pen of a single person, at least a conversation between modest numbers of people, who can hear one another and respond to the pressure of each other's thoughts.

In recent years academic political philosophers have devoted considerable attention to outlining the qualities which deserve most weight in taking public decisions of any consequence.[42] They have taken their cue from Aristotle's acknowledgement of the principal merit of democratic choice: its capacity to reach out to, and bring into play, the full breadth of knowledge and awareness of the entire citizen body.[43] The assemblage and sifting of this range of experience, as Aristotle saw it, was a process of deliberation. For a group of human beings who can communicate with one another, deliberation might hope ideally to become a common enquiry, and an exercise in public reasoning, which could bring into play every element of wisdom present in the citizen body. It could also hope to subject the less wise and more grossly partial elements within the judgement of each citizen to disciplined public scrutiny and mutually accountable criticism.

Deliberative democracy, democracy which embodies and realizes democracy at its best, attempts to prescribe how a community of human beings should wish for its public decisions to be taken. Many themes have naturally suggested themselves. It should take these decisions reflectively, attentively and in good faith. It should take them as decisions about what would be publicly good, and not as calculations of what would be personally most advantageous. It should take them non-exclusively: ensuring that all those whom they affect, and all who are sufficiently mature and rational to identify their own interests,[44] can play an active part in determining their outcome. More exactly still, it should take them in a way in which all can enter, and all who wish to in fact do enter, the deliberation as equals, and hold equal weight within it.[45]

The order of egoism clashes more drastically with some of these requirements than it does with others. But both as a form of life and a milieu within which to live, it is at best neutral, and at worst blankly indifferent, towards any of them. Towards some it is, and will always remain, quite openly hostile. Within the order of egoism a large part of the point of power is always money, and a large part of the point of money is always power.[46] Individuals can, and conspicuously do, shape their own lives in very different terms. But it is difficult (and possibly flatly impossible) for them to override the main structuring principle of the form within which they live. Democracy as a form of government and democratization as a social, cultural, economic and political process have very different rhythms. They are also subject to quite different sorts of causal pressures. Democratization is open-ended, indeterminate and exploratory. It sets out from, and responds to, the conception of democracy as a political value, a way in which whatever matters deeply for a body of human beings should in the end be decided. Democracy as a form of government is rather less open-ended, considerably more determinate and far less audacious in its explorations. Because in government some human beings always extensively control very many others in numerous ways this fundamental contrast between value and form of government has some obvious merits. It is better for there to be clear limits to how far you can be controlled by others. Democratization today can be both more exploratory and braver than democratic government because, unlike the latter, it is neither licensed by, nor responsible to or for, the order of egoism. It sits much lighter within our form of life, always searching out the limits of licence, but leaving the task of securing that form of life, with varying degrees of gratitude, firmly to others.

Representative democracy, the form in which democracy has spread so widely over the last six decades, has equipped itself for the journey by making its peace ever more explicitly with the order of egoism. It offers a framework within which that order can flourish, but also one in which the citizens at large can set some bounds both to its pretensions and to its consequences. Wealth by permission of the people may or may not present less of a practical hazard to any of them than wealth secured in open defiance of their will. At least it is less obnoxious. The battle lines between the two orders which Babeuf and his fellow conspirators saw run very differently in any actual representative democracy, losing all their starkness and most of their political plausibility. You can track the progress of representative democracy as a form of government from the 1780s until today, sticking pins into the map to record its advance, and noting not merely the growing homogenization of its institutional formats as the decades go by, but also the cumulative discrediting of the rich variety of other state forms which have competed against it throughout, often with very considerable initial assurance. The state form which advances across this time-span was pioneered by Europeans; and it has spread in a world in which first Europe and then the United States wielded quite disproportionate military and economic power.

For much of this time that state form was taken up by others for its promise to withstand or offset the power wielded by its inventors, or spurned instead in favour of rivals (above all communism or fascism) which promised more credibly to provide the same service. For most of the twentieth century, it was spurned with particular contempt in the great wounded former empires of Russia and China. But for much of the first half of the century it was spurned too in temporarily more potent and menacing states like Germany and Japan, with better immediate prospects of turning the tables on their overweening enemies. Its most decisive advances, the largest number of fresh pins moving across the map, came with three great defeats. The first was the breaking of German and Japanese military power in the Second World War. The second, which followed closely, and also required much violent struggle if of a more dispersed kind, was the collapse of western colonial empire across the world, most of it within two decades of the close of the Second World War. Representative democracy was the model imposed on their defeated enemies by that war's western victors.[47] It was also the model which, after much preliminary foot-dragging, they chose to bequeath to most of their former colonies, from the stunning precedent of imperial India,[48] to the most parlous of Caribbean or Pacific island dependencies. Only with the return of Hong Kong to the People's Republic of China was the choice firmly repudiated from the outset by the new sovereign (if scarcely by the inhabitants themselves). With the third great defeat, the end of the

Soviet Union and the collapse of the bloc of states which it had built so painstakingly around it on its own model, representative democracy shook off all remaining exemplary rivals, and became virtually an index of global normality. It was still firmly rejected in China, site of the lengthiest and proudest tradition of political autonomy of any human society, and very little dented in its rulers' sense of self-sufficiency by more than half a century of rule under the aegis of a local variant of an openly western political doctrine. It was excluded tenaciously and brutally in many other parts of the world, in most cases by the rulers of societies visibly faltering in the struggle for wealth and power. But none of its numerous and sometimes well-armed enemies could any longer confront it with a countervailing model of their own, with the power to reach out to and convince populations with different cultures and any real opportunity to decide their political arrangements for themselves. On a global scale nothing like this had ever occurred before, although there were more local precedents scattered throughout history, in the Asian states encircling the Central Kingdom of China,[49] or the long shadows cast by Rome across the continent of Europe.

In the course of this last advance, a number of plausible and widely credited assumptions have been refuted. It is clearly not true, for example, that the western provenance of this political model makes it somehow ineligible for other parts of the world or for populations with sharply contrasted cultural traditions. It can be (and has been) adopted with some success in every continent, in societies with long and cruel experiences of arbitrary rule, cultures of great historical depth, and religious traditions which insist on the profound inequality of human beings and the duty of most of them to view their superiors with the utmost deference, in East and South and South East Asia, in Latin America, and more sporadically and precariously, in Sub-Saharan Africa and even the Middle East. In itself this is scarcely surprising. Every element in these supposed disqualifications had prominent counterparts over most of the history of the

European continent. Behind the resistance to its advance there lies sometimes antipathy towards the western societies from which it originated, and sometimes a more urgent hatred of the immediate power and arrogance of the United States itself. But accompanying both there is also always an understandable reluctance on the part of those who hold power within them on other bases and by different means at the prospect of being subverted openly and from within.

This advance has occurred in a world of intensifying trade and ever-accelerating communication, in which people, goods and information traverse the globe incessantly. It is a world in which human populations are drawn more tightly together, and depend more abjectly for their security and prosperity on the skills and good intentions of those who rule them than they have ever done before. That world certainly needs many facilities which it has yet to acquire, and not a few which it has yet even to invent or imagine. But one facility which it clearly needs all the time, and with the utmost urgency, is a basis on which its human denizens can address the task of ensuring the skill and good intentions of their rulers for themselves. This task has many different components. It requires the searching out and assemblage of a vast range of information, the strenuous exercise of critical judgement, the permanent monitoring of the performance of those who devote most of their lives to competitive politics or public administration. There are no cheap or reliable recipes for guaranteeing a successful outcome, and little evidence that institutional design on its own can hope to shoulder most of the burden. There are also a great many sites, including numerous formally independent nation states, in which the rulers show little sign of recognizing any such responsibility, and the great majority of the population has little, if any, effective power to protect themselves against the fecklessness or malignity of those who do for the moment rule them.

In the midst of impotence and despair, representative democracy is scarcely an impressive recipe for building order, peace, security, prosperity or justice. No one could readily mistake it for a solution to the Riddle of History. But, in its simple unpretentious way, it has by now established a clear claim to meet a global need better than any of its competitors. The fact that the need itself is still so urgent, and now so evidently confronts every human population of any scale, make the question of how to meet it genuinely global. They also make it a question to which, for the first time, there might be a truly global answer. The fact that none of representative democracy's surviving rivals acknowledges the need as clearly, and none at all volunteers to provide the question with a global answer, lend it a unique status, fusing timeliness and well-considered modesty with a claim for the present to something very close to indispensability.

It is hard to judge how long this claim will hold up. There are many ineliminable limitations to the form of government, and much that it cannot in principle ensure for any human population. It cannot hope to render professional politics ingratiating to most of us anywhere for any length of time; and it duly fails to do so. It guarantees a disconcerting combination of shabbiness of motive and pretence to public spirit throughout most of the cohorts of practising politicians. That shabbiness might be veiled in more closed and less audibly competitive conditions; but it is bound to be highlighted mercilessly throughout the political arena by the vigorous efforts of competitors, inside and outside their own political groupings. All of this was seen from democracy's outset in Athens itself; and its key elements were described with unsurpassed panache and scorn by Plato himself.

It fashions a world in which political leaders call incessantly for the rest of us to trust them, and rely implicitly on their competence, integrity and good intentions. But within that world they must press their appeal permanently in the teeth of their rivals' indefatigable explanations of just how misplaced such trust would be, and how naïve it must be to confer it. For many decades, in many settings, the mass political party served to some degree to generate and sustain this kind of trust, at least between particular groups of the citizens and the party itself as an organization. It lent a political shape to communities of residence or occupation, helped to define a sense of shared interest across them, and established salient outlines for political conflict over the exercise of governmental power.[50] But in the long run many different influences have dissipated most of the plausibility of party structures. The struggle to sustain a trust in political leadership has been submerged increasingly by the rising waters of popular disbelief. Schumpeter's electoral entrepreneurs[51] must trade now on a market where trust is more elusive and expensive than ever, and the grounds for distrust easier and cheaper than ever to disseminate effectively. Even the more insistent of their newer weapons, the skills of the advertising profession and the ever-extending facilities of the media of communication, are far better suited to dispelling trust than to nurturing it or creating it in the first place. Whatever you should learn from advertisements, it can scarcely be a generalized credulity.

Seen as a whole, this is a disenchanted and demoralized world, all too well adjusted to lives organized around the struggle to maximize personal income. But it is also a world permanently in quest of opportunities for re-enchantment, and often ready to identify and respond to the most fugitive and unreliable of cues: not just the youth, energy and determination of Tony Blair, but the cinematic vigour of Arnold Schwarzenegger, or the entrepreneurial momentum of Silvio Berlusconi.[52] Viewed with charity the modern democratic politician's world is a strenuous ordeal, scanned intermittently by most citizens, often querulously and always with some suspicion. It is a world from which faith, deference and even loyalty have largely passed away, and the keenest of personal admiration seldom lasts for very long.

If this is the triumph of democracy, it is a triumph which very many will always find disappointing. It carries none of the glamour which Pericles invoked for its Athenian namesake. Over the two centuries in which it has come to triumph, some have seen it simply as an impostor, bearer of a name which it has stolen, and instrument for the rule of the people by something unmistakably different. No one anywhere nowadays can plausibly see it as rule by the people. In itself, this is no occasion for regret. Had it really been rule by the people, as Madison and Sieyes, Robespierre and even Buonarroti, all warned, it would assuredly not have triumphed, but dissolved instead, immediately and irreversibly, into chaos. The least ambitious case which can be made for it is that it is so very far from the worst that we have to fear: that it offers the inhabitants of the world in which we find ourselves the safest and least personally offensive basis on which to live together with our fellow citizens within our own states. That service is not one which we have yet learned to provide at all reliably by any other means; and no one could reasonably deny its fundamental importance. But that is a case essentially for the practical merits of representative democracy as a form of government. It shows no evident appropriateness in our selection of the word *democracy* as the name for this form of government.

For that name to be appropriate, it must mean more than this. More stirringly perhaps, it must also imply that representative democracy as it now is cannot be all for which we can reasonably hope. There must be some link between the historical fact that the word itself means so much more (or means something so different) and the possibility that the way in which we are now governed can be altered to fit that word better, or at least recover some imaginative contact with it. This may or may not prove to be so. (It will depend, amongst other things, on how we act politically in the future.) There are at least two drastic ways in which the democracy of today might perhaps be altered in this direction. One is in the flow and structuring of information amongst citizens, and the degree to which all governments restrict and withhold information from the governed. Governmental seclusion is the most direct and also the deepest subversion of the democratic claim,[53] sometimes prudent, but never fully compatible with the literal meaning of the form of rule. The more governments control what their fellow citizens know the less they can claim the authority of those citizens for how they rule. The more governments withhold information from their fellow citizens the less accountable they are to those who give them their authority. Even to fit its own name, modern representative democracy would have to transform itself very radically in this respect. The struggle for that transformation will certainly be arduous because the interests in obstructing it are both so huge and so well positioned to impede it. But the case against transforming it has now become merely one of discretion. No powerful imaginative pressures still survive to challenge the judgement that this is how it plainly should be altered.

The second drastic way in which our existing practice of rule might converge more with its democratic title finds itself for the present in very different circumstances. But it is just as simple, and not obviously any less compelling. As a word, *democracy* has won this global competition to designate legitimate rule largely by courtesy of Buonarroti's order of egoism, the thought-through self-understanding and endorsement of a capitalist economy. For Buonarroti himself its victory in this guise would have been a single vast act of theft. But since he had so little comprehension of the basis on which that economy had grown in his own day, and no foreknowledge of the utterly different world which it has since constructed, his assessment carries very little weight. What still retains most of its original force is the simple perception that a ruling people cannot confront one another in conditions of acute inequality, where a few control many before, during and after every governmental choice or action. For well over a century capitalist economies faced fierce political pressure from well-organized mass political parties, representing many millions of citizens, to compress these inequalities and place all citizens on something closer to an equal political footing. At least for the moment those pressures have largely disappeared. But their disappearance does nothing to lessen the anomaly of the chasm between the meaning of democracy as a word and the substance of contemporary representative democracy in action. At present that chasm seems unbridgeable even in principle. It could be spanned at all only if we came to understand economies well enough to establish some real control over them, an idea which may not even make sense, and an achievement which certainly seems practically quite beyond our reach.

For the moment, therefore, democracy has won its global near-monopoly as basis for legitimate rule in a setting which largely contradicts its own pretensions. It remains blatantly at odds with many of the most obtrusive features of existing practices of rule. It still clashes systematically and fundamentally with the defining logic of economic organization. But its victory is no mere illusion. It clashes with each as an independent power in its own right, and with an appeal altogether warmer than either. It may for the present have less power than either (certainly far less than the logic of economic organization). But it still mounts a permanent challenge to each. Melodramatically but not essentially misleadingly, you can see the relations between the three as a long drawn-out war of position, in which the fronts are always under pressure, and no one can foresee quite where they will run even a few years ahead.[54]

Beyond (or beneath) this war of position runs another and older struggle, to which democracy as yet barely applies even in the breach. The main elements of rule amongst human beings still occur within the individual politically sovereign units of the nation state. Democracy has won its global near-monopoly as an answer to the question of how a nation state should be governed. Much else is adjusted, co-operatively or quarrelsomely, among groups of nation states in the endless variety of arenas constructed for the purpose. But the scope of the adjustment is still determined by (and its enforcement still overwhelmingly left to) individual states.

Many hope (and a few even believe)[55] that in the long run democracy can and will provide a good name for a quite different basis both for adjustment and for enforcement. It will keep its global title to define the conditions for legitimate rule, but it will also itself enforce those conditions, unitarily and comprehensively, across the entire globe. In this vision democracy would become global not just in pretension or aspiration but in simple fact. One *demos*, the human population of the whole globe, would not merely claim a shared political authority across that globe, but literally rule it together. This is a natural yearning (with a lengthy Christian and pre-Christian past).[56] It reflects powerful and wholly creditable sentiments. But it is an extremely strained line of thought.

It ignores the direct link between adjudication and coercion in defining what a state is. It thinks away (or temporarily forgets) the vast chasm of power and wealth between different populations across the world. It sets aside not merely the victory of the order of egoism, but also the factors which have caused it to win. It grossly sentimentalizes the sense in which democracy ever does rule even in an individual nation state. As an expectation about the human future it is little better than absurd. But it gets one key judgement exactly right. Democracy may or may not provide either a compelling or a reliable recipe for organizing political choice and its enforcement within one country. It certainly cannot hope, just by doing so, to provide at the same time a compelling or realistic recipe for organizing the political or economic relations between that country and others. Unless we can make more impressive headway in identifying and installing such a recipe within our own country and for our own country, there is little danger of hitting on a remedy for the brutal historical gap between the world's different populations. Perhaps, given world enough and time, there could be such a remedy, and not merely in moral philosophy or welfare economics, but even in economic organization and political practice. If there really could be, what is quite clear is that we are not for the present moving towards it. Until we do, we should at least expect to go on paying the price for the scale of our failure to do so.

NOTES

NOTES TO THE PREFACE

1.   This movement of transliteration and translation across the
      languages and societies of the world is a piece of genuinely global
      intellectual and political history which has yet to be traced with
      any care. Until we know why and how it has happened, we cannot
      hope to understand one of the central features of modern politics
      (or perhaps simply to understand modern politics?). For a
      stimulating comparative study centring on concepts and practices
      of freedom see Robert H. Taylor (ed), *The Idea of Freedom in Asia
      and Africa* (Stanford: Stanford University Press, 2002), especially
      Sudipta Kaviraj's superb analysis of India's experience. The most
      ambitious attempt to assess the significance of its impact in the key
      case of China (oldest, densest, most defiantly autonomous of the
      world's cultures, and globalizer in its own right and in its own
      terms very long ago) has been made over the last thirty years by
      Thomas A. Metzger. (See conveniently his 'The Western Concept
      of Civil Society in the Context of Chinese History', Sudipta
      Kaviraj & Sunil Khilnani (eds), *Civil Society: History and*

Possibilities (Cambridge: Cambridge University Press, 2001), 204–31.) For classic studies of parts of the journey, see Hao Chang, *Liang Ch'I-Chao and Intellectual Transition in China 1890–1907* (Cambridge, Mass.: Harvard University Press, 1971) and Benjamin Schwartz, *In Search of Wealth and Power: Yen Fu and the West* (New York: Harper, 1964). For Japan see chapters by Kenneth B. Pyle (on 'Meiji Conservatism'), Peter Duus & Irwin Scheiner (on 'Socialism, Liberalism, Marxism'), and by Andrew E. Barshay (on 'Postwar Social and Political Thought 1945–1990') in Bob Tadashi Wakabayashi (ed), *Modern Japanese Thought* (Cambridge: Cambridge University Press, 1998), esp 122–25, 297–98 and 326–27; Andrew Barshay, 'Imagining Democracy in Postwar Japan: Reflections on Maruyama Masao and Modernism', *Journal of Japanese Studies*, 18, 1992; Nobutaka Ike, *The Beginnings of Political Democracy in Japan* (Baltimore: Johns Hopkins University Press, 1950). For transliteration into Arabic see, for example, James L. Gelvin, 'Developmentalism, Revolution and Freedom in the Arab East', in Taylor (ed), *Idea of Freedom*, especially (for Gamal Abdul Nasser) 85–86; or into Wolof, in Senegal, Frederick Schaffer's exemplary *Democracy in Translation: Understanding Politics in an Unfamiliar Culture* (Ithaca: Cornell University Press, 1998).

2. It is important to underline how recently this has become a well-secured judgement. Even now, the relative scale of China's population means that only the countervailing weight of India's numbers makes it obviously true. Even twenty-five years ago the presumption that India was as likely to remain democratic as Holland would have seemed (and perhaps been) quixotic.

NOTES TO CHAPTER 1

1. Since we have come by now to mean so many different things by it, and since there is so much about the past of which we are blankly ignorant, you cannot really say when democracy in that sense began, or even, in any interesting sense, when it might have done so.

2. Someone who earned their living from composing speeches or teaching others how to do so. For all three of these roles Athens, at the time and later, offered pre-eminent examples, figures who still tower over the entire history of western culture: Aeschylus, Sophocles, Euripides, Plato, Aristotle, Demosthenes. Some were more friend than enemy of the democracy. But even these did not take the trouble, or see the occasion, to praise Athens's political regime and way of life with the same zest and amplitude in any text which has come down to us. One, at least, went out of his way to do exactly the opposite.

3. Thucydides, *History of the Peloponnesian War Books I & II*, tr Charles Forster Smith (Cambridge, Mass.: Harvard University Press, 1928), Bk I, xxii, 1, pp 38–39. For the novelty and self-consciousness of Thucydides's method at this point see Simon Hornblower, *A Commentary on Thucydides, Vol 1* (Clarendon Press: Oxford, 1997), 59–61.

4. Thucydides, *History*, I, xxii, 4, pp 40–41. Thucydides's claim was to have composed it as a possession for all time, rather than a prize essay to be heard for the moment (Hornblower, *Commentary*, 61–62).

5. Josiah Ober, *Mass and Elite in Democratic Athens* (Princeton: Princeton University Press, 1989); Harvey Yunis, *Taming*

Democracy: Models of Rhetoric in Classical Athens (Ithaca: Cornell University Press, 1996). He did not, of course, hold power solely by making speeches (cf M.I. Finley, *Politics in the Ancient World* (Cambridge: Cambridge University Press, 1983); Finley, 'Athenian Demagogues', *Past and Present*, 21, 1962, 3–24), but the speeches were essential to his capacity to hold it. The principal sources for the career of Pericles are Thucydides's *History* and Plutarch's *Life*. For an excellent brief summary see the article by David Lewis, *Encyclopedia Britannica*, 15th ed, 1974.

6. Thucydides, *History*, II, lxv, 9, pp 376–77: Athens 'became something that was a democracy by name, but actually a rule by the first man'. (See Hornblower, *Commentary*, 346, and for critical assessment of the claim, 344–47.)

7. Buried where they fell, on the battlefield where Athens, standing virtually alone, saved Greece from the massive land forces of the first great Persian invasion in 490BC.

8. For Pericles's speech, see Thucydides, *History*, II, xxxv–xlvi, pp 318–41. For the significance of the funeral oration as a public ceremony, and its determined use in defining Athens as a political community, both to itself and to others, see Nicole Loraux's impressive *The Invention of Athens*, tr Alan Sheridan (Cambridge, Mass.: Harvard University Press, 1986).

9. Thucydides, *History*, II, xxxviii, 1, pp 322–23

10. Thucydides, *History*, II, xxxvii, 1–2, pp 322–23. The translation is disputed, see Hornblower, *Commentary*, 298–99.

11. Thucydides, *History*, II, xli, 1, pp 330–31: 'In a word, then, I say that our city as a whole is the school (*paideusin*) of Hellas.' Hornblower (*Commentary*, 307–8) has a thoughtful discussion of what Thucydides intended Pericles to convey, and commends the translation 'a living lesson'.

12. Thucydides, *History*, II, xl, 2, pp 328–29. Hornblower, *Commentary*, 305–6 & 77–78, citing L.B. Carter, *The Quiet Athenian* (Oxford: Clarendon Press, 1985), 45. Note the balance between committed public concern and the levels of mutual respect and civility which Pericles emphasizes alongside it.

13. As Loraux's work shows excellently.

14. *Metics (metoikoi)* were resident aliens.

15. For the range of intellectual criticism prompted by Athens's democratic experience, see especially Josiah Ober, *Political Dissent in Democratic Athens: Intellectual Critics of Popular Rule* (Princeton: Princeton University Press, 1998).

16. Pseudo-Xenophon, *The Constitution of Athens*, tr G. Bowersock (Cambridge, Mass.: Harvard University Press, 1968). No doubt the main reason for continuing so to call him is, as Mogens Hansen says (Mogens H. Hansen, *The Athenian Democracy in the Age of Demosthenes* (Oxford: Blackwell, 1991), 5), because that is what he sounds like. See too: A.W. Gomme, 'The Old Oligarch', in *More Essays in Greek History and Literature* (Oxford: Basil Blackwell, 1962), 38–69.

17. Cf his repeated formula: 'I do not praise *(ouk epaino)*…' (Pseudo-Xenophon, I, 1, pp 474–75; III, 1, pp 498–99 etc).

18. Pseudo-Xenophon, I, 4 , pp 476–77

19. Pseudo-Xenophon, I, 2, pp 474–75

20. Pseudo-Xenophon, I, 4, pp 476–77

21. Pseudo-Xenophon, I, 1, pp 474–75; 'in making their choice they have chosen to let the worst people be better off than the good *(chrestous)*. Therefore on this account I do not think well of their constitution. But since they have decided to have it so, I intend to point out how well they preserve their constitution and accomplish those things for which the rest of the Greeks criticize them.'

22. Pseudo-Xenophon, I, 2, pp 474–75

23. Pseudo-Xenophon, I, 5, pp 476–77: *to beltiston* – literally, the best bit.

24. Pseudo-Xenophon, I, 5, pp 476–77

25. Pseudo-Xenophon, I, 6–8, pp 478–79

26. Pseudo-Xenophon, I, 3, pp 476–77

27. Pseudo-Xenophon, I, 7, pp 478–79

28. Cf John Dunn, *The Cunning of Unreason: Making Sense of Politics* (London: HarperCollins/New York: Basic Books, 2000).

29. Compare the status of 'spin' in assessments of the political merits and limitations of the Blair government.

30. Compare, to take distasteful recent examples, the task of capturing the political realities of Taliban Afghanistan, Kim Jong Il's North Korea, or Saddam Hussein's Iraq.

31. Cf A.H.M. Jones, *Athenian Democracy* (Oxford: Basil Blackwell, 1957); M.I. Finley, *Democracy Ancient and Modern*, 2nd ed (London: The Hogarth Press, 1985) & *Politics in the Ancient World* (Cambridge: Cambridge University Press, 1983); Hansen, *The Athenian Democracy*; Robin Osborne, 'Athenian Democracy: something to celebrate?', *Dialogos*, 1, 1994, 48–58; 'The Demos and its Divisions in classical Athens', Oswyn Murray & S.R.F. Price (eds), *The Greek City* (Oxford: Clarendon Press, 1990), 265–93; 'Ritual, finance, politics: an account of Athenian democracy', R. Osborne & S. Hornblower (eds), *Ritual, Finance, Politics: Athenian Democratic Accounts presented to David Lewis* (Oxford: Clarendon Press, 1994),1–21.

32. They do not make those realities unreal (somehow cancel them), still less render them inconsequential. They merely make them, in many respects and for many purposes, inaccessible to us.

33. Compare three classic pictures: H.L.A. Hart, *The Concept of Law* (Oxford: Clarendon Press, 1961); Ronald Dworkin, *Law's Empire* (London: Fontana, 1986); Michel Foucault, *Power* (London: Allen Lane Penguin Press, 2001).

34. Josiah Ober, *Political Dissent in Democratic Athens*

35. Compare the reactions of Western Europe and North America to the military suspension of elections in Algeria in 1991, and the hideous consequences which followed from that suspension.

36. Hansen, *Athenian Democracy*, 29–32; Simon Hornblower, 'Creation and Development of Democratic Institutions in Ancient Greece', J. Dunn (ed), *Democracy: The Unfinished Journey* (Oxford: Oxford University Press, 1992), 1–16.

37. Only wealthier (and invariably male) Athenians continued, for almost a century, to be eligible to hold such office.

38. Hansen, *Athenian Democracy*, 29–32. G.E.M. de Sainte Croix, *The Class Struggle in the Ancient Greek World* (London: Duckworth, 1981) is the most ambitious modern attempt to place the Athenian experience in the perspective of the history of the Greek world as a whole; but he does not offer a systematic assessment of Solon's purposes or achievements.

39. Plato, Machiavelli, James Harrington, Rousseau, James Madison, Sieyes, Robespierre, Jeremy Bentham, even, as it turned out, somewhat self-contradictorily, Lenin.

40. All Lawgivers/Legislators were men. Contrast, according to Plato (who blandly credited Pericles's to his mistress Aspasia), the real authors of funeral orations (Plato, *Menexenus*, tr R.G. Bury (Cambridge, Mass.: Harvard University Press, 1929), 329–81, 336–39, 380–81).

41. As far as we now know. But compare the argument of Hansen, *Athenian Democracy*, 69–70.

42. Herodotus, *History*, tr A.D. Godley (Cambridge, Mass.: Harvard University Press, 1922), V, 66, 2, pp 72–73; Hansen, 33–34

43. Thucydides, *History*, II, xxxvi, 1–2, pp 320–21; Loraux, *Invention of Athens*

44. Thucydides, *History*, I, ii, 3–6, pp 4–7

45. Hansen, *Athenian Democracy*, 92–93. Hansen's outstanding book provides the best contemporary account of the institutions of the democracy at work.

46. Hansen, *Athenian Democracy*, 90–94

47. Hansen, *Athenian Democracy*, 94

48. In the fourth century BC this may have ceased to be so, at least for some, because of the institution of the *misthos*, a daily rate of pay not merely for acting as a juror on the popular courts but also for attending the Assembly itself. The members of the Council, serving in effect throughout an entire year, had always needed to have their own meals provided for them at public expense. The *misthos* was loathed by critics of the democracy for coarsening the social composition of its principal institutions, supplementing the motives for political participation by grossly material incentives, and altering the democracy's natural political balance by so doing: precisely the consequences which appealed to the citizen majority who opted for it.

49. Hansen, *Athenian Democracy*, chapter 6

50. Hansen, *Athenian Democracy*, chapter 10

51. With some of the smaller units there may have been an element of duress in the volunteering (Hansen, *Athenian Democracy*, 249), as there often still is in small political units to this day.

52. This was not a position which could be held twice by the same person in any given year (Hansen, *Athenian Democracy*, 250), perhaps ever.

53. Plutarch, *Lives*, Vol 2, tr Bernadotte Perrin (Cambridge, Mass.: Harvard University Press, 1916); *Pericles*, 32, pp 92–95; 35, p 103; Thucydides, *History*, II. lxv, 3–5, pp 374–75

54. Although modern historians have sometimes employed the term to analyse aspects of Athenian politics, the Athenians had nothing which distantly resembled a modern political party.

55. See, especially, Finley, *Politics in the Ancient World* & W. Robert Connor, *The New Politicians of Fifth-Century Athens* (Princeton: Princeton University Press, 1971). We can certainly assume, as all the finest historians of Athens always have, that this hard political labour of co-ordination, persuasion, reward, and threat must have gone on all the time.

56. Slave-dependent, women-excluding, unabashedly ethnocentric. No one any longer would care to defend these confines openly.

57. In the case of Plato this remains a partisan judgement. He certainly had personal and family links with men who did try to subvert it; and no one could fail to recognize that he viewed many aspects of it with visceral revulsion. But the reason we still read him today is that he understood some features of it all too well, and can still help us to understand them too, should we happen to wish to.

58. Aristotle, *Politics*, tr H. Rackham (Cambridge, Mass.: Harvard University Press, 1932); *The Athenian Constitution*, tr H. Rackham (Cambridge, Mass.: Harvard University Press, 1935)

59. George Grote, *A History of Greece from the Earliest Period to the Generation Contemporary with Alexander the Great* (London, 1846–56): and for the longer-term historical context see Jennifer Tolbert Roberts, *Athens on Trial: The Antidemocratic Tradition in Western Thought* (Princeton: Princeton University Press, 1994).

60. Which are the words we reach for when we try hardest to steady ourselves intellectually and politically in face of the greatest trauma of modern history? Cf the volume subtitles chosen by Ian

Kershaw for his magisterial study of Hitler's impact: *Hitler: A Life*, Vol 1 *Hubris*; Vol 2 *Nemesis* (London: Allen Lane, 1998 & 2000).

61. Cf Cynthia Farrar, *The Origins of Democratic Thinking* (Cambridge: Cambridge University Press, 1988)

62. Thomas Hobbes, *Hobbes's Thucydides*, ed Richard Schlatter (New Brunswick, N.J.: Rutgers University Press, 1975)

63. Pseudo-Xenophon, I, 5, pp 476–77

64. It would be more accurate to say jury murder. But this is too odd a phrase in modern English to introduce, without explaining it at the same time. The mass juries of the Athenian courts were one of the most potent instruments of its democracy in action. When they voted for Socrates's death, they were making as definite a political choice as when they voted in the Assembly to savage Mitylene, or voted again, a few hours later, to reprieve it (Thucydides, *History*, III, xxxvi, i–xlix, 4, pp 54–87).

65. Plato, *Crito*, tr H.N. Fowler (Cambridge, Mass.: Harvard University Press, 1914), 150–91

66. Plato, *Apology*, tr H.N. Fowler (Cambridge, Mass.: Harvard University Press, 1914), 68–145

67. Whatever his own personal flirtations with incumbents of that role (cf Plato, *Epistles*, tr R.G. Bury (Cambridge, Mass.: Harvard University Press, 1929), Seventh Letter, 476–565)

68. Just what practical conclusions to draw from this (or even what practical conclusions Plato himself went on to draw from it) remains far from obvious – far enough from obvious to provide the main intellectual stock in trade for an entire school of political thought, the extended *clientela* of Leo Strauss, an important element in American (and hence in world) politics over the last three decades: Ann Norton, *Leo Strauss and the Politics of American Empire* (New Haven: Yale University Press, 2004).

69. Thomas Hobbes, *De Cive* (1642) & *Leviathan* (1651).

70. Plato, *The Republic*, tr Paul Shorey, 2 vols (Cambridge, Mass.: Harvard University Press, 1930–35), 559D–562, Vol 2, 295–303

71. *Republic*, 561D, 302–03

72. *Republic*, 561D, 302–03

73. *Republic*, 561C–E, 300–03

74. *Republic*, 562B–C, 304–05

75. *Republic*, 562C, 304–05

76. *Republic*, 562D–563 D, 304–11

77. *Republic*, 563D, 310–11

78. *Republic*, 564A, 312–13

79. *Republic*, 564A, 312–13, 566D–580C, 322–69

80. Plato's later political writings, *The Laws* and *The Politicus* (or *Statesman*), have less to say about democracy and left far less imprint on subsequent political perception or judgement.

81. Aristotle, *Politics*, 1279b, II 19–20, pp 208–09

82. Aristotle, *Politics*, 1279a, II 37–39, pp 206–07

83. Aristotle, *Politics*, 1279a, I 18, 1279b, I 10, 204–07

84. Cf, helpfully, Martha C. Nussbaum, *The Fragility of Goodness* (Cambridge: Cambridge University Press, 1986), Pt 3, 235–394

85. Cf David Bostock, *Aristotle's Ethical Theory* (Oxford: Oxford University Press, 2001)

86. Compare Hegel's dazzling portrait, 'The Political Work of Art', in *The Philosophy of History*, Pt II, chapter 3, tr J. Sibree (New York: Dover, 1956), 250–76. E.M. Butler, *The Tyranny of Greece over Germany* (Cambridge: Cambridge University Press, 1935).

Contrast the findings on the classical Greek *polis* itself of Mogens Hansen's massive collaborative study of the city state form across time and space: '95 Theses about the Greek Polis in the Archaic and Classical Periods', *Historia*, 52 (2003), 257–82.

87. Cf Finley, *Politics in the Ancient World* with Farrar, *Origins of Democratic Thinking*.

88. Cf e.g. Quentin Skinner, *Visions of Politics* (Cambridge: Cambridge University Press, 2002), Vol 1, chapters 8–10

89. Cf Dunn, *The Cunning of Unreason*

90. Cf John Dunn, *Western Political Theory in the Face of the Future* 2nd ed (Cambridge: Cambridge University Press, 1993), chapter 1

91. Cf Neil Harding, 'The Marxist-Leninist Detour', in Dunn (ed), *Democracy: The Unfinished Journey* (Oxford: Oxford University Press, 1992), 155–87

92. For the fate of the San Bushmen (a periphery of the periphery) see Leonard Thompson, *Survival in Two Worlds: Moshoeshoe of Lesotho* (Oxford: Clarendon Press, 1975), chapter 1, esp 13 & 19, or C.W. de Kiewiet, *A History of South Africa: Social and Economic* (Oxford: Oxford University Press, 1957), chapter 1, 19–20; for the Nuer as British anthropologists liked to think of them see E.E. Evans-Pritchard, *The Nuer* (Oxford: Clarendon Press, 1940). For their more recent fate see Douglas H. Johnson, *The Root Causes of Sudan's Civil Wars* (London: James Currey & Bloomington: Indiana University Press, 2004).

93. One of the bravest attempts to do so is Mark Elvin, *The Pattern of the Chinese Past* (Stanford: Stanford University Press, 1972). See also G.E.R. Lloyd & N. Sivin, *The Way and the Word* (New Haven: Yale University Press, 2002), and, in more breathless outline, Jared Diamond, *Guns, Germs and Steel* (London: Jonathan Cape, 1997), chapter 16, 'How China became Chinese', 322–33.

94. Mogens Hansen (*The Athenian Democracy*) claims something close to this for fourth-century Athens, but as a political outcome, and certainly not as a verbal implication of the term *demokratia* itself.

95. See particularly Fergus Millar, *The Crowd in Rome in the Late Republic* (Ann Arbor: University of Michigan Press, 1998) & *The Roman Republic in Political Thought* (Hanover: University Press of New England, 2002), an exceptionally illuminating study of the development of Roman political thought and its historical impact.

96. Though see, still, Ronald Syme, *The Roman Revolution* (Oxford: Clarendon Press, 1939), or Christian Meier, *Caesar*, tr David McLintock (London: Fontana, 1996).

97. Though Vergil's adamantine formula – *Tu regere imperio populos, Romane, memento*: Remember, O Roman, that it is for you to rule peoples with empire (Vergil, *Aeneid*, VI, 851) – scarcely suggests the latter.

98. The great historian of this endless circling back is John Pocock. See, especially, J.G.A. Pocock, *The Machiavellian Moment* (Princeton: Princeton University Press, 1975) and his recent magnum opus on the context of Edward Gibbon's late-eighteenth-century masterpiece, *The Decline and Fall of the Roman Empire*: J.G.A. Pocock, *Barbarism and Religion*, thus far Vols 1–3 (Cambridge: Cambridge University Press, 1999–2003).

99. Millar, *The Roman Republic in Political Thought*

100. Millar, *The Roman Republic*, 48–49

101. Millar, *The Roman Republic*, 23–36; F.W. Walbank, *Polybius* (Berkeley, Calif.: University of California Press, 1972); Kurt von Fritz, *The Mixed Constitution in Antiquity* (New York: Columbia University Press, 1954); Claude Nicolet, 'Polybe et les institutions romaines', E. Gabba (ed), *Polybe* (Geneva, 1973), 209–58. There is an interesting study of Polybius's acutely ambivalent attitude to Roman power and Roman culture by Craige B. Champion, *Cultural*

Politics in Polybius's Histories (Berkeley, Calif.: University of California Press, 2004).

102. Polybius, *The Histories*, tr W.R. Paton, 6 vols (Cambridge, Mass.: Harvard University Press, 1922–27), XXXVIII, 22, Vol 6, 438–9: 'Scipio, when he looked upon the city as it was utterly perishing and in the last throes of its complete destruction, is said to have shed tears and wept openly for his enemies. After being wrapped in thought for long, and realizing that all cities, nations, and authorities must, like men, meet their doom; that this happened to Ilium, once a prosperous city, to the empires of Assyria, Media, and Persia, the greatest of their time, and to Macedonia itself, the brilliance of which was so recent, either deliberately, or the verses escaping him, he said:

> A day will come when sacred Troy shall perish
> And Priam and his people shall be slain.
> (Homer, *Iliad* VI, 448–9)

And when Polybius speaking with freedom to him, for he was his teacher, asked him what he meant by the words, they say that without any attempt at concealment he named his own country, for which he feared when he reflected on the fate of all things human. Polybius actually heard him and recalls it in his history.'

(This fragment survives only in Appian, *Punica*, 132, though see also *Histories*, XXXVIII, 21, 436–37.) Walbank is sceptical of the significance of this fulsome passage (*Polybius*, 11). There is a careful discussion of the grounds for doubt in A.E. Astin, *Scipio Aemilianus* (Oxford: Clarendon Press, 1967), 282–87.

103. Aristotle, *Politics*, esp 1281b–1284a, 220–24 cf Polybius, *Histories*, VI, 10–18, Vol 3, 292–311. For his central aim see *Histories*, I, 5–6, Vol 1, 2–5: 'For who is so worthless or indolent as not to wish to know by what means and under what system of polity the Romans in less than fifty-three years have succeeded in subjecting the whole inhabited world to their sole government – a thing unique in

history?' A good sense of how far the category of democracy was from suggesting itself as an immediate description of Rome's politics can be derived from Andrew Lintott, *The Constitution of the Roman Republic* (Oxford: Oxford University Press, 1999) and Claude Nicolet, *The World of the Citizen in Republican Rome*, tr P.S. Falla (London: Batsford, 1980).

104. Millar, *Roman Republic*, 170

105. Hansen, *The Athenian Democracy*; compare Millar, *Roman Republic*, 166–67; Polybius, *Histories*, VI, 13, Vol 3, 298–301 (on Senate and diplomacy).

106. Polybius, *Histories*, VI, 57, 396–99: esp 'When this happens, the state will change its name to the finest sounding of all, freedom and democracy *(demokratia)*, but will change its nature to the worst thing of all, mob-rule *(ochlokratia)*.' Millar insists, convincingly, that Polybius at this point can only have had Rome in mind, *Roman Republic*, 30, 35–36.

107. Polybius, *Histories*, VI, 57, 398–99

108. Polybius, *Histories*, VI, 10, 12–14, 292–93

109. Millar, *Roman Republic*, 55–58; Joseph Canning, *A History of Medieval Political Thought* (London: Routledge, 1996), 125–26; Janet Coleman, *A History of Political Thought from the Middle Ages to the Renaissance* (Oxford: Blackwell, 2000), 62; Coleman, 50–80, is excellent on the background of educational practice into which Aristotle's *Politics* was absorbed; Anthony Black, *Political Thought in Europe 1250–1450* (Cambridge: Cambridge University Press, 1992), 20–21.

110. Coleman, *History of Political Thought*, 55. There proved to be effective demand at the apogee of Islamic civilization for many aspects of Aristotle's thinking. But nothing about the political organization of any Islamic society gave pressing occasion for addressing his exploration of the significance of politics. (Dimitri

Gutas, *Greek Thought, Arabic Culture: The Graeco Arabic Translation Movement in Baghdad and Early Abbasid Society* (London: Routledge, 1998); Muhsin Mahdi, *Alfarabi and the Foundation of Islamic Political Philosophy* (Chicago: University of Chicago Press, 2001); Muhsin Mahdi, 'Avicenna', *Encyclopedia Iranica*, Vol 3 (London: Routledge, 1989), 66–110; Richard Walzer, *Greek into Arabic* (Oxford: Bruno Cassirer, 1962), chapter 14, 'Platonism in Islamic Philosophy'.

111. Quentin Skinner, 'The Italian City-Republics', in J. Dunn (ed), *Democracy: The Unfinished Journey*, 57–69; Hans Baron, *The Crisis of the Early Italian Renaissance*, revised ed (Princeton: Princeton University Press, 1966); Philip Jones, *The Italian City State: From Commune to Signoria* (Oxford: Clarendon Press, 1997)

112. Millar, *Roman Republic*, 58–59

113. Millar, *Roman Republic*, 60–61

114. Millar, *Roman Republic*, 62–63

115. Andreu Bosch, *Summari, index o epitome des admirables y nobilissims titols de honor de Cathalunya, Rossello I Cerdanya* (1628), facsimile Barcelona 1974, cited by Xavier Gil, 'Republican Politics in Early Modern Spain: the Castilian and Catalano-Aragonese Traditions', in Martin Van Gelderen & Quentin Skinner (eds), *Republicanism: A Shared European Heritage* (Cambridge: Cambridge University Press), Vol 1, 263–88 at p 280.

116. Wyger R.E. Velema, '"That a Republic is Better than a Monarchy": Anti-Monarchism in Early Modern Dutch Political Thought', in Skinner & Van Gelderen, *Republicanism*, Vol 1, 9–25, esp 13–19; Martin Van Gelderen, 'Aristotelians, Monarchomachs: Sovereignty and *respublica mixta* in Dutch and German Political Thought, 1580–1650', Skinner & Van Gelderen, *Republicanism*, Vol 1, 195–217.

117. *Vrye Politijke Stellingen en Consideratien van Staat*, 172–73, ed Wim Klever, Amsterdam 1974, cited by Martin Van Gelderen, 'Aristotelians, Monarchomachs and Republics', Skinner & Van Gelderen (eds), *Republicanism*, Vol 1, 195–217, at 215–16.

118. Hans Erich Bödeker, 'Debating the *respublica mixta*: German and Dutch Political Discourses around 1700', in Skinner & Van Gelderen (eds), *Republicanism*, Vol 1, 219–46, esp 222–28; Jonathan Scott, 'Classical Republicanism in Seventeenth-Century England and the Netherlands', in Skinner & Van Gelderen, *Republicanism*, Vol 1, 61–81, esp 76–80; Warren Montag, *Bodies, Masses, Power: Spinoza and his Contemporaries* (London: Verso, 1999); Jonathan I. Israel, *Radical Enlightenment: Philosophy and the Making of Modernity, 1650–1750* (Oxford: Oxford University Press, 2001); Hans Blom, *Morality and Causality in Politics: the Rise of Materialism in Seventeenth-Century Dutch Political Thought* (Utrecht: University of Utrecht Press, 1995)

119. The key setting was the Putney debates inside the parliamentary armies: A.S.P. Woodhouse (ed), *Puritanism and Liberty* 2nd ed (London: J.M. Dent & Sons, 1950); David Wootton, 'The Levellers', in Dunn (ed), *Democracy: The Unfinished Journey*, 71–89, & 'Leveller Democracy and the English Revolution', in J.H. Burns & Mark Goldie (eds), *Cambridge History of Seventeenth-Century Political Thought* (Cambridge: Cambridge University Press, 1991), 412–42. The best overall study of the movement remains H.N. Brailsford, *The Levellers and the English Revolution*, 2nd ed (Nottingham: Spokesman Books, 1976).

120. Hobbes, *Behemoth, or the Long Parliament*, 2nd ed, F. Toennies (London: Frank Cass, 1969), 21: 'For after the Bible was translated into English, every man, nay every boy and wench, that could read English, thought they spoke with God Almighty, and understood what he said.'

121. Hobbes, *Behemoth*, 26–44

122. Hobbes, *Behemoth*, 43; *De Cive: the English Version*, ed Howard Warrender (Oxford: Clarendon Press, 1983)

123. Cf Dunn, *Western Political Theory in the Face of the Future*, chapter 1

124. Blair Worden, *Roundhead Reputations* (London: Penguin, 2002), 100. Worden gives a spirited portrait of Toland in action, 95–120, stressing above all his youthful ebullience and manipulative opportunism (p 119). See also Sullivan, *John Toland and the Deist Controversy* (Cambridge, Mass.: Harvard University Press, 1982) and Chiara Giuntini, *Panteismo e ideologia repubblicana: John Toland (1676–1722)* (Bologna: Il Mulino, 1979); Blair Worden, 'Republicanism and the Restoration 1660–1683', in David Wootton (ed), *Republicanism and Commercial Society 1649–1776* (Stanford: Stanford University Press, 1994), 139–93; and Israel, *Radical Enlightenment.*

125. The contemporary translation, Thomas Hobbes, *De Cive: The English Version*, captures the flavour of Hobbes's writing better, despite some inaccuracy. For a more analytically and historically reliable version see Thomas Hobbes, *On the Citizen*, ed Richard Tuck & tr Michael Silverthorne (Cambridge: Cambridge Univesity Press, 1998). For the centrality of Hobbes's engagement with classical rhetoric, see Quentin Skinner, *Reason and Rhetoric in Hobbes's Philosophy* (Cambridge: Cambridge University Press, 1996).

126. Hobbes, *De Cive: The English Version*, X, ix, p 136

127. Benjamin Constant, *Political Writings*, ed Biancamaria Fontana (Cambridge: Cambridge University Press, 1988), 313–28

128. Hobbes, *De Cive: The English Version*, chapter VII, 1, and 5–7: pp 106–07, 109–10; Chapter XII, 8: pp 151–52. Richard Tuck has emphasized the importance of this judgement in shaping Hobbes's vision of politics from the beginning: Richard Tuck, *Philosophy*

and Government 1572–1651 (Cambridge: Cambridge University Press, 1993, 310–11).

129. Hobbes, *De Cive: The English Version*, chapter VII, 1: pp 106–07

130. C.V. Wedgwood, *The Trial of Charles I* (London: Fontana, 1964), 71

131. See particularly *The Correspondence of Thomas Hobbes*, ed Noel Malcolm, 2 vols (Oxford: Clarendon Press, 1994). There is a striking picture of his work fanning out amongst Europe's intelligentsia in Malcolm's *Aspects of Hobbes* (Oxford: Clarendon Press, 2002), chapter 14, 457–545, but as yet no especially illuminating biography. The biography to wait for, once again, is Noel Malcolm's, in preparation for the Clarendon Press.

132. There are two interesting recent biographies of Spinoza by Steven Nadler, *Spinoza: A Life* (Cambridge: Cambridge University Press, 1999) and Margaret Gullan-Whur, *Within Reason: A Life of Spinoza* (London: Pimlico, 2000). Much the most ambitious and learned presentation of his impact on European thought and feeling at large is Israel's remarkable *Radical Enlightenment: Philosophy and the Making of Modernity* (Oxford: Clarendon Press, 2000), always interesting but not invariably convincing in its judgements. Contrast, for example, on the impact of Hobbes, Malcolm's chapter in his *Aspects of Hobbes*.

133. His biographer John Aubrey records Hobbes as saying of Spinoza's *Tractatus Theologico-Politicus* that he had 'cut through him a bar's length, for he durst not write so boldly'. John Aubrey, *Brief Lives*, ed Andrew Clark, 2 vols (Oxford: Clarendon Press, 1898), I, 357.

134. Nadler, *Spinoza*, 44

135. Israel, *Radical Enlightenment*, 166

136. Nadler, *Spinoza*, chapter 6, esp 127–29

137. Nadler, *Spinoza*, 182–83

138. Spinoza, *Political Works*, ed & tr A.G. Wernham (Oxford: Clarendon Press, 1958). For helpful assessments of Spinoza's political thought see especially Malcolm, *Aspects of Hobbes*, 40–52; Wernham's Introduction; and Theo Verbeek, *Spinoza's Theologico-Political Treatise: Exploring 'The Will of God'*, (Aldershot: Ashgate, 2003). For the Dutch background to Spinoza's political thought see, besides Israel's *Radical Enlightenment*, also his The Intellectual Origins of Modern Democratic Republicanism, *European Journal of Political Theory*, 3 (2004), 7–36.

139. Spinoza, *Political Works (Tractatus)*, Chapter XI, 440–43

140. Spinoza, *Political Works (Tractatus)*, 316–17

141. Spinoza, *Political Works (Tractatus Theologico-Politicus)*, 276–78. Compare Hobbes, *De Cive*, VII, 1, 106–7

142. Spinoza, *Political Works (Tractatus Theologico-Politicus)*, 284

143. Spinoza, *Political Works (Tractatus Theologico-Politicus)*, 288

144. Spinoza, *Political Works (Tractatus Politicus)*, 376

145. Spinoza, *Political Works (Tractatus Politicus)*, chapter X, 440: '*tertium et omnino absolutum imperium*'. It is not clear what the intended force of this formula is. For Spinoza all sovereignty is by definition absolute. The sovereign is entitled to (and potentially needs to) judge everything about how human beings should or should not act: *Tractatus Politicus*, IV, 2, pp 300–01. It sometimes appears that he wishes to argue that democracy differs from monarchy and aristocracy in that it will never be (or is incapable of proving) self-frustrating or self-undermining (*Tractatus Politicus*, VIII, 3, 4, 6 & 7, pp 370–73: 'If there is such a thing as absolute sovereignty, it is in reality what is held by the entire multitude'). But in practice democratic sovereigns are every bit as capable of misjudging their own interests or even their future tastes as aristocracies or monarchs. At no point does Spinoza offer any grounds for denying this; nor is there any evidence that he felt the

least inclination to deny it. Under a democracy, there is indeed nothing but the *demos* itself to stop the state doing whatever it then chooses. But this gives no guarantee that the *demos* will judge coherently or accurately, nor that it will appreciate over time the consequences of its own actions. Did Spinoza not see this? Did he wish to deny it? I cannot see that we know.

146. Spinoza, *Political Works (Tractatus Politicus)*, 440, 442

147. Spinoza, *Political Works (Tractatus Theologico-Politicus)*, 136

148. *Atque hac ratione omnes manent ut antea in statu naturali aequales.* (Spinoza, *Political Writings (Tractatus Politicus)*, 135–36)

149. Polybius, *Histories*, VI, 57, 398–99. Nadler, *Spinoza: A Life*, chapters 10 & 11.

150. Nadler, *Spinoza: A Life*, 306.

151. Spinoza, *Political Works (Tractatus Theologico-Politicus)*, XX, pp 240–243: 'I have thus shown: I. That it is impossible to deprive men of the freedom to say what they think. II. That this freedom can be granted to everyone without infringing the right and authority of the sovereign; and that everyone can keep it without infringing that right as long as he does not use it as a licence to introduce anything into the state as a law, or to do anything contrary to the accepted laws. III. That it is no danger to the peace of the state; and that all troubles arising from it can easily be checked. IV. That it is no danger to piety either. V. That laws passed about speculative matters are utterly useless; and finally, VI. That this freedom not only can be granted without danger to public peace, piety, and the right of the sovereign, but actually must be granted if all are to be preserved.'

152. Compare Hobbes, *De Cive*, X, 8: p 135: 'although the word *liberty*, may in large, and ample letters be written over the gates of any City whatsoever, yet it is not meant the *Subjects*, but the *Cities* liberty, neither can that word with better Right be inscribed on a

City which is governed by the *people*, then that which is ruled by a *Monarch*.' The city which Hobbes had in mind was Lucca: (Hobbes, *Leviathan*, ed Richard Tuck (Cambridge: Cambridge University Press 1991), Chapter 21, 149: 'there is writ on the Turrets of the city of Luca in great Characters at this day, the word *LIBERTAS*; yet no man can thence inferre, that a particular man has more Libertie, or Immunitie from the service of the Commonwealth there, than in *Constantinople*.' The inscription still stands. But contrast Quentin Skinner, *Liberty before Liberalism* (Cambridge: Cambridge University Press, 1998) for the tradition of political understanding which Hobbes sought to overthrow. For the substantial degree of overlap between Spinoza's views and this judgement of Hobbes, see Spinoza, *Political Works (Tractatus Theologico-Politicus)*, XVI, the lengthy penultimate sentence of p 136. As Spinoza himself concludes: '*Nec his plura addere opus est.*' There is no need to say more...

153. Spinoza, *Political Works (Tractatus Politicus)*, VII, 5, p 338–39 insists stoutly that it is stupid to be willing to live as slaves in peace in order to wage war more effectively: '*inscitia sane est, nimirum quod, ut bellum felicius gerant, in pace servire.*' But he does not choose to dispute the common charge against democracy that its virtue is far more effective in peace than it is in war '*ejus virtus multo magis in pace quam in bello valet*'.

154. Algernon Sidney, *Discourses on Government* 2nd ed (London:J. Darby, 1704), 146: 'That is the best Government, which best provides for war'

155. Spinoza, *Political Works (Tractatus Politicus)*, VII, 338–39. This was a judgement in itself which would have astounded any Athenian.

156. Spinoza, *Political Works (Tractatus Politicus)*, chapter XI, 440–41: '*Reliqua desiderantur*'. The rest is missing...

157. The diary of the Leiden scholar Gronovius records that Spinoza requested an audience with Johan de Witt to discuss the latter's (rumoured) negative reactions to the *Tractatus Theologico-Politicus*, and that de Witt responded, unambiguously enough, that he 'did not want to see him pass his threshold' (W.N.A. Klever, 'A New Document on De Witt's Attitude to Spinoza', *Studia Spinoziana*, 9 (1993), 379–88; Nadler, *Spinoza*, 256.)

158. See especially Hansen, *Athenian Democracy*; 71–2, 228–29, 266–68 (on *ho boulomenos*), 81–85 (on *isonomia* and *isegoria*); Finley, *Politics in the Ancient World*; and cf Martin Ostwald, *From Popular Sovereignty to Sovereignty of Law: Law, Sovereignty and Politics in Fifth-Century Athens* (Berkeley, Calif.: University of California Press, 1986).

159. The political significance of this is well captured by Quentin Skinner in 'From the State of Princes to the Person of the State', *Visions of Politics*, Vol 2, 368–413. For its longer-term implications see especially Istvan Hont, 'The Permanent Crisis of a Divided Mankind', in J. Dunn (ed), *Contemporary Crisis of the Nation State?* (Oxford: Blackwell, 1994), 166–231.

160. This great phrase comes from the dying speech (a more individualist genre than the funeral oration) of an unreconstructed Leveller leader, Colonel Richard Rumbold, decades after the movement itself had been crushed by Oliver Cromwell. He delivered the speech (as much of it as he was permitted to, and in face of considerable resistance from his captors) at the Market Cross in Edinburgh in June 1685, shortly before he was hung, drawn and quartered for designing the death of the King in the Rye House Plot against Charles II. (*The Dying Speeches of Several Excellent Persons who Suffered for their Zeal against Popery and Arbitrary Government,* London, 1689 (Wing 2957), 24): 'I am sure there was no Man born marked of God above another; for none comes into the World with a Saddle on his Back, neither any Booted and Spurred to ride to him.'

The plot itself drew its name from its intended setting, Rumbold's own house in the Kentish town of Rye, with its conveniently high garden wall, ideal for an ambush: Richard Ashcraft, *Revolutionary Politics and Locke's 'Two Treatises of Government'* (Princeton: Princeton University Press, 1986), 352–71, esp 364.

NOTES TO CHAPTER 2

1. Franco Venturi, *Saggi sull'Europa Illuminista*, Vol 1, *Alberto Radicati di Passerano* (Turin: Einaudi, 1954), 'Deismo, cristianesimo e democrazia perfetta', 248–69; Jonathan I. Israel, *Radical Enlightenment* (Oxford: Clarendon Press, 2001). For a notable example earlier in the seventeenth century (expressed in Latin, as far as we know in strict seclusion, and not yet reliably dated) see the resolute rejection of Hobbes's critique of democracy by William Petty, as a young man a close acquaintance and admirer of Hobbes: Frank Amati & Tony Aspromourgos, 'Petty *contra* Hobbes: a previously untranslated manuscript', *Journal of the History of Ideas*, 46 (1985), 127–32, esp 130 'Whether it is more pleasant to human nature to transfer their power forever into the hands of a single person (that is, for those who hold power to give it away) or whether it is better to serve the very same person but only appointing him to office after a gradual process and for a brief period? I propose that power should be shaped and drawn up by the people themselves; otherwise the monarch will be susceptible to the daily change of affairs and to his temperament.' A cogent line of thought.

2. Gordon S. Wood, *The American Revolution: A History* (London: Weidenfeld & Nicolson, 2003)

3. Alexis de Tocqueville, *Democracy in America*, tr & ed Harvey C. Mansfield & Delba Winthrop (Chicago: University of Chicago Press, 2002)

4. Sheldon Wolin, *Tocqueville Between Two Worlds: The Making of a Political and Theoretical Life* (Princeton: Princeton University Press, 2001)

5. Bernard Bailyn, *The Ideological Origins of the American Revolution* (Cambridge, Mass.: Harvard University Press, 1967). For the variations in political structure and culture from one colony (or State) to another see helpfully Richard Beeman, *The Varieties of Political Experience in Eighteenth-Century America* (Philadelphia: University of Pennsylvania Press, 2003).

6. Bernard Bailyn, *To Begin the World Anew* (New York: Alfred Knopf, 2003), 106

7. Bailyn, *To Begin the World Anew*; Jack N. Rakove, *James Madison and the Founding of the American Republic* 2nd ed (New York & London: Longman, 2002); Gordon S.Wood, *The Creation of the American Republic* (Chapel Hill: University of North Carolina Press, 1969)

8. Bailyn, *To Begin the World Anew*, 106

9. Bailyn, *To Begin the World Anew*, 107

10. Wood, *Creation of the American Republic*; Jackson Turner Main, *The Antifederalists: Critics of the Constitution 1781–1788* (Chicago: Quadrangle Books, 1964)

11. Jacob E. Cooke (ed), *The Federalist* (Alexander Hamilton, John Jay & James Madison) (Cleveland: Meridian Books, 1961) Introduction, xix–xxx

12. Rakove, *James Madison*, 11. Besides Rakove's clear and thoughtful study, and his rich analysis of the intellectual and political background to the Constitution, *Original Meanings* (New York: Vintage, 1997), see especially Lance Banning, *The Sacred Fire of Liberty: James Madison and the Founding of the Federal Republic* (Ithaca: Cornell University Press, 1995). One month earlier, in April 1787, Madison had summarized his conclusions in a striking diagnosis of 'The Vices of the Political System of the United States' (*Papers of James Madison*, ed Robert A. Rutland et al, Chicago: University of Chicago Press (1975), IX, 345–58, esp 354–57)

13. Rakove, *James Madison*, 64–5

14. Rakove, *Madison*, 61–2

15. Rakove, *Madison*, 63

16. Cooke (ed), *Federalist*, 56. Jefferson was Ambassador in Paris at the time. For Madison's letter of 24 October 1787, see *Papers of James Madison*, ed Rutland, University of Chicago Press, 1977, X, 205–220. Like its two predecessors (p 206), it was delayed by the difficulties of finding a reliable transatlantic carrier and the pressing concerns of America's leading naval officer, John Paul Jones (pp 218–19). On the relation of democracy to America's political predicament see especially 212–13:

    'Those who contend for a simple Democracy, or a pure republic, activated by the sense of the majority, and operating within narrow limits, assume or suppose a case which is altogether fictitious. They found their reasoning on the idea, that the people composing the Society, enjoy not only an equality of political rights; but that they have all precisely the same interests, and the same feelings in every respect. Were this in reality the case, their reasoning would be conclusive... The interest of the majority would be that of the minority also; the decision could only turn on mere opinion concerning the good of the whole, of which the major voice would be the safest criterion; and within a small sphere, this voice could be most easily collected, and the public affairs most accurately managed. We know however that no Society ever did or can consist of so homogeneous a mass of Citizens. In the savage State indeed, an approach is made towards it; but in that State little or no Government is necessary. In all civilized Societies, distinctions are various and unavoidable. A distinction of property results from that very protection which a free Government gives to unequal faculties of acquiring it. There will be rich and poor; creditors and debtors; a landed interest, a mercantile interest, a manufacturing interest.' etc.

17. *Federalist*, 59

18. *Federalist*, 60

19. *Federalist*, 60–61

20. *Federalist*, 61

21. *Federalist*, 65

22. *Federalist*, 65

23. *Federalist* (Number 63), p 427

24. *Federalist*, 427

25. *Federalist*, 428

26. *Federalist* (Number 48), p 333

27. *Federalist*, 335–36. Compare Thomas Jefferson, *Notes on the State of Virginia* (New York: Harper, 1964), 113–24: 'An *elective despotism* was not the government we fought for, but one which should not only be founded on free principles, but in which the powers of government should be so divided and balanced among several bodies of magistracy, as that no one could transcend their legal limits, without being effectually checked and restrained by the others...'

28. Wood, *The American Revolution, 62*

29. Wood, *American Revolution*, 67

30. Wood, *American Revolution*, 66

31. Wood, *American Revolution*, 40–41

32. Madison to Edward Everett, 14 November 1831: Drew R. McCoy *The Last of the Fathers: James Madison and the Republican Legacy* (Cambridge: Cambridge University Press, 1989), 133

33. McCoy, *Last of the Fathers*, 116–17. Madison to Thomas Ritchie, 18 December 1825: 'All power in human hands is liable to be abused. In Governments independent of the people, the rights and interests of the whole may be sacrificed to the views of the Government. In Republics, where the people govern themselves, and where, of course, the majority govern, a danger to the minority arises from opportunities tempting a sacrifice of their rights to the interests, real or supposed, of the majority. No form of government, therefore, can be a perfect guard against the abuse of power. The recommendation of the republican form is, that the danger of abuse is less than in any other; and the superior recommendation of the

federo-republican system is, that while it provides more effectually against external danger, it involves a greater security to the minority against the hasty formation of oppressive majorities.' [James Madison, *Letters & Other Writings*, ed William C. Rives & Philip R. Fendall, Philadelphia, 1865, III, 507

34. McCoy *Last of the Fathers*, 193–206: James Madison, *Notes on Suffrage* c 1821

35. Gordon S.Wood, *The Radicalism of the American Revolution* (New York: Vintage, 1993), 270

36. McCoy, *Last of the Fathers*, 195

37. McCoy *Last of the Fathers*, 195

38. Wood, *Radicalism of the American Revolution*, 295–96

39. Wood, *Radicalism*, 296

40. Simon Schama, *Patriots and Liberators* (London: Fontana, 1992); R.R. Palmer, *The Age of the Democratic Revolution* Vol 1 (Oxford: Oxford University Press, 1959). There is an incisive analysis of the trajectory of the Dutch Republic from the Patriot Revolt through to the creation and fall of the Batavian Republic in Jonathan I. Israel, *The Dutch Republic: Its Rise, Greatness and Fall 1477–1806* (Oxford: Oxford University Press, 1995) chapters 42–44. For the very limited Dutch zest for democracy as a regime form earlier in the century see Leonard Leeb, *The Ideological Origins of the Batavian Revolution* (The Hague: Nijhoff, 1973), 114, 132, 144–45 etc.

41. Schama, *Patriots and Liberators*, 80–135

42. Schama, *Patriots and Liberators*, 94

43. Schama, *Patriots and Liberators*, 81

44. Schama, *Patriots and Liberators*, 94

45. Schama, *Patriots and Liberators*, 127

46. Schama, *Patriots and Liberators*, 94–95

47. Schama, *Patriots and Liberators*, 95

48. Schama, *Patriots and Liberators*, 2

49. Palmer, *Age of the Democratic Revolution*, Vol 1, 17; and see further R.R. Palmer, 'Notes on the Use of the Word "Democracy" 1789–1799', *Political Science Quarterly*, LXVIII, 1953, 203–26

50. Palmer, *Democratic Revolution*, I, 15

51. Schama, *Patriots and Liberators*, 127

52. Schama, *Patriots and Liberators*, 630–48

53. Palmer, *Democratic Revolution*, I, 341

54. Palmer, *Democratic Revolution*, I, 342

55. Palmer, *Democratic Revolution*, I, 345–46

56. Palmer, *Democratic Revolution*, I, 346

57. Palmer, *Democratic Revolution*, I, 347

58. Palmer, *Democratic Revolution*, I, 347–57

59. Palmer, *Democratic Revolution*, I, 479–502

60. Palmer, *Democratic Revolution*, I, 349

61. Palmer, *Democratic Revolution*, I, 349–50

62. This is the summary of Suzanne Tassier, the leading Belgian historian of the revolt (*Revue de l'Université de Bruxelles*,1934, 453, cited by Palmer, *Age of the Democratic Revolution*, I, 350)

63. Palmer, *Age of the Democratic Revolution*, I, 351

64. Suzanne Tassier, *Les Démocrates Belges de 1789: étude sur le Vonckisme et la Révolution brabançonne* (Brussels: *Mémoires de l'Academie royale de Belgique*, classe des letters, 2nd ser, XXVIII), 190

65. Arno J.Mayer, *The Furies* (Princeton: Princeton University Press, 2000), 323–70

66. Palmer, *Age of the Democratic Revolution*, I, 355–56. See also Janet Polasky, The Success of a Counter-Revolution in Revolutionary Europe: the Brabant Revolution of 1789, *Tijdschrift fur Geschiednis*, 102, 1989, 413–21; her *Revolution in Brussels* (Brussels: Académie Royale de Belgique, 1985). J. Craeybeckx, 'The Brabant Revolution: a conservative revolt in a backward country?', *Acta Historiae Neerlandica*, 4 (Leiden: E.J. Brill, 1970), 49–83 disputes the emphasis on Belgium's relative economic and social backwardness.

67. Frederic Volpi, *Islam and Democracy: The Failure of Dialogue in Algeria* (London: Pluto Press, 2003)

68. Richard Wrigley, *The Politics of Appearances: Representations of Dress in Revolutionary France* (Oxford: Berg, 2002)

69. René-Louis de Voyer de Paulmy, Marquis d'Argenson, *Considérations sur le gouvernment ancien et présent de la France*, 2nd ed 1784 Amsterdam

70. Nannerl O. Keohane, *Philosophy and the State in France* (Princeton: Princeton University Press, 1980), 376

71. Argenson, *Considérations sur le gouvernement ancien et présent de la France* (Amsterdam: Marc Michel Rey, 1764). Keohane, *Philosophy and the State*, 377

72. *Considérations* 1784, iv–v. The son saw fit to interpolate a considerable amount of material apparently of his own into this (officially) second edition.

73. Franklin L. Ford, *Sword and Robe* (Cambridge, Mass.: Harvard University Press, 1953, chapter 12)

74. Keohane, *Philosophy and the State*, 376

75. Keohane, *Philosophy and the State*, 390

76. Roger Tisserand (ed), *Les Concurrents de J.J. Rousseau à l'Académie de Dijon* (Paris, 1936), 130–31

77. *Considérations*, 1784, chapter 7, 192–297. The first edition, 215–328, is much sparser.

78. *Considérations*, 1784, 195. Cf first edition, 303–4. '*Le Roi ne peut-il régner sur des Citoyens sans dominer sur des esclaves?*' Can the King not reign over Citizens without dominating slaves?

79. *Considérations*. 1784, 272. Cf 1764 ed, 305–10. Compare Montesquieu's classic defence of intermediary powers as devices through which one power can obstruct another throughout *L'Esprit des Loix* (1748) (esp Bk XI, chapter 6), and the defence of the delaying function of the separation of powers in the *Federalist*. Cf Bernard Manin, 'Checks, Balances and Boundaries: the Separation of Powers in the Constitutional Debate of 1787', Biancamaria Fontana (ed), *The Invention of the Modern Republic* (Cambridge: Cambridge University Press, 1994), 27–62.

80. *Considérations*, 1784, 296. Argenson's original formulation (1764 ed, 314) was considerably more tactful towards the monarch's own authority, but just as confident of the indispensability of the people

Notes

as a source of information, both to the monarch and to one another, about the real scope of their interests.

81. Michael Sonenscher, 'The Nation's Debt and the Birth of the Modern Republic', *History of Political Thought*, 18, 1997, 64–103 & 267–325. For the pressures behind this, see especially John Brewer, *The Sinews of War: War, Money and the English State 1688–1783* (London: Unwin Hyman, 1989).

82. *Considérations*, 1784, 199. None of these details appears in the 1764 edition.

83. *Considérations*, 1784, 199. This phrase does not appear in the 1764 edition. The galvanizing effects of his Plan on rural productivity and prosperity figure prominently in the original edition (1764, 274–95).

84. *Considérations*, 1764, 7; the 1784 edition, 12 adds emphasis on the common interest in the good government of the kingdom.

85. *Considérations*, 1764, 7–8; 1784, 15

86. *Considérations*, 1764, 8; 1784, 15. The original edition (p 12) does note that Switzerland is a pure Democracy, since, although the Nobility enjoys a measure of distinction, this furnishes it with no governmental authority.

There is no compelling synoptic view of the scale, distribution or quality of Swiss democracy from canton to canton in the eighteenth century. For an assessment of an individual canton see Benjamin Barber, *The Death of Communal Liberty: A History of Freedom in a Swiss Mountain Canton* (Princeton: Princeton University Press, 1974). For Geneva, a far from democratic instance, see two chapters by Franco Venturi, *The End of the Old Regime in Europe: The First Crisis*, tr R.B. Litchfield (Princeton: Princeton University Press, 1989), 340–50, and *The End of the Old Regime in Europe: Republican Patriotism and the Empires of the East* (Princeton: Princeton University Press, 1991), 459–96; Linda Kirk, 'Genevan Republicanism', David Wootton (ed), *Republicanism, Liberty and Commercial Society 1649–1776* (Stanford: Stanford University Press, 1994), 270–309; and Helena

219

Rosenblatt, *Rousseau and Geneva: From the 'First Discourse' to the 'Social Contract'* (Cambridge: Cambridge University Press, 1997).

D'Argenson's assumption that Switzerland provided the only protracted modern European experience of democracy in action was still compelling enough a hundred years later for George Grote, the great Victorian historian of Athenian democracy, to make 'an excursion to Switzerland, in order to observe, close at hand, the nearest modern analogue of the Grecian republics', to draw conscious lessons from its experience in interpreting Athenian democracy in action, and to publish his conclusions in *Letters on Switzerland*. (See Alexander Bain, 'The Intellectual Character and Writings of George Grote', *The Minor Works of George Grote* (London: John Murray, 1873), 102–03.)

87. Franklin L. Ford, *Sword and Robe*, chapter 12. Charles-Louis de Secondat, Baron de Montesquieu, hereditary Président à Mortier of the Parlement of Bordeaux and author of the great *L'Esprit des Loix* (1748) is a classic instance.

88. Charles-René D'Argenson (ed), *Mémoires du Marquis d'Argenson* (Paris: P. Jannet, 1857–58), V, 129, Reading note on *Lettres historiques sur le Parlement*. See also the amplification in 1756, pp 349–50 etc. and cf *Considérations*, 1784, 272

89. An exception amongst its foreign admirers should perhaps be made in the case of Tom Paine. Cf *The Rights of Man* Pt II (London: J.M. Dent, 1916), 176–77 etc.

90. For Sieyes see especially his *Political Writings*, ed Michael Sonenscher (Indianopolis: Hackett, 2003); Murray Forsyth, *Reason and Revolution: the Political Thought of the Abbé Sieyes* (Leicester: Leicester University Press, 1987); and Pasquale Pasquino, *Sieyes et l'Invention de la Constitution en France* (Paris: Odile Jacob, 1998)

91. D'Argenson, *Considérations*, 1764, 7; 1784, 15

92. The most vivid and economical synoptic picture of France's movement towards revolution remains Georges Lefebvre's pre-war *The Coming of the French Revolution*, tr R.R. Palmer (New York:

Vintage, 1957). See also Jacques Godechot, *The Taking of the Bastille, July 14th 1789*, tr Jean Stewart (London: Faber, 1970), and more recently Simon Schama's swashbuckling, *Citizens: A Chronicle of the French Revolution* (New York: Alfred Knopf, 1989). There are well-balanced treatments in two books by William Doyle, *The Origins of the French Revolution* (Oxford: Oxford University Press, 1980) and *The Oxford History of the French Revolution* (Oxford: Oxford University Press, 1995), and in Colin Jones, *The Great Nation: France from Louis XV to Napoleon* (London: Allen Lane Penguin Press, 2002), 395–580.

93. On the *cahiers* see the classic analysis by Beatrice Hyslop, *Guide to the General Cahiers of 1789* (New York: Columbia University Press, 1936), and George V. Taylor, 'Revolutionary and Non-revolutionary Content in the *Cahiers*', *French Historical Studies*, 7, 1972, 479–502.

94. Goya's *Disasters of War*. And see Arno J. Mayer, *The Furies* (Princeton: Princeton University Press, 2000)

95. Edmund Burke, *The Writings and Speeches*, Vol VIII *The French Revolution 1790–1794*, ed L.J. Mitchell (Oxford: Clarendon Press, 1989)

96. Despite the fact that he is often credited with just this contribution, for drawing the young General, Napoleon Bonaparte, to the centre of Parisian politics and collaborating with him in killing off the First Republic. For Sieyes's life see Jean-Denis Bredin, *Sieyes: la Clé de la Révolution française* (Paris: Éditions du Fallois, 1988). For his ideas see Murray Forsyth, *Reason and Revolution*. The most accessible English-language version of his political works is now Michael Sonenscher's edition of his *Political Writings* (Indianapolis: Hackett, 2003) which contains all three of the key pamphlets written in 1788, along with a very subtle and suggestive Introduction. For French originals of these see Marcel Dorigny (ed), *Oeuvres de Sieyes* (Paris: Éditions d'Histoire Sociale, 1989), Vol 1.

97. Forsyth, *Reason and Revolution*, 2

98. *Vues sur les moyens d'exécution*, 2 (*Oeuvres*, ed Dorigny, Vol 1) *Political Writings*, ed Sonenscher, 5

99. Plato, *Republic*, tr Paul Shorey (Cambridge, Mass.: Harvard University Press, 1935), 558C, Vol 2, 290–91: 'assigning a kind of equality indiscriminately to equals and unequals alike'

100. Adam Smith, *Lectures on Jurisprudence*, ed R.L. Meek, D.D. Raphael, & P.G. Stein (Oxford: Clarendon Press, 1978), esp 311–30, 401–4, 433–36. John Dunn, *Rethinking Modern Political Theory* (Cambridge: Cambridge University Press, 1985), chapter 3.

101. *Vues*, 127 (*Oeuvres*, ed Dorigny, Vol 1); *Political Writings*, 54

102. *Vues*, 124–29 (*Oeuvres*, Vol 1); *Political Writings*, 53–55. I have modified the translation here, and elsewhere, to make it more literal.

103. *Vues*, 112–13 (*Oeuvres*, Vol 1); *Political Writings*, 48

104. *Vues*, 114 (*Oeuvres,* Vol 1); *Political Writings*, 49

105. *Vues*, 3; 1 (*Oeuvres*, Vol 1); *Political Writings*, 4

106. *Vues*, 3–4 (*Oeuvres*, Vol 1); *Political Writings*, 5

107. *Essai sur les privilèges*, 1–2 (*Oeuvres*, Vol 1); *Political Writings*, 69. The *Essai* was an essay on the idea of privilege; but it was also very much an assault on the highly particular array of privileges which dominated the status system of *ancien régime* France. The definite article, in this case, carries both senses.

108. *Essai*, 2 (*Oeuvres*, Vol 1); *Political Writings*, 70

109. *Essai*, 1–5 (*Oeuvres*, Vol 1); *Political Writings*, 69–71

110. *Essai*, 14 (*Oeuvres*, Vol 1); *Political Writings*, 76. Sieyes cites as evidence the shocked complaint of the Order of Nobility from the last preceding meeting of the Estates General in 1614 that the Third Estate, 'almost all the vassals of the first orders' should have had the temerity to describe themselves as younger siblings of their superiors (*Political Writings*, 90).

111. *Essai*, 53 (*Oeuvres*, Vol 1); *Political Writings*, 74–5

112. *Essai*,18–25 (*Oeuvres*, Vol 1); *Political Writings*, 76–78

113. *Essai*, 29 (*Oeuvres*, Vol 1); *Political Writings*, 80. This is, of course, equally true of the inheritance of wealth in a capitalist economy

and has remained an element of ideological vulnerability (or, at the
very least, of implausibility).

114. *Essai*, 37 (*Oeuvres*, Vol 1); *Political Writings*, 84

115. *Essai*, 40 (*Oeuvres*, Vol 1); *Political Writings*, 85

116. *Qu'est-ce que le tiers état?*, 1, 6, 9 (*Oeuvres*, Vol 1); *What is the
    Third Estate?* (*Political Writings*, 94, 96, 98). See Karl Marx,
    *Contribution to the Critique of Hegel's Philosophy of Law:
    Introduction* (Karl Marx & Frederick Engels, *Collected Works*, Vol
    3 (London: Lawrence & Wishart, 1975), 184–85).

117. George V. Taylor, 'Non-capitalist Wealth and the Origins of the
    French Revolution', *American Historical Review*, 62, 1967, 429–96;
    Colin Lucas, 'Nobles, Bourgeois and the Origins of the French
    Revolution', *Past and Present*, 60, 1973, 84–126; Patrice Higonnet,
    *Class, Ideology and the Rights of Nobles during the French
    Revolution* (Oxford: Clarendon Press, 1981); Guy Chaussinand-
    Nogaret, *The French Nobility in the Eighteenth Century: From
    Feudalism to the Enlightenment*, tr William Doyle (Cambridge:
    Cambridge University Press, 1985). For a powerful presentation of
    the realities of the First Estate in its eighteenth-century setting see
    John McManners, *Church and Society in Eighteenth-Century
    France*, 2 vols (Oxford: Oxford University Press, 1998),
    summarizing a lifetime's research.

118. Sieyes, *Essai*, 53 (*Oeuvres*, Vol 1); *Political Writings*, 90

119. Sieyes, *Tiers état*, 1 (*Oeuvres*, Vol 1); *Political Writings*, 94

120. Sieyes, *Tiers état*, 1; *Political Writings*, 94

121. Sieyes, *Tiers état*, 2; *Political Writings*, 94

122. Sieyes, *Tiers état*, 2–3; *Political Writings*, 95

123. Sieyes, *Tiers état*, 6; *Political Writings*, 96

124. Sieyes, *Tiers état*, 4; *Political Writings*, 95

125. Sieyes, *Tiers état*, 10; *Political Writings*, 98

126. Sieyes, *Tiers état*, 10; *Political Writings*, 99

127. Sieyes, *Tiers état*, 98; *Political Writings*, 147

128. Sieyes, *Tiers état*, 6–9; *Political Writings*, 97

129. Sieyes, *Tiers état*, 9; *Political Writings*, 98

130. Sieyes, *Tiers état*, 16; *Political Writings*, 102

131. Sieyes, *Tiers état*, 27; *Political Writings*, 107. As the bloodshed of the next twenty-five years placed beyond reasonable doubt, this was not a comparison to take lightly. (Cf R.R. Palmer, *Twelve who Ruled: The Year of Terror in the French Revolution* (New York: Athenaeum, 1965), 218)

132. Sieyes, *Tiers état*, 110; *Political Writings*, 158

133. *What is the Third Estate?*, ed S.E. Finer (London: Pall Mall, 1963), 177. The note does not appear in the Dorigny edition.

134. Sieyes, *Political Writings*, 147n. The note does not appear in the Dorigny edition.

135. Sieyes, *Political Writings*, 147n. Finer, *Third Estate*, 196–97 translates vividly.

136. Sieyes, *Tiers état*, 51; again Finer's translation: *Third Estate*, 96

137. R.R. Palmer, *Political Science Quarterly*, 1953

138. A. Dufourcq, *Le Régime Jacobin en Italie: étude sur la République romaine 1798–99* (Paris: Perrin, 1900), 30; Palmer, *Political Science Quarterly*, 1953, 221 translates more of the relevant text.

139. Thomas Paine, *The Rights of Man*, 176–77

140. Bredin, *Sieyes*, 525

141. M. Crook, *Élections in the French Revolution* (Cambridge: Cambridge University Press), 11. On the development of elections during the Revolution see, in addition to Crook, Patrice Gueniffey, *Le Nombre et la Raison: la révolution française et les elections* (Paris: Gallimard, 1993).

142. Forsyth, 162–65; E.-J. Sieyes, *Écrits politiques*, ed R. Zappéri (Paris: Archives Contemporaines, 1985), 189–206; Crook, 30

143. Crook, *Elections*, 31

144. Crook, *Elections*, 33

145. Crook, *Elections*, 33

146. Crook, *Elections*, 34

147. Maximilien Robespierre, *Discours et rapports à la Convention*, (Paris: Union Générale des Éditions, 1965), 213

148. Robespierre, *Discours*, 214

149. Robespierre, *Discours*, 216

150. Robespierre, *Discours*, 218

151. Robespierre, *Discours*, 221

152. Robespierre, *Discours*, 222

153. Robespierre, *Discours*, 223

154. Robespierre, *Discours*, 227. For a spirited but impressively level-headed analysis of this government in action see Palmer, *Twelve who Ruled*.

155. Robespierre, *Discours*, 236

NOTES TO CHAPTER 3

1. Cf John Dunn, *The Cunning of Unreason* (London: HarperCollins, 2000)

2. Jean-Jacques Rousseau, *The Social Contract*, Bk 1, chapter 1: 'Man is born free; and everywhere he is in chains. One thinks himself the master of others, and still remains a greater slave than they. How did this change come about? I do not know. What can make it legitimate? That question I think I can answer.' (*The Social Contract and Discourses*, tr G.D.H. Cole (London: J.M. Dent), 5; *Political Writings*, ed C.E. Vaughan (Oxford: Blackwell, 1962)

3. Raymond Geuss, *Public Goods, Private Goods* (Princeton: Princeton University Press, 2003), chapter 3 *Res Publica*. For the historical trajectory of the distinction between public and private law see Peter Stein, *Roman Law in European History* (Cambridge: Cambridge University Press, 1999), 21 etc.

4. Maximilien Robespierre, *Discours et rapports à la Convention* (Paris: Union Générale des Éditions, 1965), 213

5. M.I. Finley, *Democracy Ancient and Modern* (London: Hogarth Press, 1985); *Politics in the Ancient World* (Cambridge: Cambridge University Press, 1983); M.H. Hansen, *The Athenian Democracy in the Age of Demosthenes* (Oxford: Blackwell, 1991)

6. George Rudé, *The Crowd in the French Revolution* (Oxford: Clarendon Press, 1959); Albert Soboul, *The Parisian Sans-Culottes and the French Revolution 1793–94*, tr G. Lewis (Oxford: Clarendon Press, 1964)

7. Alexander Hamilton, Letter to Gouverneur Morris, 19 May 1777 (*Papers of Alexander Hamilton*, Vol 1, ed Harold C. Syrett & Jacob E. Cooke (New York: Columbia University Press, 1961), 255): 'When the deliberative or judicial powers are vested wholly or partly in the collective body of the people, you must expect error, confusion and instability. But a representative democracy, where the right of election is well secured and regulated & the exercise of the legislative, executive and judiciary authorities, is vested in select persons chosen *really* and not *nominally* by the people, will in my opinion be most likely to be happy, regular and durable.' Not a bad judgement as prophecies go.

8. Robespierre, *Discours*, 213

9. Sylvain Maréchal, *Manifesto of the Equals* (Filippo Michele Buonarroti, *Conspiration pour l'égalité, dite de Babeuf* (Paris: Éditions Sociales, 1957), Vol 2, 94–95: 'The French Revolution is only the precursor of another revolution, far greater, far more solemn, which will be the last.'

10. Richard Cobb, *The Police and the People: French Popular Protest 1789–1820* (Oxford: Clarendon Press, 1970), 3–81

11. Elizabeth Eisenstein, *The First Professional Revolutionist: Filippo Michele Buonarroti* (Cambridge, Mass.: Harvard University Press, 1959)

12. Jean Bruhat, 'La Révolution Française et la Formation de la Pensée de Marx', *Annales Historiques de la Révolution Française*, 48, 1966, 125–70

13. Buonarroti, *Conspiration*, 26

14. Buonarroti, *Conspiration*, 25

15. Buonarroti, *Conspiration*, 26

16. Buonarroti, *Conspiration*, 26–27

17. Buonarroti, *Conspiration*, 28

18. Buonarroti, *Conspiration*, 33

19. Buonarroti, *Conspiration*, 114

20. Buonarroti, *Conspiration*, 114n

21. Alexis de Tocqueville, *Democracy in America*, tr & ed Harvey C. Mansfield & Delba Winthrop (Chicago: University of Chicago Press, 2000)

22. For the sheer length of the time-span see Alexander Keyssar, *The Right to Vote: The Contested History of Democracy in the United States* (New York: Perseus Books, 2000). For the complexity and ambivalence of the protracted and still severely incomplete process of political reconciliation to the outcome see especially Rogers Smith, *Civic Ideals: Conflicting Visions of Citizenship in US History* (New Haven: Yale University Press, 1997), and James H. Kettner, *The Development of American Citizenship 1608–1870* (Chapel Hill: University of North Carolina Press, 1978).

23. Cf Bernard Williams, 'External and Internal Reasons', in his *Moral Luck* (Cambridge: Cambridge University Press, 1981), 101–13

24. For a classic exposition of this point, see Adam Przeworski, *Capitalism and Social Democracy* (Cambridge: Cambridge University Press, 1985)

25. Elizabeth Eisenstein, *The First Professional Revolutionist*

26. Cobb, *The Police and the People* gives a withering verdict. For the subsequent fate of the Democrats see Isser Woloch, *The Jacobin Legacy: The Democratic Movement under the Directory* (Princeton: Princeton University Press, 1970), esp chapter 6 'The Democratic Persuasion'.

27. David Hume, 'Of the First Principles of Government', *Essays Moral, Political and Literary*, ed Eugene F. Miller (Indianapolis: Liberty Press, 1985), 32: 'Nothing appears more surprising, to those who consider human affairs with a philosophical eye, than the easiness with which the many are governed by the few; and the implicit submission, with which men resign their own sentiments and passions to those of their rulers. When we enquire by what means this wonder is effected, we shall find, that, as FORCE is

always on the side of the governed, the governors have nothing to support them but opinion. It is therefore, on opinion only that government is founded; and this maxim extends to the most despotic and most military governments, as well as to the most free and most popular.' The best picture of the conclusions which Hume drew from this insight is still Duncan Forbes, *Hume's Philosophical Politics* (Cambridge: Cambridge University Press, 1975).

28. François Furet, *Interpreting the French Revolution*, tr Elborg Forster (Cambridge: Cambridge University Press, 1982). The best attempt to tell the story continuously in relation to a single political community has been made (unsurprisingly) in relation to France itself. See Pierre Rosanvallon, *Le Sacre du citoyen: Histoire de la suffrage universel en France* (Paris: Gallimard, 1992), *Le Peuple introuvable: histoire de la représentation démocratique en France* (Paris: Gallimard, 1998); *La Démocratie inachevée: Histoire de la souveraineté du peuple en France* (Paris: Gallimard, 2000); *Le Modèle Politique Français: la société civile contre le jacobinisme de 1789 à nos jours* (Paris: Le Seuil, 2004). For the context of modern politics see John Dunn (ed), *The Economic Limits to Modern Politics* (Cambridge: Cambridge University Press, 1990) (especially the chapter by Istvan Hont).

29. Josiah Ober, *Mass and Elite in Democratic Athens* (Princeton: Princeton University Press, 1989); and Harvey Yunis, *Taming Democracy: Models of Rhetoric in Classical Athens* (Ithaca: Cornell University Press, 1996)

30. Thucydides, *History of the Peloponnesian War*, Bks I & II, tr Charles Forster Smith (Cambridge, Mass.: Harvard University Press, 1928), II, lxv, 9, pp 376–77

31. Joseph Schumpeter, *Capitalism, Socialism and Democracy* 3rd ed (London: George Allen & Unwin, 1950), 285

32. See, for example, Ronald Dworkin, *Sovereign Virtue* (Cambridge, Mass.: Harvard University Press, 2000)

33. The country of which this is least clearly true is still the United States of America; and the obstacles which stand in the way of its

doing so are still a plain legacy from the efforts by Madison and his colleagues to ensure that the United States should not be what they understood as a democracy (cf Manin, 'Checks, Balances and Boundaries', in Biancamaria Fontana (ed), *The Invention of the Modern Republic* (Cambridge: Cambridge University Press, 1994), 27–62).

34. Jack Goody, *The Domestication of the Savage Mind* (Cambridge: Cambridge University Press, 1977)

35. Cf Ronald Dworkin, *Sovereign Virtue*; John Rawls, *A Theory of Justice* (Oxford: Clarendon Press, 1972); *Political Liberalism* (New York: Columbia University Press, 1993)

36. G.A. Cohen, *If You're an Egalitarian, How Come You're So Rich?* (Cambridge, Mass.: Harvard University Press, 2000)

37. The idea of fixed and objective standards enjoyed an intense glamour in the course of the Revolution. The view that measures of time and space can and should be drawn directly from the fabric of the world itself, and not from antique superstitions or habits, led, amongst other things, to the creation of a new calendar and the invention of the metric system: cf Denis Guedj, *Le Mètre du monde* (Paris: Editions du Seuil, 2000); Ken Alder, *The Measure of All Things* (London: Abacus, 2004).

38. 'US Leader appeals to closest friend in the world', *Financial Times*, 20 November 2003, p 4

39. Joseph de Maistre, *Works*, ed & tr Jack Lively (New York: Macmillan, 1964), 93 : 'It is said that the people are sovereign; but over whom? Over themselves, apparently. The people are thus subject. There is surely something equivocal if not erroneous here, for the people which *command* are not the people which *obey*.'

40. C.V. Wedgwood, *The Trial of Charles I* (London: Fontana, 1964), 217

41. Wedgwood, *Trial of Charles I*, 71

42. Bruce Cumings, *North Korea: The Hermit Kingdom* (London: Prospect, 2003)

43. Peter Holquist, *Making War, Forging Revolution* (Cambridge, Mass.: Harvard University Press, 2002); Philip Short, *Pol Pot: The History of a Nightmare* (London: John Murray, 2004)

44. Plato, *The Republic*, 558C, tr Paul Shorey (Cambridge, Mass.: Harvard University Press, 1935), Vol 2, 290–91

45. Benjamin Constant, *Political Writings*, ed Biancamaria Fontana (Cambridge: Cambridge University Press, 1988), 313–28

NOTES TO CHAPTER 4

1. The best picture of Babeuf's political life, the botched conspiracy to which he gave his name, his defiant defence of a lifetime's aims and convictions before the tribunal at Vendôme, failed suicide attempt and prompt execution is R.B. Rose, *Gracchus Babeuf: The First Revolutionary Communist* (London: Edwin Arnold, 1978). There is no good reason to doubt Babeuf's commitment to democracy under less extreme conditions throughout his life: 68, 160–61, 380. On 4 July 1790, from the Conciergerie prison, in the third number of his *Journal de la Confédération*, he gave classic expression to the most drastic vision of what democracy means: 'If the People are the Sovereign, they should exercise as much sovereignty as they absolutely can themselves... to accomplish that which you have to do and can do yourself use representation on the fewest possible occasions and be nearly always your own representative' (p 77). Easier said than done. For the final stage of his life see 325–26.

2. Neil Harding, *Lenin's Political Thought*, 2 vols (London: Macmillan, 1977 & 1981)

3. Cf Jeremy Bentham's verdict on full-fledged natural rights: *Anarchical Fallacies*, in J. Bentham, *Rights, Representation and Reform: Nonsense upon Stilts and Other Writings on the French Revolution*, ed Philip Schofield, Catherine Pease-Watkin & Cyprian Blamires (Oxford: Clarendon Press, 2002), 317–434, esp 330.

4. Dorothy Thompson, *The Chartists: Popular Protest in the Industrial Revolution* (Aldershot: Wildwood House, 1986) ; Gareth Stedman Jones, Rethinking Chartism, *Languages of Class* (Cambridge: Cambridge University Press, 1983), 90–178; Mark Hovell, *The Chartist Movement* (Manchester: Manchester University Press, 1918); Logie Barrow & Ian Bullock, *Democratic Ideas and the British Labour Movement 1880–1914* (Cambridge: Cambridge University Press, 1996)

5. For Cavour see Dennis Mack Smith, *Italy: A Modern History* (New Haven: Yale University Press, 1997), chapters 1–3; Denis Mack Smith, *Cavour and Garibaldi: A Study in Political Conflict* (Cambridge: Cambridge University Press, 1985); Anthony Cardozo, 'Cavour and Piedmont', John A. Davis (ed), *Italy in the Nineteenth Century* (Oxford: Oxford University Press, 2000), 108–31. For Bismarck, A.J.P. Taylor, *Bismarck: The Man and the Statesman* (London: Arrow Books, 1961); Fritz Stern, *Gold and Iron: Bismarck, Bleichroder and the Building of the German Empire* (London: George Allen & Unwin, 1977). For Disraeli, Paul Smith, *Disraeli: A Brief Life* (Cambridge: Cambridge University Press, 1996); Edgar Feuchtwanger, *Disraeli* (London: Arnold, 2000); Maurice Cowling, *1867: Disraeli, Gladstone & Revolution* (Cambridge: Cambridge University Press, 1967).

6. Proudhon thought and wrote about this issue over several decades, usually in a state of some anxiety and dismay. For key episodes see Pierre-Joseph Proudhon, *Idée Générale de la Révolution au xixe siècle*, ed Aimé Berthod (Paris: Marcel Rivière, 1923), 210–14 and 344–45. For characteristic notes see, e.g. p 211: '*Je veux traiter directement, individuellement pour moi-même; le suffrage universel est à mes yeux une vraie loterie*' (a complete lottery); p 208 'Gouvernement démocratique *et* Religion naturelle *sont des contradictions, à moins qu'on ne préfère y voir deux mystifications. Le peuple n'a pas plus voix consultative dans l'État que dans l'Église: son rôle est d'obéir et de croire.*' *La Révolution Sociale démontrée par le coup d'état du deux decembre*, ed Edouard

Dolléans & Georges Duveau (Paris: Marcel Rivière, 1936), chapter 3 & pp 288–97; *De la Capacité Politique des Classes Ouvrières*, ed Maxime Leroy (Paris: Marcel Rivière, 1924), Pt II, chapter 15 & Pt III. For helpful presentations of his thinking as a whole see Robert J. Hoffman, *Revolutionary Justice: The Social and Political Thought of P-J Proudhon* (Urbana: University of Illinois Press, 1972) and K. Steven Vincent, *Pierre-Joseph Proudhon and the Rise of French Republican Socialism* (New York: Oxford University Press, 1984).

7. Cf Michael Mandlebaum, *The Ideas that Conquered the World: Peace, Democracy and Free Markets in the Twenty-first Century* (Oxford: Public Affairs Press, 2002) Tony Smith, *America's Mission: The United States and the Worldwide Struggle for Democracy* (Princeton: Princeton University Press, 1995); John A. Thompson, *Woodrow Wilson* (London: Longman, 2002) gives a lucid and balanced account. Note the firmness of Wilson in stating America's war aims to Congress, 2 April 1917: 'We shall fight for the things we have always carried closest to our hearts, – for democracy, for the right of those who submit to authority to have a voice in their own governments, for the rights and liberties of small nations, for a universal dominion of right by such a concert of free peoples as shall bring peace and safety to all nations and make the world itself at last free' (149–50). But note also the prudent reservation a year later (remarks to foreign correspondents, 8 April 1918): 'I am not fighting for democracy except for the peoples who want democracy. If they don't want it, that is none of my business' (169, 185). Some Presidents learn slower than others: if at all.

8. Paul Bracken, *The Command and Control of Nuclear Forces* (New Haven: Yale University Press, 1982)

9. John Erickson, *The Road to Stalingrad* & *The Road to Berlin* (both London: Panther, 1985)

10. Tony Judt, *La Réconstruction du parti socialiste 1921–1926* (Paris: Presses de la Fondation Nationale des Sciences Politiques, 1976); *Socialism in Provence 1871–1914: A Study of the Origins of the Modern French Left* (Cambridge: Cambridge University Press,

1979); *Marxism and the French Left: Studies in Labour and Politics in France 1830–1981* (Oxford: Clarendon Press, 1986); George Lichtheim, *Marxism: An Historical and Critical Study* (London: Routledge, 1961); *Europe in the Twentieth Century* (London: Weidenfeld & Nicolson, 1972) Annie Kriegel, *Aux Origines du communisme français*, 2 vols (Paris: Mouton, 1966); Richard Lowenthal, *World Communism: The Disintegration of a Secular Faith* (New York: Oxford University Press, 1964).

Behind this quarrel lay, amongst much else, the thorny question of Marx's own attitude towards democracy, in theory and in practice. This epitomizes the opacity of the story which we need to recover, shrouded in the dense competing smoke screens laid down by well over a century of global struggle. For representative disagreements, see besides the works of Lichtheim and Furet, Shlomo Avineri, *The Social and Political Thought of Karl Marx* (Cambridge: Cambridge University Press, 1968); Oscar J. Hammen, *The Red 48-ers* (New York: Charles Scribner, 1969); Alan Gilbert, *Marx's Politics* (Oxford: Martin Robertson, 1981); Richard N. Hunt, *The Political Ideas of Marx and Engels*, 2 vols (London: Macmillan, 1974); Hal Draper, *Karl Marx's Theory of Revolution*, 2 vols in 4 (New York: Monthly Review Press, 1977–78); Leszek Kolakowski, *Main Currents of Marxism*, tr P.S. Falla (Oxford: Clarendon Press, 1978); Michael Levin, *Marx, Engels and Liberal Democracy* (Basingstoke: Macmillan, 1989) & *The Spectre of Democracy: The Rise of Modern Democracy as Seen by its Critics* (Macmillan: Basingstoke, 1992) and the Introduction by Gareth Stedman Jones to Karl Marx & Friedrich Engels, *The Communist Manifesto* (London: Penguin Books, 2002).

11. François Furet, *The Future of an Illusion*, tr Deborah Furet (Chicago: University of Chicago Press, 1999)

12. Cf J. Dunn, *The Politics of Socialism* (Cambridge: Cambridge University Press, 1984); *The Cunning of Unreason* (London: HarperCollins, 2000)

13. George W. Bush, *Financial Times*, 11 November 2003. Cf Woodrow Wilson, note 7 above.

14. Cf Paul Kennedy, *The Rise and Fall of the Great Powers* (London: Fontana, 1989)

15. Orlando Figes, *A People's Tragedy: The Russian Revolution 1891–1924* (London: Pimlico, 1997), chapter 6, esp 232–41; Teodor Shanin, *The Awkward Class: Political Sociology of Peasantry in a Developing Society: Russia 1910–1925* (Oxford: Clarendon Press, 1972); Geroid T. Robinson, *Rural Russia under the Old Regime* (Berkeley, California: University of California Press, 1967).

16. Louis Antoine de Saint-Just, *Oeuvres Complètes*, ed Charles Vellay (Paris: Charpentier & Fasquelle, 1908), II, 238 Speech of 8 Ventôse An II (26 Feb 1794), a report to the Convention on the contents of its prisons: *'les malheureux sont les puissances de la terre; ils ont le droit de parler en maîtres aux gouvernements qui les négligent.'* [The unfortunate (the poor) are the powers of the earth; they have every right to speak as masters to governments which neglect them.]

17. Alexis de Tocqueville, *Democracy in America*, ed & tr Harvey Mansfield & Delba Winthrop (Chicago: University of Chicago Press, 2000)

18. Cf J. Dunn (ed), *Contemporary Crisis of the Nation State?* (Oxford: Blackwell, 1995)

19. Cf Samuel Finer, *The History of Government* 3 vols (Oxford: Clarendon Press, 1997)

20. J. Dunn, *The Cunning of Unreason* (London: HarperCollins, 2000)

21. Mogens H. Hansen, *The Athenian Democracy in the Age of Demosthenes* (Oxford: Blackwell, 1991)

22. Benjamin Constant, *Political Writings*, ed Biancamaria Fontana, (Cambridge: Cambridge University Press, 1988), 313–28

23. Joseph Schumpeter, *Capitalism, Socialism and Democracy* 3rd ed (London: George Allen & Unwin, 1950), chapters 20–23; esp chapter 23, 'The Inference'. For the life from which these judgements emerged see Richard Swedberg, *Schumpeter: A Biography* (Princeton: Princeton University Press, 1991).

24. Schumpeter, *Capitalism*, 285. And see p 247: 'the people never really rule but they can always be made to do so by definition.' Compare the force of two aphorisms gleaned from his private diary: aphorism 3: 'Democracy is government by lying' (Swedberg, 200); and aphorism 18: 'To lie – what distinguishes man from animals' (Swedberg, 201).

25. Cf Robert Putnam, *Bowling Alone* (New York: Simon & Schuster, 2001). For what may be some of the consequences see Thomas Patterson, *The Vanishing Voter* (New York: Vintage, 2003) & Russell J Dalton, *Democratic Challenges, Democratic Choice: The Erosion of Political Support in Advanced Industrial Societies* (Oxford: Oxford University Press, 2004). For the ecological context within which this seepage of interest is occurring see Harold L. Wilensky, *Rich Democracies: Political Economy, Public Policy & Performance* (Berkeley, California: University of California Press, 2002).

26. For a particularly vivid example see Paul Ginsborg, *Italy and its Discontents 1980–2001* (London: Penguin, 2001)

27. Georges Sorel, *Reflexions on Violence*, tr T.E. Hulme & J. Roth (New York: Collier Books, 1961), 222. The whole of chapter 7, 'The Ethics of the Producers', remains a powerful indictment.

28. Pierre Rosanvallon, *Le Sacre du Citoyen: histoire du suffrage universel en France* (Paris: Gallimard, 1992). Cf M.H. Hansen, *The Athenian Democracy in the Age of Demosthenes* (Oxford: Blackwell, 1991).

29. Ronald Dworkin, *Sovereign Virtue* (Cambridge, Mass.: Harvard University Press, 2000)

30. Cf Thomas Hobbes, *The Elements of Law*, chapters 8 & 9 (Hobbes, *Human Nature and De Corpore Politico*, ed J.C.A. Gaskin (Oxford: Oxford University Press, 1994), 48–60, 138–39), and for the strategic judgement which issues from this vision Thomas Hobbes, *Leviathan*, ed Richard Tuck (Cambridge: Cambridge University Press, 1991), chapter 11, p 70.

31. Cf Adam Smith, *The Theory of Moral Sentiments*, ed D.D. Raphael & A.L. Macfie (Oxford: Clarendon Press, 1976). To the cool eye of the order of egoism in its heyday, the moral sentiments have no privileged place amongst other sentiments; and their causal power, or motivational pressure, falls plainly short of sundry other sentiments.

32. Francis Hutcheson, *An Essay on the Nature and Conduct of the Passions and Affections with Ilustrations on the Moral Sense* 3rd ed (London: A. Ward etc, 1742). First ed 1728. The more sophisticated diagnosticians of the order of egoism are disinclined to believe that there is a moral sense. There is good reason to believe that they are right. Bernard Williams, *Ethics and the Limits of Philosophy* (London: Fontana, 1985); *Shame and Necessity* (Berkeley: University of California Press, 1993).

33. Robert B. Westbrook, *John Dewey and American Democracy* (Ithaca: Cornell University Press, 1991). Alan Ryan, *John Dewey and the High Tide of American Liberalism* (London & New York: W.W. Norton, 1995).

34. Cf Geoff Eley, *Forging Democracy: The History of the Left in Europe 1850–2000* (New York: Oxford University Press, 2002)

35. Tocqueville, *Democracy in America*

36. Hansen, *The Athenian Democracy in the Age of Demosthenes* (Oxford: Blackwell, 1991); Marcel Detienne, *Qui veut prendre la parole?* (Paris: Seuil, 2003)

37. John Stuart Mill, *Considerations on Representative Government* (London: J.M. Dent, 1910), 180

38. Paul Ginsborg, *Silvio Berlusconi: Television, Power and Patrimony* (London: Verso, 2004)

39. Bernard Manin, *The Principles of Representative Government* (Cambridge: Cambridge University Press, 1997)

40. David Butler & Austin Ranney (eds), *Referendums: A Comparative Study of Practice and Theory* (Washington, DC: American Enterprise Institute, 1980) and *Referendums around the World: The Growing Use of Direct Democracy* (Basingstoke: Macmillan, 1994)

41. Yannis Papadopoulos, *Démocratie Directe* (Paris: Economica, 1998)

42. Amy Gutmann & Denis Thompson, *Why Deliberative Democracy?* (Princeton: Princeton University Press, 2004); James S. Fishkin, *Democracy and Deliberation* (New Haven: Yale University Press, 1991), accessible samples from a very large body of recent academic writing.

43. Aristotle, *Politics*, tr H. Rackham (Cambridge, Mass.: Harvard University Press, 1932), 1281b–1284a, pp 220–41 (esp III, vi, 4–10 & III, vii, 12)

44. These remain intensely controversial criteria; and it is hard to see how they could ever cease to be so.

45. Far the most elaborate and pertinacious attempt to think this idea through has come in the massive oeuvre of Jürgen Habermas. For an impressively clear and sceptical assessment of the limits to its coherence see Raymond Geuss, *The Idea of a Critical Theory* (Cambridge: Cambridge University Press, 1980).

46. Thomas Hobbes, *Elements of Law*, chapter 8 (*Human Nature*, 48–49)

47. John Dower, *Empire and Aftermath: Yoshida Shigeru and the Japanese Empire 1878–1954* (Cambridge, Mass.: Harvard University Press, 1979) & *Embracing Defeat: Japan in the Aftermath of World War II* (Harmondsworth: Penguin, 2000); Alan S. Milward, *The Reconstruction of Western Europe 1945–51* (London: Methuen, 1984)

48. Sunil Khilnani, *The Idea of India* (London: Hamish Hamilton, 1997); Sarvepalli Gopal, *Jawaharlal Nehru: A Biography* 3 vols (London: Jonathan Cape, 1975–84); Granville Austin, *The Indian Constitution: Cornerstone of a Nation* (Oxford: Clarendon Press, 1966)

49. John K Fairbank (ed), *The Chinese World Order: Traditional China's Foreign Relations* (Cambridge, Mass.: Harvard University Press, 1968)

50. For a particularly illuminating discussion see Adam Przeworski, *Capitalism and Social Democracy* (Cambridge: Cambridge

University Press, 1985). For a vivid sketch of a great political leader deeply dedicated to this world and to the party as its central form of agency see Tony Judt, *The Burden of Responsibility* (Chicago: University of Chicago Press, 1998), 29–85 on Léon Blum.

51. Schumpeter, *Capitalism, Socialism and Democracy*

52. Paul Ginsborg, *Silvio Berlusconi: Television, Power and Patrimony* (London: Verso, 2004)

53. J. Dunn, 'Situating Democratic Accountability', in Adam Przeworski, Susan C. Stokes & Bernard Manin (eds), *Democracy, Accountability and Representation* (Cambridge: Cambridge University Press, 1999), 329–44

54. J. Dunn (ed), *The Economic Limits to Modern Politics* (Cambridge: Cambridge University Press, 1990); Dunn, *Cunning of Unreason*

55. David Held, *Global Covenant* (Cambridge: Polity, 2004); *Democracy and the Global Order* (Cambridge: Polity, 1995)

56. It asks in effect for the re-creation of the Garden of Eden, to harbour the great and natural community of mankind (John Locke, *Two Treatises of Government*, II, para 128, ed Mark Goldie (London: J.M. Dent, 1993), 179; 'he and all the rest of mankind are one community... this great and natural community') in punctilious shared observance of the Law of Nature itself. Or, if that for some reason proves unavailable, for equally punctilious and spontaneous observance of 'known standing laws' which raise no contentious issues of judgement in their interpretation and provoke no quarrels in their enforcement. Compare J. Dunn, 'The Contemporary Political Significance of John Locke's Conception of Civil Society', Sunil Khilnani & Sudipta Kaviraj (eds), *Civil Society: History and Possibilities* (Cambridge: Cambridge University Press, 2001), 39–57.

INDEX